Church in Motion

Missional Church, Public Theology, World Christianity

Stephen Bevans, Paul S. Chung, Veli-Matti Kärkkäinen, and Craig L. Nessan, Series Editors

IN THE MIDST OF globalization there is crisis as well as opportunity. A model of God's mission is of special significance for ecclesiology and public theology when explored in diverse perspectives and frameworks in the postcolonial context of World Christianity. In the face of the new, complex global civilization characterized by the Second Axial Age, the theology of mission, missional ecclesiology, and public ethics endeavor to provide a larger framework for missiology. It does so in interaction with our social, multicultural, political, economic, and intercivilizational situation. These fields create ways to refurbish mission as constructive theology in critical and creative engagement with cultural anthropology, world religions, prophetic theology, postcolonial hermeneutics, and contextual theologies of World Christianity. Such endeavors play a critical role in generating theological, missional, social-ethical alternatives to the reality of Empire—a reality characterized by civilizational conflict, and by the complex system of a colonized lifeworld that is embedded within practices of greed, dominion, and ecological devastation. This series—Missional Church, Public Theology, World Christianity—invites scholars to promote alternative church practices for life-enhancing culture and for evangelization as telling the truth in the public sphere, especially in solidarity with those on the margins and in ecological stewardship for the lifeworld.

Church in Motion
The History of the Evangelical Lutheran Mission in Bavaria

Translation of *Kirche in Bewegung: Die Geschichte der evangelischen Mission in Bayern*. Neuendettelsau: Erlanger Verlag, 2014.

Hermann Vorländer

Foreword by Craig L. Nessan

☙PICKWICK *Publications* · Eugene, Oregon

CHURCH IN MOTION
The History of the Evangelical Lutheran Mission in Bavaria

Missional Church, Public Theology, World Christianity 8

Copyright © 2018 Hermann Vorländer. All rights reserved. Except for brief quotations in critical publications or reviews, no part of this book may be reproduced in any manner without prior written permission from the publisher. Write: Permissions, Wipf and Stock Publishers, 199 W. 8th Ave., Suite 3, Eugene, OR 97401.

Pickwick Publications
An Imprint of Wipf and Stock Publishers
199 W. 8th Ave., Suite 3
Eugene, OR 97401

www.wipfandstock.com

PAPERBACK ISBN: 978-1-5326-1431-6
HARDCOVER ISBN: 978-1-5326-1433-0
EBOOK ISBN: 978-1-5326-1432-3

Cataloguing-in-Publication data:

Names: Vorländer, Hermann, author. | Nessan, Craig L., foreword.

Title: Church in motion : the history of the Evangelical Lutheran Mission in Bavaria / Hermann Vorländer ; foreword by Craig L. Nessan.

Description: Eugene, OR : Pickwick Publications, 2018 | Missional Church, Public Theology, World Christianity 8 | Includes bibliographical references and index.

Identifiers: ISBN X978-1-5326-1431-6 (paperback) | ISBN 978-1-5326-1433-0 (hardcover) | ISBN 978-1-5326-1432-3 (ebook)

Subjects: LCSH: Neuendettelsau Mission. | Missions, German—History. | Protestant churches—Missions—History. | Protestant churches--Germany—Bavaria—History. | Missions, German. | Protestant churches. | Protestant churches—Missions. | Germany—Bavaria.

Classification: BX4844 V68 2018 (paperback) | BX4844 V68 (ebook)

Manufactured in the U.S.A.   05/15/18

In loving memory of my dear wife, Dorothea (1940–2018)

Mission is therefore nothing else than the one church of God in its motion—the actualization of the one universal Catholic church. Where mission penetrates, fences collapse that separate nations from nations.
—WILHELM LOEHE

Contents

Foreword by Craig L. Nessan | xi
Preface and Acknowledgments | xiii
Abbreviations | xvii

1 The History of the Protestant Mission in Bavaria | 1
   The Struggle for Mission in the Beginning of the Nineteenth Century: 1819 to
      1845 | 1
   The Foundation of the Lutheran Missionary Work in North America by Wilhelm Loehe
      and Friedrich Bauer: 1842–1874 | 4
      Life and Work of Wilhelm Loehe as the Initiator of the Neuendettelsau
         Mission | 4
      Friedrich Bauer: Loehe's Closest Friend and Coworker | 21
   Consolidation and Crisis of the Neuendettelsau Mission: 1875–1933 | 29
   Missionary Work during Times of Conflict and Failure: 1933–1945 | 42
      Mission and National Socialism | 42
      The Position of the Neuendettelsau Mission under the Leadership of Friedrich
         Eppelein | 48
   New Beginnings and Challenges: 1945–1972 | 66
   The Department for World Mission within an Ecumenical Network: 1972–2007 | 71

2 The History of Cooperation of the Bavarian Lutheran Mission with
   Overseas Churches | 94
   Pacific and East Asia | 94
      Australia | 95
      New Guinea | 98
      Pacific | 121
      China | 122

       Hong Kong | 129
       Korea | 132
       Malaysia | 134
       Singapore | 137
       Relations with Other Churches and Organizations in Southeast Asia | 138
  Africa | 138
       General | 138
       Tanzania | 140
       Kenya | 150
       Congo / Zaire | 152
       Mozambique | 155
       Liberia | 156
       Relations with Other Churches and Organizations in Africa | 159
  Latin America | 162
       Brazil | 162
       Central America | 167
       Relations with Other Lutheran Churches in Latin America | 172

3 **Priorities and Developments of Bavarian Mission Work in the Twentieth Century | 174**
  Understanding of Mission | 174
  Mission and Church | 181
  People in God's Mission | 183
  Mission and Partnership | 188
  Mission and Money | 192
  Mission and Media | 194
  Mission and Development Service | 198
  Mission and Colonialism | 199
  Mission and Culture | 202
  Mission, Religions, and Interreligious Dialogue | 203
  Mission in Germany | 206
  Mission and Diakonia (Social Services) | 207

4 **Summary | 210**

Appendices
Chronologies | 215
List of Persons and Translations of Titles and Institutions | 234
Map of Bavaria | 237

Author Biography | 239
Bibliography | 241
Index of Persons | 247
Index of Places, Countries, Rivers | 253
Index of Institutions | 259

Foreword

OUT OF AN OBSCURE village in Germany emerged a church in motion that has changed the globe! This is at the heartbeat of the amazing story documented in this book. Neuendettelsau was the site of the rural parish where Wilhelm Loehe lived out his pastoral ministry from 1837 until his death in 1872, a place where he did not willingly choose to serve. However, devoted to God's Word and undertaking the duties of a local pastor in leading worship, offering pastoral ministry, and taking his context seriously, Loehe sowed seeds that took root near and far, in vastly different global contexts, that are bearing fruit to this day.

The Loehe legacy comes to expression through seven features that characterize this narrative of the evangelical mission that emanated from Bavaria to partner churches in North America, East Asia, and the South Pacific, Africa, and Latin America: 1) worship-centered community lived out in life-giving relationships, 2) the discipline of a faith informed by the practices of Pietism, 3) Lutheran confessional commitments, 4) the allowance for "open questions" that distinguish between the center of Christian faith and matters of adiaphora, 5) engagement in care for the needs of the world through diaconal service, 6) a heart for Christian mission by serving others in word and deed, and 7) a global horizon for extending the church's work.

Loehe was not only a dedicated pastor and formidable theologian but a stellar administrator, whose organizational abilities managed not only to found deaconess institutions at home but generated the international connections fostered by his spirit as carried forth by his successors in leading the mission work abroad. Hermann Vorländer is one of these successors, who knows this history from the inside out, having served many years as director of the missional institution grounded by Loehe, which under his leadership became known as Mission EineWelt (https://mission-einewelt.de/en/).

The author details the historical developments in all the countries reached as partner churches through the relationships of accompaniment extending from Neuendettelsau, locating these efforts in relationship to many other mission institutions that also were at work during this fruitful period. This in itself is a major contribution. Even more insightful is the analysis of the meanings of mission as these came to expression through this particular effort. The book explores the multifaceted significance of mission in relation to an understanding of God, church, partnership, finances, media, development projects, colonialism, culture, interfaith relationships, and diakonia. The book includes relevant chronologies and an accounting of personnel that will be of service to researchers for years to come.

On behalf of the editors of the series Missional Church, Public Theology, World Christianity, and as one who proudly identifies with the Loehe legacy as it came to expression through Wartburg Theological Seminary in Iowa, one of the global institutions launched in partnership with the mission efforts of Loehe in Neuendettelsau, I am pleased to commend this book to readers across the world, who themselves have been blessed by this history. Moreover, I endorse the book to the many other readers who will be informed and stirred by the work of the Spirit documented in this volume.

Craig L. Nessan
Wartburg Theological Seminary
Dubuque, Iowa, USA

Preface and Acknowledgments

IN 2017, THE PROTESTANT churches around the world remembered the beginning of the Reformation five hundred years ago. On October 31, 1517, Martin Luther published in Wittenberg his Ninety-five Theses and became the leader of a movement that had great influence on the history of Europe. The Lutheran churches around the world base their life and theology on Luther´s teachings.

A special national exhibition in Wittenberg portrayed ninety-five personalities who had a special relationship to Martin Luther. Among them is Pastor Wilhelm Loehe, who was not the first but the most influencial initiator of missionary work not only in Bavaria but in all of Germany. He understood himself as a disciple of Luther and tried to implement his teachings into the practice of the church of his time. He was also active in spreading the Lutheran faith to other countries, starting in North America.

The Reformation developed from the beginning as an international movement that expanded into other European countries. Students from many countries came to Wittenberg to get to know Luther and his interpretation of the Bible. After their return they founded Lutheran congregations and churches in their homelands. Initially the Lutheran movement was restricted to Europe, because only the Catholic countries of Spain and Portugal had colonies overseas where they did missionary work among the natives. Worldwide mission was out of sight for Lutheran theologians and church leaders. Luther himself understood the Great Commission in Matthew 28:18–20, according to his Small Catechism, not as the mission to bring the gospel to the whole world, but to baptize infants within the local congregations.

It took nearly two hundred years until, in 1705, August Hermann Francke, as a member of the Danish Halle Mission, sent the first Protestant missionaries from Germany to India. He was followed by Nikolaus Ludwig Graf von Zinzendorf, a Moravian and member of the Bretheren's Congregation of Herrnhut (Herrnhuter Brüdergemeine), who sent missionaries to the Caribbean since 1732 and later also to other parts of the world. In the beginning of the nineteenth century, under the influence of Pietism and the revival movement, public interest in foreign mission awoke in the wider public of Germany. The Great Commission in Matthew 28:18–20 was now generally understood as a commission for world mission.

Within this movement the small town of Neuendettelsau in Bavaria played an important role under the leadership of Pastor Wilhelm Loehe. He began missionary work in North America by sending missionaries to the German emigrants. He founded missionary congregations that brought the gospel to the Native Americans. He is considered a founding father of the two big Lutheran churches in the USA. His missioners actively participated in 1847 in the foundation of the Lutheran Church–Missouri Synod (LCMS). Other missioners from Neuendettelsau founded in 1854 the Iowa Synod, which later became part of what is now the Evangelical Lutheran Church in America (ELCA). The chapel at Wartburg Theological Seminary in Dubuque, Iowa, and an academic building at Concordia Theological Seminary in Fort Wayne, Indiana, are dedicated to Wilhelm Loehe.

He was supported by Friedrich Bauer, who in 1846 started a mission seminary in Nuremberg, which operated from 1853 to 1985 in Neuendettelsau. Until 1985 nearly nine hundred graduates were trained and sent to churches overseas in North America, Australia, Papua New Guinea, Brazil, Ukraine, Africa, and elsewhere. They did missionary work on the basis of the Lutheran doctrine that they learned in the seminary with the emphasis on Bible, Lutheran confession, liturgy, Holy Communion, church discipline, and ordination of the pastor.

Mission work in Bavaria and all over Germany did not start from "above" but from "below," initiated not by the church and state authorities but by individuals, both pastors and lay persons. Only recently the Evangelical Lutheran Church in Bavaria has taken over the full responsibility for mission work.

The book is the translation of my book *Kirche in Bewegung: Die Geschichte der evangelischen Mission in Bayern* (Neuendettelsau: Erlanger

Verlag, 2014). It covers the period until 2007, when the new Center Mission One World began with its operations. Therefore also this English version ends mainly with 2007, except that some new developments are added.

This study is the first attempt to describe the history of the Lutheran mission in Bavaria, not only the Neuendettelsau Mission, but also other mission activities. During my time as director of the Department for World Mission since 1992, I planned to write such a book when I retire. This is the result of my efforts. But my time available for research was limited, therefore only part of the scholarly literature could be consulted. The book is written for pastors and lay persons active in church and mission.

The first part describes the history of the missionary work in the Evangelical Lutheran Church in Bavaria (ELCB) between 1819 and 2007. Not all periods are dealt with equally. There is a certain emphasis on the relationship between the Neuendettelsau Mission and National Socialism, because this period was often neglected in publications. National Socialism was not only dominant in Neuendettelsau, but also in Papua New Guinea and Brazil.

The second part of the book describes the history of the missionary activities of ELCB in Asia/Pacific, Africa, and Latin America. Papua New Guinea and Tanzania were and are the countries in which Bavarian missionaries invested the most work, therefore they are treated more extensively than others. Mission churches developed into partner churches where often American Lutherans are also active. I gained the information for this part mainly from many visits during my service in the Department for World Mission.

The third part describes important developments in missionary work and theology in recent years, e.g., the concept of missio dei, role of mission personnel, mission and church, communio and partnership, development service, money and media, colonialism and culture, interreligious encounter and diakonia.

The last two centuries were not only the era of enormous scientific and technological developments and terrible wars, but also the era of the mission. The gospel reached, by missionary work, the most remote corners of the earth. Now the majority of Christians live in the countries of the global South.

The title of the book is taken from Wilhelm Loehe's discourse *Three Books on the Church*: "Mission is nothing else than the one church of God in its motion." Under God's guidance men and women moved the Bavarian church to cross its borders and bring the gospel to foreign countries. They also brought motion into the local congregations to vitalize church life on the basis of the Lutheran confession. This movement continues until today within the worldwide communion of churches.

I did the translation work by myself, including all texts quoted from authors and documents. Ms. Laurel Vogl, MA, helped me to put the text into correct English. For bibliographical references please consult the German version.

I owe thanks to my colleagues who supported me with valuable advices: Horst Becker, DD, Dr. Wolfgang Döbrich, Rev. Friedrich Durst, Rev. Gernot Fugmann, MA, Rev. Reinhard Hansen, Dr. Hans Rössler, Dr. Johannes Triebel, and Dr. Herwig Wagner. My wife, Dr. Dorothea Vorländer, supported me in numerous advises and proof-reading. I received technical assistance from Daniela Denk, Susanna Endres, Brigitte Hagelauer, Matthias Honold, MA, Günter Kohlmann, Helge Neuschwander-Lutz, Hans Spalt, and Roland St.Pierre. I owe thanks to Dr. Craig L. Nessan, who encouraged me to publish this study in English.

Neuendettelsau, Easter 2018
Dr. Hermann Vorländer

Abbreviations

DMW	Department for World Mission of the Evangelical Lutheran Church in Bavaria (Missionswerk)
EKD	Protestant Church in Germany (Evangelische Kirche in Deutschland)
ELCB	Evangelical Lutheran Church in Bavaria
ELCA	Evangelical Lutheran Church in America
ELCPNG	Evangelical Lutheran Church of Papua New Guinea
ELCT	Evangelical Lutheran Church in Tanzania
EMW	Association of Protestant Churches and Missions in Germany (Evangelisches Missionswerk in Deutschland)
FELM	Finnish Evangelical Lutheran Mission
IECLB	Evangelical Church of the Lutheran Confession in Brazil
KED	Church Development Service (Kirchlicher Entwicklungsdienst)
LCA	Lutheran Church of Australia
LCMS	Lutheran Church–Missouri Synod
LMC	Lutheran Mission Cooperation (Tanzania)
MEW	Mission One World – Center for Partnership, Development and Mission of the Evangelical Lutheran Church in Bavaria (Mission EineWelt – Centrum für Partnerschaft, Entwickung und Mission der Evangelisch-Lutherischen Kirche in Bayern)
NSDAP	National Socialist German Workers Party
PCC	Pacific Council of Churches
PNG	Papua New Guinea
PTC	Pacific Theological College

1

The History of the Protestant Mission in Bavaria

The Struggle for Mission in the Beginning of the Nineteenth Century: 1819 to 1845

THE HISTORY OF THE Protestant mission in Germany started in 1705 when August Hermann Francke sent the first Protestant missionaries to India in cooperation with the Danish king. He was followed by Nikolaus Ludwig Graf von Zinzendorf, whose Herrnhuter Brüdergemeine ("Moravians") since 1732 sent missionaries to the Caribbean and later to other parts of the world. The first Moravian missionary, Johann Leonhard Dober (1706–1766), came from Mönchsroth near Ansbach in present Bavaria.

Since the end of the eighteenth century missionary societies were founded in England. Under the influence of Pietism and the revival movement, Protestant Christians in Germany also wanted to start missionary work abroad in the beginning of the nineteenth century. But the foundation of missionary associations was regarded with suspicion by many governments in Germany, because they were presumed to be conspiratorial, subversive associations. In Bavaria one could be sentenced to fines or imprisonment if members of a congregation met with the pastor in a house to sing hymns or read from a prayer book. Therefore, the mission friends in Württemberg chose the Swiss city of Basel in 1815 to start the Protestant Mission in Basel under the leadership of Friedrich Spittler. Since 1816, Christoph Blumhardt edited the *Magazine for the Newest History of the Protestant Missionary and Bible Society*. The magazine became so widespread in Bavaria that the Protestant Christians in

Bavaria assembled to establish auxiliary associations for the support of the Basel Mission.

At that time the Protestant church in Bavaria had just been constituted in 1817 after the reorganization of Germany following the Napoleon era. Bavaria originally consisted only of the southern part around Munich and was predominantly Catholic. In 1806, Bavaria was enlarged by mostly Protestant territories in Franconia. Franconia is the name of the northern part of Bavaria with Nuremberg as its biggest city. The Catholic king of Bavaria remained the head of the Protestant church until 1918 according to the agreements in the time of the Reformation. Since 1945, the church has carried the official name Evangelical Lutheran Church in Bavaria. It has about 2.5 million members in 1,500 congregations taken care of by about 2,500 pastors. The leadership consists of the four governing bodies: (head) bishop, general synod, synod committee, and supreme church council.

The first local missionary association in Bavaria was founded in 1819 in Erlangen. It was followed by foundations in Nuremberg, Fürth, Hersbruck, Würzburg, etc. In particular, in Erlangen the professor of mineralogy Karl von Raumer; the Lutheran theology professors Adolf von Harless, Friedrich Höfling, Franz Delitzsch, and Gottfried Thomasius; and the Reformed professor Christian Krafft promoted the work of the local missionary society. Students of theology and artisans met in homes to read the Bible and exchange mission news. The church authorities, which were part of the state administration at that time, disapproved of these associations. They suspected them of sectarianism and criticized the distribution of pamphlets as an interference with parochial law.

In 1822, Heinrich Holzschuher from Wunsiedel applied for an exit visa to attend Basel Mission Seminary. This was postponed by the government until the applicant proved "that, after finishing the mission course, he would work permanently abroad so that after a possible return to Bavaria he would not become a burden for the Bavarian authorities." The candidate subsequently withdrew his plan.

Collections in congregations and public collections for mission were not permitted. Only private donations were allowed because they "emerge from the inner spirit and essence of Christianity," as a decision of the Royal Protestant Supreme Consistory in Munich told mission friends in Nuremberg in 1822. However, it added that "their charity should be directed to objects of the fatherland" rather than "to the Tartar tribes in Asia, the Kaffirs in Africa, and the savages in South and North America."

Criticism also came from the ranks of Nuremberg liberals and influential rationalists. The "mission thing," as it was called, led to a controversial discussion within the Protestant church in Bavaria.

Adolf von Harless (1806–1879), who attended the same grammar school (gymnasium) as Loehe in Nuremberg, taught as a professor of theology in Erlangen beginning in 1833. He opened access to Luther's theology for both Wilhelm Loehe and Friedrich Bauer. Harless promoted the "mission thing" in Erlangen and, starting in 1845, taught at Leipzig University. He also belonged to the board of Leipzig Mission und encouraged its Lutheran orientation. Since 1850, he worked as a court preacher in Dresden and was appointed president of the Royal Supreme Protestant Consistory in Munich in 1852. He supported the struggle for the Lutheran confession in the Bavarian church and in 1853 accomplished the renaming of the Central Missionary Association to the "Central Evangelical Lutheran Missionary Association."

For a long time, the Royal Protestant Supreme Consistory, as part of the Bavarian government, refused permission to found a central missionary society. In a communication of 1828, the consistory stated as follows:

> Bavarians go abroad and devote themselves to missionary work, arousing concern that once when they can no longer work, they return to the homeland and drop burdens on the municipalities.... All conventicles, missionary prayer meetings and special services remain forever prohibited. When the members gather to thank God and Christ for the promotion of their work with prayer and hymn, they can do this using one of the churches at the time of public services.

The Bavarian government also feared that through a connection with the Basel Mission "disadvantages of various kinds for the internal order of our kingdom are generated."

Parallel with the efforts to establish a central missionary society, negotiations were undertaken to establish a Bible society, which was often supported by the same individuals. The commitment to the dissemination of the biblical message inside and to the mission outside went hand in hand. But already in 1824 the establishment of the Bavarian Central Bible Association (Bayerischer Zentralbibelverein) was approved by the government.

In the Roman Catholic Church, there were also efforts to start missionary societies. In 1837, King Ludwig I approved the establishment of the Ludwig Missionary Society, which is now part of Missio Munich.

Finally, on January 17, 1843 "His Majesty the King allowed the establishment of a Protestant Missionary Association in Bavaria." It was to "support local missionary associations and institutions in their goal to convert Gentiles" and to be under the supervision of the Protestant Supreme Consistory. It allowed the setting up of Lutheran and Reformed district and local missionary associations. Beginning in 1844 the *Nuremberg Mission Journal* (*Nürnberger Missionsblatt*) appeared. In 1845, the first mission festival was held in Nuremberg, which for many years was the most important public event in the church. The Central Missionary Association (Zentralmissionsverein) closely cooperated with the Central Bible Society. Both saw their common task in spreading the word of God "to all people for the sake of the salvation of their souls." Until recently the director of the Neuendettelsau Mission was a "born" member of the executive board of the Central Bible Association.

At that time the village pastor of Neuendettelsau, Wilhelm Loehe, went his own way without caring for the rules of the state or the church. He started missionary work within his congregation and its lasting effects are now described.

The Foundation of the Lutheran Missionary Work in North America by Wilhelm Loehe and Friedrich Bauer: 1842–1874

Life and Work of Wilhelm Loehe as the Initiator of the Neuendettelsau Mission

Wilhelm Loehe (1808–1872), a pastor in Neuendettelsau, began missionary work in North America in 1842. After a confrontation with the Lutheran Church–Missouri Synod, he left the mission training mainly to his friend Friedrich Bauer and thereafter devoted himself especially to the work in the Deaconess Institute (Diakonissenanstalt), which he founded in 1854. (Wilhelm Löhe Archive of the Society for Inner and Outer Mission)

Johann Konrad Wilhelm Loehe (Löhe) was born on February 21, 1808, in the city of Fürth. His father, a shopkeeper, died in 1816, thus the young man was mainly influenced by his pietistic mother. He attended the grammar school (gymnasium) in Nuremberg and was admitted to the study of theology at the University of Erlangen in 1826. He was especially influenced by the Reformed professor of theology Christian Krafft (1784–1845). In 1828 he spent a term at the University of Berlin, where he did studies with the professors Ernst Wilhelm Hengstenberg and Friedrich Schleiermacher. After his return to Erlangen in 1830 he finished his theological studies with the church entrance exam. He became a vicar in Fürth and worked as an assistant pastor in several Franconian congregations. In 1835 he met his later wife, Helene Andreä, from Frankfurt. They married in 1837 after Loehe became pastor in the small village of Neuendettelsau. After the birth of their four children his wife died suddenly in 1843 at the age of only twenty-four. He then took care of his children as a single father and never married again. His applications for parishes in Erlangen, Augsburg, Nuremberg, and Fürth remained unsuccessful.

In his parish work he emphasized liturgical education in the spirit of Lutheranism and church discipline. Later he fought for the Lutheran character of his church. At times he thought about joining an independent Lutheran church. He was discontent with the structure of his church, in which the Catholic king of Bavaria was the head of the church, who could give orders to the pastors. In 1854 he founded the Deaconess Institute (Diakonissenanstalt) in Neuendettelsau and left the work in the Mission Seminary and the connections to North America to his friend Friedrich Bauer. He sent deaconesses also to America, France, and Eastern Europe. During his last years he suffered from severe illnesses before he died on January 2, 1872. For his funeral on January 5, 1872 he had given the instruction that it should be handled like that of deaconesses, without a sermon or speech.

Since his early youth Wilhelm Loehe was filled with enthusiasm for mission. At the age of nineteen, under the influence of his professor Christian Krafft, he founded in Fürth a missionary society to support the Basel Mission. He studied intensively the missionary work of the Moravians in North America. During his time in Kirchenlamitz he promoted evangelistic activities.

In 1836, the Evangelical Lutheran Mission in Saxony was founded in Dresden. It emerged from an auxiliary organization for the Basel Mission and has now been converted into a Lutheran mission society. In 1848, it was moved to Leipzig because of the proximity to the faculty of theology of the university and has since been the Evangelical Lutheran Mission Leipzig–Leipzig Mission. It received significant donations from Bavaria for many years, partly more than from Saxony, because it saw itself as missionary society for all Lutheran churches and invited them to join.

In 1838, Wilhelm Loehe visited the mission festival in Dresden and also took part in the testing of seminarians. He, however, did not believe that the Dresden Mission brought forth well-trained missionaries. They knew less than "well-informed confirmands," Loehe wrote in his travel report. Therefore, in 1841, he began his own missionary training within the Neuendettelsau parish. From 1846, he worked with the Mission Preparation Institute for Fort Wayne, which was founded in Nuremberg by Friedrich Bauer. Loehe continued to support the Leipzig Mission with donations, but only half-heartedly: "If I knew where my people should turn with their love for the mission and their laboriously saved bag, I would be warned of Dresden, not to support an institution from which achievements are not to be expected that could give honor to our church."

The picture shows Neuendettelsau at the time of Loehe with the six-hundred-year-old village church of St. Nikolai, which in 1898 was demolished and replaced by a new building. On the right is seen the parsonage, in which Loehe in 1841 prepared the first two "emergency helpers" for missionary service in North America. (Wilhelm Löhe Archive of the Society for Inner and Outer Mission)

Loehe began missionary work as a private activity within his parish in Neuendettelsau, which the church and state authorities could not prohibit. The year 1840 was decisive for Loehe. He was particularly concerned with the situation of German immigrants to North America. The German American pastor Friedrich Wynecken (1810–1876) in an "emergency call" urged German Lutherans to send pastors and teachers to the scattered Lutherans in North America to assist the settlers and to help with the conversion of the Native Americans. The settlers often lived not only a materially but also spiritually poor life. Since they mostly did not have pastors, their children were not baptized, their couples were not blessed, and the dead did not receive a church funeral.

On January 10, 1841, Loehe published this call in the *Nördlingen Sunday Journal* (*Nördlinger Sonntagsblatt*), which was edited by his friend Rev. Friedrich Wucherer. Wynecken described the "The Distress of the German Lutherans in North America" with impressive words:

> Thousands of families, your co-religionists, perhaps according to the flesh, your brothers and sisters hunger for the strong supply of the gospel; they plead to you with pity crying: O plead for us! Give us preachers who strengthen us with the bread of life and edify us through the word of the Lord, who teach our children in the doctrine of salvation of Jesus. O plead for us, or we are lost! Why do you help not? Is this the love of Jesus? Is this keeping his commandment? Bear in mind the words: As you did it to one of the least of these my brothers, you do to me.

Loehe published this call under the heading "The Lutheran Emigrants in North America: An Address to the Readers of the Sunday Journal." Through additions and reinforcements he intensified the emergency call:

> Thousands, hundreds of thousands, are driven from Germany across the sea to find new homes. German fathers, mothers, German children, German brothers, sisters, relatives, comrades of young Germans, walk in large numbers under another sky on another planet. Did, with their bodies, also love disappear? Did the memory of distant loved ones die? Fathers, do you not ask for your children? Mothers, do you not worry about those who have sucked your breasts? . . . Most German emigrants are members of the Protestant church. . . . We believe in one holy Catholic church which wraps around the heavens and the earth! We love across the ocean, to the forests of America, to the distant mountains, to the broad streams—anywhere where people settle who are committed to the pure word and the unchanged administration of the sacraments! Our brothers walk in the wilderness of North America–without food for their souls. . . . And we should not provide assistance? Should we watch how our

fellow believers are deceived due to the lack of shepherds and observe as the evangelical church of North America dissolves? Shame on us if we did not do to her what we can! . . . I beg you for Christ's sake take your hands, get quickly together! Counsel not for long! It is important to save immortal souls!

After this call not only many donations came, but also two young men. Adam Ernst (1815–1895), a shoemaker from Baldingen, and Georg Burger (1816–1847), a weaver from Oettingen, were ready to follow this call. For one year they were instructed in the parsonage of Neuendettelsau by Loehe and Heinrich Brandt, the dean of Windsbach district. Finally on July 11, 1842, farewell was given to them during a prayer service in St. Nikolai in Neuendettelsau. This was the beginning of the Neuendettelsau Mission. It began as a personal initiative of this congregation pastor who did not wait for state or church approval. Only later in 1849, the Society for Inner Mission in the Sense of the Lutheran Church (Gesellschaft für Innere Mission im Sinne der lutherischen Kirche) was established, to provide an institutional framework for the missionary work.

Loehe gave instructions to his "emergency helpers" Ernst and Burger. He exhorted them to remain artisans and to earn their own living. They should avoid "all noisy, drumming, overrunning preaching of the Methodists . . . The Lord . . . let you plant and water in peace." He called them "the first swallows that were to proclaim a rich spring." They should go as "emergency helpers" because Loehe could not find academically trained theologians. As teachers and catechists, they should work and hold reading services.

Adam Ernst (1815–1895, left) and Georg Burger (1816–1847, right) were the first "emergency helpers" whom Loehe sent to North America on July 11, 1842. They later turned away from Loehe and joined the Lutheran Church–Missouri Synod. (Archive Mission One World)

The first two emergency helpers began an adventurous journey. On a farmer's wagon they went to Erlangen, then on foot to Gotha, later on a wagon and on foot via Göttingen to Bremen. There they arrived exhausted and with wounded feet. The sea voyage to America was also not very enjoyable. They had to drink undrinkable water and eat inedible meat and sauerkraut with worms. The two men then reached New York and, after several months, came to Ohio, where they attended a Lutheran seminary in Columbus in order to become pastors. Ernst worked as a pastor in the congregation of "New Dettelsau" in Union County, Ohio, and later in other Lutheran congregations in USA and Canada. Burger also worked as a pastor in the Ohio Synod but died only a few years later, in 1847. Both turned away from Loehe and became founding members of the Lutheran Church–Missouri Synod. After them, other young men were trained by Loehe and sent as "emergency helpers" to North America.

Located in Michigan, the city of Frankenmuth was founded in 1845 by immigrants from Franconia with Loehe's support. It is now a tourist attraction with Franconian-Bavarian flair. (Privately owned)

In 1845, a group of emigrants from Neuendettelsau and the surrounding region left their homes under the leadership of Pastor August Friedrich Crämer (1812–1891), who was born in Kleinlangheim (Bavaria). Loehe not only arranged the voyage to America but also provided the emigrants with two bells, a picture, paraments, and a Bible for an altar, and Communion vessels. They went to Michigan, where they built the settlement of Frankenmuth ("Courage of Franconians"). They were sent to start a congregation and do missionary work among native Americans. "Through them, the American Indians should realize with their eyes, how beautiful and good it is with Jesus," Loehe wrote. For the indigenous children a school was built. In 1846, the first Native American children were baptized. In 1847, missionary Eduard Baierlein from Leipzig Mission came to assist Rev. Crämer. Baierlein was called to serve in India in 1853, while Crämer later helped to found the Lutheran Church–Missouri Synod and taught as a professor in Fort Wayne. The colonies of Frankentrost ("Consolation of Franconians") in 1847, Frankenlust ("Joy of Franconians") in 1848, and Frankenhilf ("Help of Franconians") in 1850 were founded. With a "wandering capital" Loehe funded these settlements.

In St. Lorenz Church in Frankenmuth, named after the main church in Nuremberg, a window remembers Wilhelm Loehe. (Privately owned)

In a lecture at the annual general meeting of the Central Missionary Association in 1846, Loehe emphasized the need to "shine the way to eternity with the torch of the eternal gospel for the disappearing Indian tribes." He did not evoke the end of Native American life, but wanted to promote missionary work among them and point to grievances: "You could reach the hearts of Christians, when you remember the debt which Protestants loaded on them by driving those Indians from their homes and act with terrible cruelty against them." He concludes by stating: "I wish that all congregations of the Lutheran confession may realize their task to be missionary congregations for the Indians."

 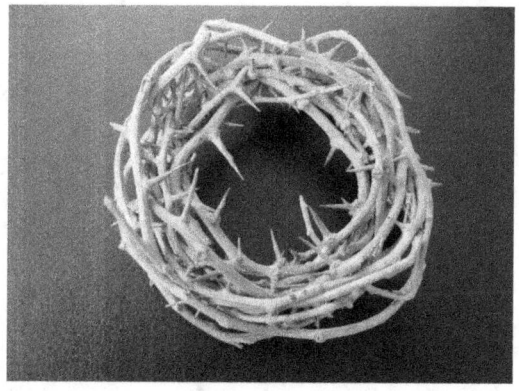

Moritz Bräuninger (1836–1860) was sent to do missionary work among Native Americans and was murdered by them in 1860. In the Loehe Era Museum in Neuendettelsau the woven crown of thorns remembers him as the first martyr of the Neuendettelsau Mission. (Archive Mission One World)

In 1860, the missionary work of the Neuendettelsau missionaries Moritz Bräuninger and Jacob Schmidt among the Upsaroka Native Americans came to a tragic end. Bräuninger, only twenty-three years old, came originally from Saxony and was trained as a carpenter. He was sent to North America in 1858 and started missionary work together with Jakob Schmidt in Montana. On July 23, 1860, he was killed on the Powder River, probably due to misunderstandings and lack of local knowledge. In the Loehe Era Museum in Neuendettelsau a crown of thorns woven by him prior to his departure stands in remembrance of the first martyr of the Neuendettelsau Mission. Loehe wrote in his obituary: "Moritz Bräuninger was destined to be able to offer his life unto the Lord Jesus. The circumstances of his death are of the kind that we can feel happy: our mission is consecrated with martyr's blood. Therefore, our mission will not perish. Far from holding Bräuninger's murder a misfortune, we now believe in a coming blessing for the Indians." His wish was not fulfilled. The Iowa Synod continued missionary work among Native Americans for a while but the situation, due to the suppression and murder of the Native Americans by the whites, became increasingly difficult. During the American Civil War in 1864 several mission stations at Deer Creek were destroyed by Native Americans. In 1866 the Iowa Synod decided to end the mission among Native Americans, which had been so highly encouraged and financially supported by Loehe. Only after Loehe's death the Neuendettelsau Mission resumed classic Gentile mission, namely since 1875 in Australia and since 1886 in New Guinea.

Missionary work in North America became a complicated and very painful matter for Loehe. In 1847, most of his emergency helpers, together with Lutheran immigrants from Saxony, founded the German Lutheran Synod of Missouri, Ohio and Other States, from which the Lutheran Church–Missouri Synod developed. Its theologians considered Loehe even as a heretic and did not agree with his understanding of the ministry.

Rev. Dr. Carl F. Walther (1811–1887) was one of the founders of the Lutheran Church–Missouri Synod in 1847 and became its first president. During his visit to Neuendettelsau in 1851 he could not agree with Loehe on important theological issues, which led to the final break between Loehe and the Missouri Synod. (Archive Mission One World)

In 1839, Dr. Carl Ferdinand Walther (1811–1887), the first president of the Lutheran Church–Missouri Synod, emigrated to North America from Saxony. In 1847, he and a few others founded the Lutheran Church–Missouri Synod. He came in 1851 to Neuendettelsau to clarify theological issues with Loehe. The two could not, however, agree in regard to the questions of ministry, eschatology, and the status of the confessional writings. Loehe understood the ministry not as part of the general priesthood of all believers, but as a special gift of God that is rooted in baptism and by ordination receives its specific dignity. Walther came from Saxony and had suffered long enough under the rule of the church government. He would not tolerate a dominance of the pastor over the congregation. He understood the ministry as part of the general priesthood and ordination as a human act and order. He referred to Martin Luther, who had emphasized the right and power of the congregation to settle, install, and depose pastors. In Walther's opinion, the ordination does not constitute a specific consecration, but is derived from the baptismal service in a congregation.

Another point of dispute was the doctrine of the millennial kingdom and its imminent expectation, which Loehe emphasized but Walther rejected with Article 17 of the Augsburg Confession. Loehe also criticized that, for Walther, the confessional writings are above or at least equal to the Scriptures, while Loehe looked at them as inferior to the Bible. Without an agreement, Walther returned to America in 1851. When Loehe opened a school teachers college in 1852 in Saginaw, Michigan, he initially did not want to pass its control to the Missouri Synod, thus he renounced the cooperation causing the final break in 1853. Even Rev. Wynecken, who had initiated Loehe's mission to America, joined the Missouri Synod and later became its second president.

The graduates of the Neuendettelsau Mission Seminary Georg Grossmann (1823–1897), Johannes Deindörfer (1828–1907), Dr. Sigmund Fritschel (1833–1900), and Gottfried Fritschel (1836–1889) were the founders and senior officers of the Iowa Synod. (Archive Mission One World)

A few followers of Loehe under the leadership of Georg Grossmann, Johannes Deindörfer, Sigmund Fritschel, and Michael Schüller founded the German Evangelical Lutheran Synod of Iowa and Other States on August 28, 1854 in the parsonage of St. Sebald by the Spring (St. Sebald am Quell), Iowa. By 1872 the episcopal oriented synod comprised more than 13,000 members. In 1853, Wartburg Theological Seminary was founded. It was located first in Dubuque, Iowa, until 1857, then from 1857 to 1868 in St. Sebald by the Spring, from 1868 to 1889 in Mendota, Illinois, and since 1889 again in Dubuque, Iowa. The seminary started in the Emerson Mansion and in 1916 a new seminary building was erected resembling the Wartburg castle near Eisenach, Germany, which has retained its appearance until today. Led by Grossmann until 1868, the teachers' college in Saginaw later moved to several locations. Since 1935 it has been located in Waverly, Iowa, and carries the name Wartburg College. In 1930, the Iowa Synod became part of the American Lutheran Church, which in 1988 joined the newly formed Evangelical Lutheran Church in America (ELCA).

Loehe admonished the expatriate Germans insistently not to give up their German Lutheranism, as in his "Call from Home to the German Lutheran Church of North America" (1845):

> You are Germans! You brought a beautiful language over the ocean. In the confusion of languages there is none more beautiful. Keep what you have. You have, by God's grace, the good part. Do not mix up your language with the language of the English; it is only a bad exchange. Who exchanges wealth for poverty, good sound for evil sound, and figure for shadow? . . . Your language is next to your church your greatest treasure; you have taken it across to the deserts of your forests. . . . With your language you lose your history with the simple understanding of the Reformation, also your beautiful German Bible, your hymns that sound up to the sky, your incomparable catechisms, your books of devotion, and your liturgies. Surrender neither you nor your children to foreign nations! May the German language live and reign in your houses, in your villages, in your cities, in your schools, in your churches, in your synods. May you not be punished for your despise of the German language. For truly a German who is not German, is a cursed man on earth, because all the privileges that God gave him among the nations are stolen–and will be refunded with nothing.

For Loehe, Lutheran confession and German language belong closely together. It was only much later that the Lutheran confessional writings were translated into English. Some of Loehe's students withdrew from their synods when the local majority wanted to introduce English in schools and churches.

Loehe did not want to send missionaries and did not speak of "missioners" but of "emergency helpers." He supported these "emergency helpers" during the time of preparation, departure, and the start of their work. He did not send them explicitly but held a simple farewell ceremony including the celebration of Holy Communion. An ordination was out of sight for him. He only wanted to provide the congregations in America with theologically trained men. Because mission is the task of all congregation members, missionaries can only be ordained and sent by them. Loehe had initially assigned missionary work to the general priesthood; however, from 1849 on he assigned missionaries to the ministry and understood them as "wandering presbyters."

Wilhelm Loehe recommended in 1848 to assemble the "like-minded" in a society:

> Although we are not friends of associations, because we look at it as a sign and testimony that the church, in whose sphere they were needed, is not what and how it should be. . . . Because this is the case, however, the church compels us to convene provisionally in circles and associations, until it becomes again the association of associations, and all associations are amalgamated in it.

Discipline and sacrifice should be practiced based on the catechism of apostolic life in a missionary society. In the revolution of 1848 Loehe saw the chance for the Protestant church to become independent of the state system. Therefore, he wrote the "Proposal for a Lutheran Association for Apostolic Life" and added the "Draft Catechism of Apostolic Life." Although his proposal was welcomed by many, an association was not founded immediately.

On September 12, 1849 the Society for Inner Mission in the Sense of the Lutheran Church (Gesellschaft für Innere Mission im Sinne der lutherischen Kirche) was finally established in Gunzenhausen, which was then formally constituted on October 8, 1849. The Society celebrated its first annual festival in 1850 in Nuremberg, later in Aha near Gunzenhausen, and then mainly in Gunzenhausen, traditionally held on the second

Wednesday in July, often associated with the sending of missionaries or the installation of coworkers at home. After the First World War "women and virgins" could also become members.

Since 1888, the Society has borne the extended name Society for Inner and Outer Mission in the Sense of the Lutheran Church (Gesellschaft für Innere und Äussere Mission im Sinne der lutherischen Kirche). In its best time over one thousand members belonged to the Society, among them important personalities of the Bavarian church. Currently faith seminars, retreats, Bible weeks, and lectures are offered. By the project for baptismal catechesis "Tripp Trapp" young parents are taught the Christian education of their children. Since the establishment of the Loehe Archive the Society is also active in the research on Loehe. The Free Mouth Publishing House also belonged to the Society and edited the collected works of Loehe in twelve volumes, as well as evangelistic writings, Christian fiction, etc.

The current statute formulates as follows:

> The Society is committed in all its work to the Holy Scriptures and the Lutheran confessions. It advocates for continuous and repentant examination of the life and character of the church in relationship to Scripture and the confessions. For this purpose, it seeks connection, exchange, and cooperation with such forces around the world which stand up for the pure gospel.

According to Loehe the church must be the vehicle of mission. Inner and outer mission, home and foreign mission belong together, even prioritizing mission among Christians. In America he wanted to create the counter-model to the state churches in Germany, namely, a free apostolic episcopal church of the brethren with priesthood, diaconate, and congregation. It should as soon as possible go its own way and be dedicated to the mission among the Native Americans and expatriates. It should serve as a model for the universal Lutheran church, which should form the core of a global church. He had in view the catholicity of the church. If the church turns to its inner calling, the outer mission develops automatically. The conversion of the individual is not the goal of mission, rather, the goal is his or her inclusion in the body of the church. With this perspective, Loehe became a pioneer of the ecumenical movement and the integration of church and mission, which was then realized in the twentieth century.

Wartburg Theological Seminary 1853-1854

The first home of Wartburg Theological Seminary was in rented rooms in a building on Garfield Avenue in Dubuque, Iowa. The first class was held here on 10 November 1853.

The first Wartburg Theological Seminary was located in rented premises in Dubuque, Iowa. Here in 1853 the first classes were held. (Wartburg Theological Seminary Archives, Dubuque, Iowa)

On October 17, 1866, Loehe celebrated "the twenty-fifth anniversary of our missionary work for North America mostly among fellow believers." The Iowa Synod was represented by Professor Sigmund Fritschel from Wartburg Theology Seminary. He came along with about a hundred coworkers, pastors, and mission friends, mostly from the vicinity. In his homily Loehe emphasized that there is no reason for pride and arrogance, rather for humility, sadness, and gratitude. Under the motto "failure and success," he drew his résumé after twenty-five years of working in America. In the work with emigrants many plans could not be put into effect and caused great disappointments, particularly the separation from the Missouri Synod. Loehe regretted the "termination of the ecclesial communion from the side of the Missouri Synod which had grown up with our help." The colonies were alienated from their founder by the opinion that he was a heretic. The plan to settle a part of Michigan entirely with Franconians and to found a new kind of Franconia there had failed. He also raised the question of the "theodicy of mission":

> One may dare to say, the whole history of the kingdom of God is an ongoing failure, accompanied by only a partial success. God's mercy goes forward under obstacles, which not only delay his progress, but also touch the heart of the eternal Father himself. God grieves over his own failure. Jesus weeps over Jerusalem. . . . Besides much failure, which causes humility, we still have quite a lot to thank. . . . We have been able to help the colonies to a certain extent to earthly wellbeing and to a thriving church existence. . . . Although the Missouri Synod has become at odds against us, it was not made without us, even if one does not think of it! The Missourians certainly have our applause for the things that characterize them, but not our admiration, and we are pleased there is a synod of Missouri. . . . It is better governed than any state churches in Germany.

Loehe wanted to keep up the communion fellowship with the Missourians after it had been denounced by them. His achievement is to be seen in the fact that communion is important to them. The love of the Lord's Supper was enough motivation to continue the work, even without visible success. Although the Missouri Synod has denounced the communion fellowship with Loehe, it yet celebrates Holy Communion in its congregations on a regular basis and with a perfect understanding of the sacrament, even without visible unity. Thirteen years after the separation Loehe spoke mainly of the Missourians and not of the Iowa Synod, whose representative was present at the celebration. Most human and financial resources had come to the Missouri Synod, and the separation hurt Loehe personally.

Since the 1840s Loehe and his friends fought for the enforcement of the Lutheran character of the Bavarian church. They finally achieved in 1854 the separation of Lutheran, Union, and Reformed congregations. In an audience with King Maximilian in 1853, after lengthy negotiations, it was allowed that the Central Protestant Missionary Association was renamed the Evangelical Lutheran Central Missionary Association. The decisive factor was the influence of the president of the Supreme Protestant Consistory, Adolf von Harless, who had already, as a court preacher in Dresden, worked for the Lutheran orientation of the Leipzig Mission.

The Central Missionary Association exists to this day under the name Evangelical Lutheran Central Association for Foreign Mission (Evangelisch-Lutherischer Zentralverband für Äussere Mission) and is associated with the mission center in Neuendettelsau. In 1911, it received the status of a public corporation which it holds to this day.

Loehe kept contact with the Central Missionary Association, which was initially connected to the Dresden and Leipzig Missions. Later the Central Missionary Association supported in particular the missionary work among Native Americans, which was initiated by Loehe. The Neuendettelsau Mission was probably less dependent on the financial support of the Central Missionary Association, because it achieved significant income from the sale of its journal *Church Communications from and about North America* (*Kirchliche Mittheilungen aus und über Nord-Amerika*) and from donations.

The Basel Mission regretted the strengthening of Lutheran confessionalism in Bavaria and the foundation of its own missionary societies. Although the missionary movement in Bavaria had its origin in the Basel Mission, donations for the Basel Mission diminished in favor of the Neuendettelsau and Leipzig Missions. In the beginning, Loehe and Harless had demanded that the Basel Mission join the Lutheran church, but this was rejected for obvious reasons. Rather, the Basel Mission argued that the confessional differences must step back in the proclamation of the gospel among the Gentiles. Its director, Ludwig Hoffmann, emphasized in 1842 that it is important for the teaching of the seminarians to help them love "not Luther, Calvin, Zwingli, but always Christ." The Basel Mission "has high respect for the religious peculiarities, but it considers them irrelevant to the Gentile world." Thus, the Basel Mission henceforth played a minor role in Bavaria.

Loehe could not, in the long run, manage the training of theologians in addition to his work in the parish, although he was supported by pastors in his neighborhood. He also did not want to perform a complete training, but merely to provide feeder services for the Lutheran seminary in Fort Wayne. In 1844, he proposed to transfer the training to Nuremberg. Here, Friedrich Bauer came to his help.

Friedrich Bauer: Loehe's Closest Friend and Coworker

Friedrich Bauer (1812–1874) founded in 1846 the Mission Preparation Institute for North America (Missionsvorbereitungsanstalt für Nordamerika) in Nuremberg on Loehe's suggestion which was transferred in 1853 to Neuendettelsau. The missionary work owes to him its institutional framework, without which the present mission center would not exist. Bauer also wrote the first German school grammar that was widely circulated in Germany and Austria and was continued by Konrad Duden after his death. (Archive Mission One World)

Marcus Friedrich Bauer was born on June 14, 1812 in Nuremberg. His father was a teacher and died early in 1819. Bauer attended the same grammar school (gymnasium) as Loehe in Nuremberg and began to study theology in Erlangen and Halle in 1830. There he was influenced primarily by Lutheran professors like August Tholuck (1799–1877) and Adolf von Harless (1806–1879). After his ordination, he served as a preacher and pastor at the Sebastian Hospital as well as a vicar at St. Egidien in Nuremberg. Then he taught since 1838 as a catechist and teacher of the German language at the trade school (Kreislandwirtschafts und Gewerbeschule) in Nuremberg, which was moved to Triesdorf near Ansbach in 1931. He was dragged into the conflict between rationalism, liberalism, and Lutheran confessionalism. The dean of Nuremberg district, Rev. Karl Fikenscher, wrote in a report in 1839 that "the candidate Bauer joined the strictest fraction of Lutheranism . . . and with his comrades shares the conviction that the present constitutional and confessional status of the Lutheran church is so unbearable that one must doubt, if there were a Lutheran church in Bavaria." This meant that Bauer could not expect to become a pastor in the church. He was later even forced to give up his teaching at the trade school.

In 1850, Bauer published a grammar textbook under the title *Principles of High German Grammar for the Lower and Middle Classes of Higher Educational Institutions* (*Grundzüge der neuhochdeutschen Grammatik für die unteren und mittleren Klassen höherer Bildungsanstalten*), which he improved constantly. He never held a degree in German literature or linguistics, but he was interested in language and linguistic history and driven by the love for the youth. This grammar textbook reached until 1912 a total of forty-nine editions, which was then published after Bauer's death by Konrad Duden, the famous reformer of German spelling. The textbook had decisive influence on the mother tongue grammar teaching in Germany and contributed with the linguistic unification to the political unity of Germany. For the empire of Austria-Hungary, a separate Catholic edition was published in which the quotations from the Luther Bible were replaced by quotations from the Catholic Bible translations. In 1859, Bauer added an "etymology auxiliary book" (Etymologie-Hilfsbuch) for teachers.

Bauer joined Loehe in 1841 in connection with the newly started tracts association. On Loehe's initiative, he founded in 1846 the Mission Preparation Institute for Fort Wayne (later: for North America) (Missionsvorbereitungsanstalt für Fort Wayne (later: für Nord-Amerika) as a private enterprise at the Obstmarkt, later in the Tetzelgasse in Nuremberg. Here young men could be prepared for the Concordia Theological Seminary in Fort Wayne, Indiana. After the break with the Missouri Synod in 1853, it was no longer possible to send graduates to the seminary in Fort Wayne. Therefore, and for reasons of cost, in 1853 Bauer moved the Mission Preparation Institute to Neuendettelsau and built it into an independent mission training institute with three years of training. But Bauer could take up teaching only after several months of illness. At first Bauer taught part time. After retiring as a teacher at the trade school in Nuremberg, he was paid by the newly founded Society for Inner Mission. The mission training institute became the theological, spiritual, and organizational center of the missionary work, which existed under the name Mission and Diaspora Seminary until 1985.

Bauer was originally pietistically oriented and then, like Loehe, went into the Lutheran confessional direction. "Teaching was his life, his desire, and his ambition." (Koller) He edited the dogmatics of the orthodox Lutheran theologian Nikolaus Hunnius (1585–1643). This work also served as the basis for his lectures on dogmatics and ethics, which were copied by his students and used as textbooks. They were later extended by Loehe's successors Johannes and Martin Deinzer. The dogmatics was prepared for printing by Bauer's nephew Otto Küffner and published in 1921 under the title *Christian Dogmatics on the Lutheran Foundation (Christliche Dogmatik auf lutherischer Grundlage)*. In 1904,

Bauer's *Christian Ethics on the Lutheran Foundation* (*Christliche Ethik auf lutherischer Grundlage*) appeared in print.

In his teaching Bauer followed the theological goals of his mentor Wilhelm Loehe, which Christian Weber summarizes as follows: "Presently God's plan comes to its fulfillment as the churches come to their global unity. Here, the Lutheran confession as a unifying center and North America as a free country play an important role. As Bauer is committed to mission training, he always has in mind this vision of unity." Focus on the confession and vision of the idea of unity mark his educational concept.

In 1854, Friedrich Bauer bought the Upper Inn in Neuendettelsau and started, at his own expense, the Mission Preparation Institute. In front of the house his three children, Magdalena, Friedrich, and Gottlieb, can be seen. (Archive Mission One World)

Bauer led the Mission Institute from 1846 until his death in 1874. His title was first catechist, then later inspector of the Mission Institute. After the inn Sun (Sonne) had functioned first as a transition place, Bauer bought in 1853 from his own resources the Upper Inn (Obere Wirtschaft) in Neuendettelsau. When Bauer held the service in St. Nikolai church, people said: "Today the Upper Inn keeper was preaching." The operation of the inn was going on for some time in the dining room where the mission pupils were eating. The former dance hall on the first floor Bauer used as a teaching and study room. Bauer lived with his family under one roof with his pupils, who slept under the roof on straw mattresses. In

1865, Bauer renounced the lease with the Society for Inner Mission and prompted them to buy his house.

Between him and Loehe, with regard to the seminary building, profound conceptual differences developed. While Loehe soon built a stately mother house for the deaconesses, he was of the opinion that for the mission "the principle of poverty and the restriction on the essentials should prevail" and that "mission pupils should be scattered in the farmhouses as formerly." Bauer said that under these conditions he could no longer work, because he saw his life's work endangered, and rebelled against Loehe. This rebellion against the "father friend" almost tore Bauer's heart. At the same time, he won self-confidence and eventually reached the point that the Society for Inner Mission not only bought the building of the Upper Inn from him, but also in 1867 a new building was erected. Bauer experienced this achievement as a turning point in his life: "I was amazed and had to wonder that God allowed, after so long and severe misfortune, the sun to shine on me and surpassed himself truly in kindness." In 1867, the new building was inaugurated. At the building's entrance was written the word of the Bible from Ezekiel 34:16: "I will seek what was lost and I will bring back the strayed." Later the Society for Inner Mission bought also the adjoining buildings, and an extension was added.

In 1867, the new building for the Mission Institute for North America was inaugurated. The inscription quotes, as a motto for the missionary work, Ezekiel 34:16: "I will seek what was lost and I will bring back the strayed." Friedrich and Dorothea stand near the entrance on the right. (Archive Mission One World)

Hans Rössler describes in detail the relationship between Bauer and Loehe: "Bauer's life work was the Mission Institute, his life's subject the relationship with Loehe." He called Loehe his "beloved friend and brother." He was stricter than Loehe and practiced the "authority of an edgy but warm personality." Bauer saw himself as Loehe's "shield-bearer," i.e., squire of a higher lord, or deacon, i.e., assistant pastor.

In the seminary, a simple life and a strict order were predominant. In the summer at 5 a.m. and in the winter at 5.30 a.m. the seminarians were awakened with the call: "Brethren, get up in God's name." Washing was followed by a half-hour of silence and an hour of work until 7 o'clock. Subsequently, bed making, morning prayer, and breakfast followed. From 8 to 12 and 3 to 6 o'clock classes were held, then vespers and dinner. At 10 p.m. bedtime began. On Sundays the seminarians had their place in St. Nikolai Church near the organ and served as sacristans and offering collectors. At 2 o'clock they attended the Christian doctrine teaching and were then allowed upon approval of the inspector to take a walk. At 6 o'clock was vespers, followed by an evening stroll. Before the examinations, there was a three months time of repetition.

A house and life order, which was first formulated in 1861, laid down strict rules: The noon and evening walks are to be made in groups. The correspondence is under the supervision of the inspector. No letter or package may be received or mailed but by the hand of the inspector. A weekly visitation of the inspector takes place in all these respects. Pupils are not allowed to have a relationship to women, neither personally nor by letter, as long as they are in the institute. If it happens nonetheless, the student is to expect that he is instructed to leave the institute. The elders (Riegenmeister) are appointed by the inspector to watch over the discipline.

Life was determined by a monastic character, which at that time probably was also found elsewhere. Perhaps the strict rules about relationship to women were linked to the fact that Bauer himself got married only at the age of forty-two and Martin Deinzer at the age of thirty-eight. They therefore thought that the pupils had to take time until their marriage. These were not allowed to attend the worship of the deaconesses, not even visit the area of the Institute of Deaconesses, except for performing business matters. They should not be distracted from their studies by the numerous "womenfolk."

Upon entering the seminary, the young men had to be at least seventeen years old. They came mainly from the Bavarian church, some also from other Lutheran churches. They did not only have to pay school fees, but if possible also for their travel to America. The training initially lasted three years and was later extended to seven years. The students were taught Greek, Hebrew, and Latin, the theological disciplines, German grammar, handwriting, and music. Loehe withdrew more and more from the seminary, especially after the establishment of the Institute of Deaconesses in 1854. But every Wednesday evening he invited the pupils to his house and gave lectures on practical issues, such as church building, choice of bride and engagement, marriage, and church discipline. Also, he remained the examination commissioner until his death.

Friedrich Bauer (with a black cap) sits in the middle of teachers and students of the Mission Seminary. On his right sits his successor Johannes Deinzer. (Privately owned)

Bauer's talent was to put the training of the mission students on a systematic and pedagogically sound basis. While Loehe in his early years acted spontaneously, unsystematically, and corresponding to the situation, Bauer attached to each subject a textbook, designed a curriculum and syllabi, and placed special emphasis on self-education and the mutual shaping by the spiritually oriented community of the students. "All education is education for freedom. The road to freedom is the free obedience. The one, who cannot obey, is not a man. The missionary must be educated, not only taught. No saint falls from the sky."

In 1858, the Concordia was founded as an association of pupils. It met every Sunday evening for Bible reading, singing, and prayer. Since 1859, the so-called academy evenings were held under the direction of the inspector. In 1873, both institutions were combined. Their purpose was to promote the free lecture. Since 1914, the Concordia published a quarterly under the editorship of Adam Schuster, which was continued by his son Wilhelm up to 1995.

Bauer's successor, Johannes Deinzer, summarized the significance of his teacher as follows: "Bauer was the second founder of the missionary work which through him received its stronger organization and development." Stadler added: "Friedrich Bauer was actually the leading figure of the Neuendettelsau Mission Seminary. Wilhelm Loehe was the initiator; Friedrich Bauer managed to realize it. Without the many talents of Bauer, the Mission Institute would not have come into existence. Against Loehe's will, who wanted to keep the loose form of preparation and life community with the teachers, Bauer worked for a solid institution."

Since 1854, Bauer was responsible for the cooperation with the Iowa Synod. He acted as a contact person for his former students in organizational and financial issues, as a theological advisor, counselor, and mediator in church conflicts. There was a lively correspondence between Neuendettelsau and USA. From 1869 on he took over the sole responsibility for the publication of the journal *Church Communications from and about North America*. After Loehe's death in 1872, he headed, on an interim basis for a few months, the Institute of Deaconesses until a new rector was elected.

A few months before his death, Bauer wrote a memorandum to the pastors of the Iowa Synod: "We supported you with material resources and spiritual power, working with you in great peace and with great joy, and being happy over the visible blessing that God put on our common endeavor. Here and there our relationship was disturbed, but love could heal it, and the harmony was subsequently always more cordial than before."

Bauer strongly criticized the Missouri Synod, which equated the Lutheran confession to Scripture or even put it over it. Rather, he explained his position as a "biblical Lutheran." He implored his former pupils not to desert to the Missourians and hold on to biblical Lutheranism, which he had taught them in the seminary. "The memorandum and cover letter were a theological testament, which he wrote in the consciousness of failure." (Liebenberg)

In 1854, Bauer married Julie Dorothea, née Wach, who died in 1897. Three children survived infancy. Bauer died during a recovery stay in Rothenburg on the Tauber from the effects of pneumonia on December 13, 1874 at the age of sixty-two. His funeral took place with great participation of the population on December 16. The memorial address was given by the local pastor, Dr. Ferdinand Weber, who had previously taught as a teacher at the Mission Institute. Bauer was buried right next to Loehe, as his closest companion. His life and work is summarized on his grave stone in the words of Jesus from Matthew 13:52: "A scribe trained for the kingdom of heaven."

Bauer's successor, Johannes Deinzer, rightly described the achievements of Loehe and Bauer and their relationship to each other as follows:

> As two stars which walk in neighborly tracks, although shine clearly different from each other, nevertheless walk side by side and share their light, the names of the two men now appear united in the promised sparkle of the teachers, who during their lives stood so close to each other to a certain extent and also complemented one another.

During the celebration of Bauer's hundredth birthday—one year too late—on June 14, 1913, the mother superior of the Deaconess Institute, Therese Stählin, confessed "our sins against this pious man who always stood in the shade of Loehe and nevertheless was a star himself in the heavenly church. It is strange that sometimes we realize the heart of one's life only after the life has ended."

Until Bauer's death, 190 graduates of the Mission Seminary were sent overseas for service. Ninety-three went since 1854 to the Iowa Synod. Among them were Bauer's son Friedrich Wilhelm (1858–1939) and Johann Michael Reu (1869–1943), who taught for forty-three years at Wartburg Theological Seminary. He became well known through his numerous publications about the Bible, liturgics, homiletics, and also dogmatics. The theological faculty of Erlangen University in 1910 conferred on him an honorary doctor's degree. The last of altogether 327 seminarians were sent to USA in 1925. They often held close contact to Neuendettelsau and motivated their congregations to support the Neuendettelsau Mission in the time during and after the First World War. They also decisively contributed to the forming of the two biggest Lutheran churches in

America, the Evangelical Lutheran Church in America (ELCA) and the Lutheran Church–Missouri Synod (LCMS).

Although Wilhelm Loehe and Friedrich Bauer never visited North America, they had great influence on the development of Lutheranism in the USA. They not only sent missionary personnel, but also gave theological advice to the founders of the Lutheran churches by sending them literature about the Lutheran faith and liturgy. The Lutheran churches in America later thanked the Neuendettelsau Mission by giving help in difficult times. They supported it during and after the First World War, especially by enabling Neuendettelsau missionaries to continue work in New Guinea. ELCA still supports mission work in Papua New Guinea with personnel and money.

Consolidation and Crisis of the Neuendettelsau Mission: 1875–1933

Friedrich Bauer was succeeded by mission inspector Johannes Deinzer (1842–1897) in 1875. He had previously worked as Loehe's vicar and regarded him as his spiritual father. Since 1864 he taught at the Mission Seminary and since 1870 he acted as its vice-principal. He wrote an extensive biography about Loehe.

Rev. Johannes Deinzer (1842–1897) served as successor of Friedrich Bauer from 1875 until his untimely death in 1897. Under his leadership the Neuendettelsau Mission sent the first missionaries to Australia and New Guinea. (Archive Mission One World)

Under Deinzer the work of the Neuendettelsau Mission expanded. It followed the trails of German emigrants to Australia. It must not be narrowed down to diaspora work, because already the sending to North America included the commission for the mission among the Native Americans. This particularly applies to Australia, where Deinzer in 1875 sent the first missionaries to the Immanuel Synod. They should not only work among the expatriate Germans, but also among the indigenous Aborigines. Among the missioners was also a native of Buchhof, near Nuremberg: the young seminarian Johann Flierl (1858–1947), who went to Australia in 1878 and then in 1886 to New Guinea. Deinzer also continued cooperation with the Iowa Synod by sending graduates of the Mission Seminary. He travelled to North America in 1879, where he took part in the twenty-fifth anniversary of the Iowa Synod. It had meanwhile developed from modest beginnings into a sizeable church with 136 pastors, 230 congregations, and 25,000 members. From 1886 on, Deinzer began to train missionary staff for the Hersbruck Mission working in East Africa.

The city of Hersbruck near Nuremberg played an important role in the history of the Bavarian mission. Here on January 25, 1886, the pastor in Reichenschwand, Matthias Ittameier (1847–1939), founded the Society for Evangelical Lutheran Mission in East Africa (Gesellschaft für evangelisch-lutherische Mission in Ostafrika), which was abbreviated as the Hersbruck Mission. Already since 1829 there was a local Bible society and, since 1843, a district missionary association, whose members often were connected to Loehe. Rev. Ittameier was born in Neuendettelsau, later edited the *Nuremberg Mission Journal*, and wrote in 1881 a memorandum addressed to the Evangelical Lutheran Central Missionary Association and to the Leipzig Mission. He proposed to begin missionary work in present-day Kenya near Mombasa, following the footprints of Dr. Ludwig Krapf. He had heard the news about Krapf's death, who had come from Württemberg and went in the service of the British Church Missionary Society to East Africa. Together with Johann Rebmann, he was the first European to view the Kilimanjaro. The Central Missionary Association as well as the Leipzig Mission refused to take over the missionary work in East Africa, especially because of financial reasons. Therefore, Ittameier took the initiative and began with missionary work among the Wakamba in the south of present-day Kenya. In this he followed Krapf's missionary principles: Contrary to other missionary organizations, he did not want to start with the foundation of schools, churches, and a church organization. Rather, the converts should remain totally in their families.

Ittameier got the personnel for his missionary endeavor from the Neuendettelsau Mission Institute. He signed a contract with Johannes Deinzer about the training and sending of missionaries. Altogether there were eleven. The work among the Wakamba was for various reasons not very successful mainly because of diseases, difficulties with the British colonial administration, lack of interest among the Wakamba, and hostility from the Muslims. Also, the area was finally annexed to the British colony of Kenya in connection with the Helgoland Zanzibar Treaty of 1890. So the association dissolved on December 12, 1892 and handed over the work to the Leipzig Mission, although the latter had initially criticized the establishment of the Hersbruck Mission. It probably played a role that the Leipzig Mission had recently decided on a new work in the Kilimanjaro region. After the First World War the work among the Wakamba was abandoned by the Leipzig Mission.

Johannes Deinzer revised Bauer's dogmatics and ethics, which formed the basis for teaching at the seminary. His dogmatics "moves between Lutheran orthodoxy and Pietism in line with the Lutheran renewal movement as shaped by Loehe." (Stadler) It was directed against the Missourians and against critical rationalism. The seminary put ethics into practice with emphasis on voluntary self-education within the fellowship of students. The *Church Communications from and about North America* wrote in the obituary of Deinzer: His "teaching . . . was edifying, and a sensitive person took from the lessons something for his heart and life. He was not only a teacher, but at the same time, a pastor and caretaker of his students."

Johannes Deinzer died in 1897 at the age of only fifty-five. His work was continued by his brother Rev. Martin Deinzer (1850–1917) who headed the Mission Institute from 1897 to 1917. In 1912, he was appointed mission director. His deputy, Rev. Karl Steck (1879–1952), who taught at the seminary since 1909, received the title of mission inspector. Deinzer continued the work of his brother in revising the dogmatics and ethics of Bauer.

Under his leadership, the cooperation of the Mission Institute with the Lutheran church in Brazil began. On October 31, 1897, Rev. Otto Kuhr (1864–1938) was sent in Rothenburg on the Tauber as the first Bavarian pastor to Brazil. This was the result of cooperation with the Bavarian Lutheran Treasury of God. As a nephew of the chairman of the Society for Inner and Outer Mission and chairman of the Lutheran Treasury of God Rev. Eduard Stirner, Otto Kuhr had attended the Neuendettelsau Mission

Seminary and worked for several years in Lutheran congregations in the USA. His final commitment consisted of two words: "I go." He was sent as a preacher to decidedly Lutheran congregations in the German settlements. In his official instruction it was determined that he had to "keep clear of any peace-endangering opposition" and should work "only in places where other Protestant churches have not taken root." He should "gather our coreligionists in Lutheran congregations . . . and . . . ensure that their Evangelical Lutheran confession is beyond all doubt." The model for his work was the Iowa Synod, founded by students of Loehe.

During a festive service on the occasion of the hundredth anniversary of the first sending on November 22, 1997, Bishop Hermann von Loewenich revealed a commemorative plaque in the Rothenburg St. Jacob's church, where the motto is to be read for the service of Otto Kuhr: "Strengthen your brothers" (Luke 22:32).

In 1897, the Neuendettelsau seminarian Rev. Otto Kuhr (1864–1938) was sent as the first Bavarian pastor by the Lutheran Treasury of God (now Martin Luther Association) to Brazil. There he founded the Lutheran synod, which he headed from 1905 to 1923. (Archive Mission One World)

The Lutheran Treasury of God in Bavaria for Beleaguered Coreligionists (Lutherischer Gotteskasten in Bayern für bedrängte Glaubensgenossen) had been established in Hersbruck near Nuremberg on August 29, 1860 after a similar organization already existed in Hanover since 1853. The foundation in Hersbruck was linked to conflicts with the civil and ecclesiastical authorities, since they obviously suspected subversive activities. Also, it was feared that just by its name it could lead to a "disturbance of religious peace" between the confessions. When the association finally received approval, it was decreed that it would not publicly collect money but simply "within the association and the circle of friends" in order to avoid competition with the Gustavus Adolphus Foundation, directed to all Protestants.

The purpose of the association as described in the statute applies to this day, namely: "to support the Lutheran coreligionists inside and outside Bavaria in their religious distress living in diaspora." Thus it initially supported the training of pastors for Lutheran churches in the European diaspora. From 1880 it published the paper *The Lutheran Treasury of God* (*Der Lutherische Gotteskasten*), which reached some long runs. The Bavarian Treasury of God was renamed in 1932 as the Martin Luther Association in Bavaria (Martin-Luther-Verein in Bayern). The chairman at that time was mission director Dr. Friedrich Eppelein

The Neuendettelsau Mission Institute reached an agreement with the Lutheran Treasury of God to train pastors for Brazil. It committed itself "to make its graduates available for Brazil without any compensation for the cost of training." A total of 140 graduates of Neuendettelsau Mission Seminary were sent to Brazil, who contributed decisively to the growth of today's Evangelical Church of the Lutheran Confession in Brazil (IECLB).

Rev. Martin Deinzer (1850–1917) followed his brother Johannes in 1897 as director of the Mission Institute. He extended its work and began the training of pastors for Brazil. With him the period of theologians who were still directly influenced by Loehe and Bauer ended. (Archive Mission One World)

Martin Deinzer strictly applied the paragraphs concerning engagement within the rules of the seminary. When pupils' relationships with girls came to light, they were immediately dismissed, even if they were already in the last semester of their training. "Because of premature engagement four students had to be dismissed," it says in an annual report. They have "forgotten that it is sacred ground on which they have placed themselves." An engagement could be made only after the commissioning service, but then there was only a few weeks time.

Gradually the Mission Institute expanded by purchasing neighboring plots. In 1903, the boarding house was built to make room for the growing number of seminarians. The debt could be repaid with the proportion of the National Donation for Christian Missions in our Colonies and Dependencies, which was collected all over Germany on the occasion of the twenty-fifth jubilee of Emperor Wilhelm II in 1913. It provided the Protestant missions the surprisingly high amount of 3.2 million Reich marks, out of which Neuendettelsau received almost 150,000. This was considerably more than was collected among the Bavarian Protestants for this national donation, because it was distributed according to the number of employees, schools, and students in the colonies. Rev. Rudolf Ruf thanked the emperor on behalf of the sick director Deinzer for this gift and concluded by writing: "God bless our mission and also give us the ability to provide through loyalty and strengthening of the kingdom of God among the natives of New Guinea many subjects of Your Majesty in this land who will stand together in faithful loving prayer for Your Majesty's wellbeing and blessed government."

From the remainder of the funds of this donation, the German Protestant Mission Publication Company (Deutsche Evangelische Missions-Hilfe) was founded in 1913 under the patronage of the Emperor.

In the same year, the mission ship *Bavaria* in Rabaul ran from the stack, which was used in New Guinea. From this developed the church owned company Lutheran Shipping, which provided the only regular connections to many places on the coast.

The First World Missionary Conference in Edinburgh in 1910 was attended by Rev. Otto Küffner, a nephew of Bauer and former teacher at the Mission Seminary, and Rev. Gottfried Seiler from Feucht. On behalf of the Leipzig Mission, inspector Karl Steck also attended. Rev. Küffner reported on the conference at the annual mission festival in Gunzenhausen. To prepare for the conference, questionnaires were sent to all missionary organizations. The Neuendettelsau Mission reported on the number of employees, missionaries, baptized Christians, etc. The conference was marked by the secretary of the World Student Conference, Dr. John Mott. Only a dozen women were official delegates. The Roman Catholic Church was not invited. The activities in Latin America were excluded; the focus was on Africa and Asia. Representatives of the so-called young churches could also speak. At the end of the conference, two messages were adopted: "To the Members of the Church in Christian Countries" and "To the Members of the Christian Church in non-Christian Countries." They also highlighted the need that "our national life be christianized as a whole. Inner and outer mission must therefore go hand in hand." As the goal of all missionary efforts, the "conquest of the world for the gospel" was formulated. John Mott said that now the time has come for the evangelization of the world. A "standing committee" was installed, which should coordinate further work. The work was, however, stopped little later by the erupting of the First World War. It was only in 1921 that the International Missionary Council was established. This council paved the way for the founding assembly of the World Council of Churches in Amsterdam in 1948, where John Mott took part as honorary president. Thus, today's ecumenical movement is based on the missionary movement which had the unity of the churches as its goal.

At the First World Missionary Conference in Edinburgh in 1910 three delegates from Bavaria participated. (Schreiber, *Edinburger Welt-Missions-Konferenz*, 1)

Martin Deinzer held close contact with the Iowa Synod, and for its fiftieth jubilee he travelled to America in 1904. Because of his poor health he could not visit New Guinea but sent mission inspector Karl Steck in 1913. During his last years Martin Deinzer could perform only partly his duties. He was married to Magda, a daughter of Friedrich Bauer, and had no children. With his death in 1917 ended the period of theological teachers who were still personally influenced by Wilhelm Loehe and Friedrich Bauer.

The First World War brought a drastic break in mission. The overseas connections were cut off. The Mission Seminary was closed in August 1914 and twenty-six seminarians had to go to war. On August 13, 1914 Johann Schneider was the first to be killed; he was followed by twelve other seminarians. In 1920, a cross was erected for the seminarians killed in action on the mission compound with the inscription: "For those whom God took early from his vineyard." Later, the names of those killed and missing in the Second World War were added. The cross with the names is now in the garden of the House Luther Rose in Neuendettelsau.

The Anglo-Australian troops captured New Guinea in the fall of 1914. The Neuendettelsau missionaries had to swear the so-called neutrality oath. Mission inspector Karl Steck, as a former army officer, refused to swear this oath during his visitation stay in New Guinea. He was interned by the British in 1915 and deported to Australia. He was released in 1919 and returned to Germany in 1920. Most of the other missionaries were allowed to remain and continue to work in the country during the war.

In 1919, the classes in the Mission Seminary were resumed under the commissioning leadership of Rev. Eduard Stirner, the chairman of the Society for Inner and Outer Mission. Seventeen young men were accepted, although they were temporarily prevented from working overseas as there were more applicants than places. The intensive youth work in the congregations and the revival movement motivated many young men for mission. The economic situation of the Mission Institute was extremely precarious. Because of galloping inflation, fewer and fewer donations were given. Only with the help of Lutheran friends in Australia and America could goods be exchanged during the inflation for food in order to feed the seminarians. The Lutherans in America had already supported the Neuendettelsau Mission during the war with dollar donations which were of great help. However, often only parts of the salaries could be paid.

Since the first graduates could not go abroad, the activities of the Mission Institute shifted more towards mission work at home. Mission inspector Adam Schuster (1886–1968), who could not leave for New Guinea because of the war, was committed to this work. In 1921, the graduate of the Mission Seminary, Franz Lossin, who could not go abroad for health reasons, was installed as the first professional worker in the home mission in Bayreuth. Throughout the country, mission and evangelism events were held. Slides were shown and often accompanied by the brass band of the seminarians. In 1865, the first Bavarian brass band had been founded by Loehe in Neuendettelsau. During these meetings also the conch choir, which was founded by missionary Heinrich Zahn, played hymns.

Many seminarians blew in the conch choir founded in 1932 by the former New Guinea missionary Heinrich Zahn. They presented their music until the 1980s during church services and mission events in Bavaria. (Archive Mission One World)

From 1920 to 1928 Rev. Rudolf Ruf (1868–1950) officiated as mission director. He had participated in the life of the mission from his youth as a long-time member of the Society for Inner and Outer Mission. During Martin Deinzer's illness, in 1913 he took over his duties and taught in the seminary. At his installation by the chairman of the Mission Society, Rev. Eduard Stirner, the seminarians vowed to him "loyalty and obedience." He was also responsible for home mission while Karl Steck oversaw the outer mission. He led the Mission Institute in a difficult time and was successful in continuing mission work after the First World War. He also had to cope with many conflicts within and outside the institution which he mastered only with great faith in God. He was respected as a father by his seminarians. His student Hans Neumeyer, who later became mission director, wrote in Ruf's obituary in 1950: "He allowed us, with a conscious focus on a clear line of theological work, all the freedom in researching and learning from others. . . . From him everyone could learn the holy reverence with which a servant of Jesus Christ has to manage his office, without an exaggerated concept of his office, and without false enthusiasm. He was a true Lutheran pietist for whom our church must be thankful." In 1923, Ruf attended the founding assembly of the Lutheran World Convention in Eisenach, out of which in 1947 grew the Lutheran World Federation.

The regulations of Bauer's house order which included rules about the cleaning of shoes and the filling of lamps with petroleum were concentrated by Ruf in the essentials. In 1922, the mission museum was inaugurated in a former barrack on the mission compound, and in 1931 completely renovated. Many generations of Bavarian confirmation groups visited the museum and observed there especially the rain spells presented by mission inspector Dr. Keysser. They were impressed by the exotic weapons, animal skulls, birds and insects, stones and cult objects which were displayed in the museum.

As the "homestead for the children of field missionaries" the so-called New Guinea Home in Neuendettelsau was founded in 1925. It was not always easy for the missionaries to leave their children behind. The children often suffered from homesickness and longed for their parents. They had to contend with adjustment difficulties and considered themselves sometimes like orphans. Often, they saw their parents again only after ten or more years and had become alienated from them. The mission director acted as their guardian and intermediary until they reached twenty-four years of age.

To supplement the finances, in 1922 the Small Collection of the Neuendettelsau Mission (Kleinsammlung der Neuendettelsauer Mission) was established under the direction of Maria Drexel. At the same time, the former New Guinea missionary Johann Stössel founded the Mission Aid Association (Missionshilfe), which later organized very successful collections among thousands of its members. From 1910 to 1929, Gottlieb, the son of Friedrich Bauer (born 1860), worked as accounting officer and head of the export department in the Mission Institute. He died unmarried in 1940.

Since 1922, mission candidates were sent to Brazil and some, via USA, to Australia and New Guinea. In 1925, Gustav Gareis went to the USA as the last of 327 seminarians.

In 1920, New Guinea became an Australian mandate of the League of Nations. The Treaty of Versailles of 1920 contained in Article 438 the following provision: "Allied and Associated Powers agree that where Christian religious missions were being maintained by German societies or persons in territories belonging to them, or of which the government is entrusted to them in accordance with the present Treaty, the property which these missions or missionary societies possessed, including that of trading societies whose profits were devoted to the support of missions, shall continue to be devoted to missionary purposes. In order to ensure the due execution of this undertaking the Allied and Associated Governments will hand over such property to boards of trustees appointed by or approved by the Governments and composed of persons holding the faith of the mission whose property is involved."

As a result, the United Evangelical Lutheran Church of Australia could establish a trust company and thereby prevent the Neuendettelsau missionaries from being deposed. Director Ruf was able, with the support of the Lutheran churches in America and Australia, to continually push back the deadline for the return of the Bavarian missionaries from New Guinea. This was a result of the longstanding intensive contacts of the Neuendettelsau Mission with the Lutheran churches in America and Australia. In Australia, mission director F. Otto Theile (1880–1945) was committed to reaching an agreement that the Neuendettelsau missionaries could remain in New Guinea. He was born in Australia but trained in Neuendettelsau. In 1936, he came to Germany to represent his church during the celebration of the fiftieth jubilee of the New Guinea mission and negotiate with church and government authorities. He continued to negotiate the concerns of Neuendettelsau Mission with the Australian government and was therefore later temporarily interned. He died shortly after the end of the Second World War in August 1945.

In 1925, the Australian government reported through Theile that the German missionaries were allowed to remain, if their attitude and leadership was not hostile against the country's government and against the maintenance of public order. After Germany's admission to the

League of Nations in 1926 the provision of the Versailles Treaty in regard to missions was finally repealed.

In 1922, Hans Flierl and some missionary brides could travel to New Guinea. Later, the entry of auxiliary workers was allowed; so in 1927 nurse Helene Moll could be sent to New Guinea. She was, after thirteen years, the first independent missionary to be sent directly to New Guinea, "the first swallow, which indicated the coming summer." She was soon followed by other seminarians who had been trained in difficult times.

Since 1922, Dr. Christian Keysser (1877–1961) exercised great influence as a lecturer at the Mission Seminary on the young men and shaped an entire generation of missionaries. He came from the Northern Franconian village of Geroldsgrün and was from his youth connected with the revival movement. He worked from 1899 to 1920 as a missionary in New Guinea, where he developed the particular concept of converting a whole tribe to Christianity as opposed to the individual conversion and thereby helped the mission to break through. Because he supported the hidden fleeing German captain Hermann Detzner (1892–1970) during the First World War, the British-Australian authorities banned him from returning to New Guinea, which caused him suffering throughout the rest of his life. He wrote many books and articles and gave lectures throughout Germany. He wanted to reform the church in Germany which he experienced after his return as frozen, unwilling and uninterested in mission. In 1929, he received an honorary doctorate from the University of Erlangen. Even in retirement he was active, as far as his health allowed him, particularly as a guide in the mission museum. He died in 1961 in a car accident and was buried in Neuendettelsau.

Dr. Christian Keysser (1877–1961) worked from 1899 to 1920 as missionary in New Guinea and contributed to the breakthrough of the missionary work by his concept of conversion of a whole tribe. After his involuntary return to Germany he worked since 1922 as an influencial teacher, speaker, and writer. (Archive Mission OneWorld)

Rev. Karl Steck (1873–1952) worked from 1909 on as deputy director of the Mission Institute. He saw himself as "non-pietist" and advocated the close connection between mission and church. Already in his time as a parish pastor in Nordheim he participated in the work of the Bavarian Mission Conference, partly as its chairman. The conference sent him in 1910 as official delegate of the Leipzig Mission to the World Missionary Conference in Edinburgh. In 1914, he took part in the famous missionary conference in Heldsbach in New Guinea, where, on the question of mission strategy, he supported Keysser against Flierl. At the beginning of the First World War he refused to swear the oath of neutrality as demanded by the British authorities because he felt bound, as a reserve officer, to his oath to the German emperor. He was deported to Australia and returned only in 1920 to Germany. He got into years of violent disputes over the course of the Mission Institute, in which predominantly Adam Schuster and Friedrich Eppelein were involved. He criticized their work, particularly with regard to the formation of seminarians, as outdated and called for a reorganization of mission. The seminarians should be trained not only as Lutheran pastors, but also as missionaries. He had become familiar with their work in New Guinea. Dr. Keysser supported him in this concern, and director Ruf was open to his ideas. He experienced the Neuendettelsau Mission as too narrow and only directed towards the Society for Inner and Outer Mission. It should be rather based more firmly in the congregations. Hanfried Fontius referred to him as a pioneer of the integration of mission and church.

Steck would actually be the most obvious candidate to succeed Deinzer, but he refused to become a member of the Society for Inner and Outer Mission. When Ruf was elected, he wanted to make room for Steck again. Ruf, however, was prevented in doing so until, in 1928, he finally resigned and went as a pastor to Polsingen. At his departure, he wrote: "With gratitude and joy I think back to the time in the mission house! Because it was and remains the highlight of my life."

Steck had previously submitted his letter of resignation in case he was not elected director and in 1928 he was appointed as the first so-called professional worker of the Evangelical Lutheran Central Association for Foreign Mission in Bavaria. He also became the secretary of the Bavarian Mission Conference. His task was to deepen and promote "mission interest and love within our church." This was to be done through sermons, courses, lectures, visits, literary activities, etc. Also, he should distribute the incoming general mission gifts according to a certain percentage between Neuendettelsau and Leipzig and coordinate the regular visits of all districts within a four-year cycle.

The Mission Institute was run by an executive board. It consisted of the director as head of mission, the mission inspectors, and other professional workers. Above them was the board of the Society for Inner and Outer Mission, which was headed by a chairman and his deputy. The committees for inner and outer mission formed the "united committees" which chose the director and the mission inspectors.

In 1906, the Bavarian Association for Medical Mission (Bayerischer Verein für Ärztliche Mission) was founded in Erlangen at the suggestion of the German Institute for Medical Mission (Deutsches Institut für Ärztliche Mission), founded in 1906 in Tübingen. The articles of the association state as its goal "to support Bavarian missionary institutes in the training and recruitment of mission doctors, deacons, deaconesses, and midwives on their mission fields, to promote the medical training of missionaries and the understanding of medical mission work in the Protestant circles of Bavaria." Donations were collected and initially forwarded to the Tübingen institute. Since 1920, it also supported the Neuendettelsau and Leipzig missions. In 1928, the association had more than 2,600 members, including many doctors. The State Medical Association supported the work, and the Medical Journal published free advertisements. The association promoted in 1933 the posting of Dr. Martha Koller as the first Bavarian missionary doctor to Finschhafen in New Guinea. The association also helped with reintegration of returning doctors. It still exists and promotes medical work especially in PNG and Africa.

Missionary Work during Times of Conflict and Failure: 1933–1945

Mission and National Socialism

Between mission and National Socialism, a disastrously close relationship developed. First, we shall deal with the background. The 1920s and 1930s, from the perspective of many Protestant Christians in Germany, were marked by impiety, loss of moral standards, free thinking, leaving the church, individualism, decadence, and Bolshevism risk. Many were dissatisfied with democracy and its "party bickering." The humiliation of Germany by its enemies and the Treaty of Versailles were a heavy burden on the people. In addition to the payment of reparations the financial crisis and the terrible unemployment in the 1930s worsened the situation.

The Protestant Christians felt homeless after the fall of the Empire. Their patron, the German Emperor, was no more. They lacked a political party representing their interests, while the Catholics were organized in the Center Party and the Bavarian People's Party. The fear of a Catholic Counter-Reformation was connected with the fear of the socialist-Bolshevik wicked movement. Particularly in Franconia many Protestants soon turned to the National Socialist German Workers Party (NSDAP), because they saw their fears and desires best kept there. The supporters of the Nazis recruited mainly from the rural population and the petty bourgeoisie. Anti-Semitism flourished. The Jews were often blamed for everything, both Bolshevism and capitalism.

The Neuendettelsau Mission had its traditional supporters in the same layer of society as the NSDAP and shared many of its political views. The influential church press in Bavaria helped to spread the caricatures based on the belief in the Jewish scapegoat, especially the *Free Mouth's Weekly on Church and Politics for Town and Village* (*Freimunds politisches Wochenblatt für Stadt und Land*), published by the Neuendettelsau Mission. Since 1921, it denounced the Jewish influenced government, the promotion of immorality as a signature of the new time and criticized Jews as socialists and capitalists. In his contributions in particular, Rev. Friedrich Zindel blamed the Jews, Communists, and Bolsheviks for the demise of the monarchy and the desolate state of the Weimar Republic. Parliamentary democracy with its liberal tendencies was devalued, and the call for a strong leader grew loud. In addition to the Jews, the French were blamed for the misery. In the Free Mouth journal, the unionist tendencies to establish a Protestant national Church were also criticized and an Evangelical Lutheran Church in Germany was demanded. The ecumenical activities on the international level, e.g., at the World Conference on Life and Work in 1925, which was headed by Archbishop Nathan Söderblom, were rejected because the Lutheran confession was not adequately recognized.

Bishop Hans Meiser was welcomed at the mission festival in Gunzenhausen in July 1936 by many of the faithful with the Nazi salute. (Archive Mission One World)

In Protestant Franconia, also in Neuendettelsau, in 1932 the majority of the population voted for the Nazi Party. In 1933, Hans Loscher (NSDAP) was elected mayor of Neuendettelsau, who was replaced in 1940 by the Nazi leader Adolf Traunfelder. Traunfelder initiated in the town council in September 1933 the first anti-Jewish plaque at the railway station with the inscription "Neuendettelsau—Jews are prohibited to enter this town." From today's perspective, this plaque represented a monstrosity for a place that was marked by the loving works of mission and diakonia initiated by Wilhelm Loehe. Postcards were sent from Neuendettelsau with the swastika on the St. Nikolai church.

The NSDAP declared in its party platform of 1920 the position of a "positive Christianity" and therefore gained many followers among Protestant Christians, while the Catholics behaved rather reserved. Its platform stated: "We demand freedom for all religious denominations in the state, provided they do not endanger or violate the moral sense of the German race." The party propagated service before one's self, and the break of the slave-like rule of Jews and Freemasons. In 1932, the Nazi party participated in church council elections; the SA moved into the churches. The Nazi party stood in front of St. Lorenz Church in Nuremberg, when in 1933, Bishop Meiser was installed. In order to address the concerns of the American National Lutheran Council, Eppelein wrote a letter which was published in the Free Mouth journal and cited Hitler's government declaration of March 23, 1933: "The government sees in the two Christian denominations the most important factor in the preservation of the people." Even later in the *Free Mouth* journal "key words of our leader Adolf Hitler" were quoted, such as: "National Socialism is neither anti-church, nor anti-religious, but on the contrary, it stands on the ground of real Christianity." Obviously Eppelein, as the publisher, wanted to reject fears that the Nazi regime pursued an anti-clerical course.

In his book *My Struggle* (*Mein Kampf*), Hitler expressed criticism of missionary activities. He criticized the missionary's lack of success among the "Hottentots and Zulus," while at the same time neglecting their own people. Mission, he said, uses force against non-Christian peoples, and destroys them through a supposedly "higher culture." He concluded "that it is truly a sin against all reason, and a criminal lunacy to train a born half ape long enough until you think you have made him a lawyer." Criticism raised in Protestant mission circles was dispelled by the theses of the theology professor Karl Fetzer from the University of Tübingen: "We (i.e. the movement of the German Christians) are in favor of the work of the German Protestant mission to the Gentiles, as required by the church in the mission will of Christ, and which we cherish as a sacred heritage of the fathers."

The leadership of the Neuendettelsau Mission called for a close cooperation with National Socialism. It saw it as a great opportunity for an intensive national missionary endeavor. Since the end of the First World War, graduates of the Mission Seminary initially were not allowed to leave for New Guinea and Brazil or were sick or not tropically ambient. Some of them became employed as home missionaries. The first among them was Franz Lossin (1891–1969), who, beginning in 1921, worked in Bayreuth. Since 1928 he became increasingly involved with Nazism and joined the election campaign as a party speaker. He strongly advocated anti-Semitic opinions and called on his pastor colleagues to join the Nazi movement. This seemed unsustainable to the Mission Institute, so he was dismissed in 1930. The united committees of the Society for Inner and Outer Mission resolved: "The political convictions of all our professional workers are a matter of conscience of the individual; the freedom of political beliefs may not be touched in any way. Since persons of all political parties are entrusted to our mission, any pronounced political agitation is ruled out by itself. No employee can work in a leading position of a party or participate in any propaganda activities." There was no explicit criticism of Lossin's anti-Semitism. He later worked in organizations of the Nazi party and acted as its speaker. His dismissal and following polemics against the Neuendettelsau Mission roused public sensation.

On March 25, 1931 the Mission Institute, as the first Protestant institution in Germany, invited Nazi leaders for talks in Nuremberg with the consent of the later bishop Hans Meiser. The delegation of the NSDAP was headed by the member of parliament and later Bavarian Minister of Culture Hans Schemm, whom Eppelein knew through his former teaching in a school in Bayreuth. He mediated between the Lutheran church and the anti-clerical tendencies in the NSDAP and summarized his position in the sentence: "My policy is Germany, my religion is Christ." On the part of the Mission Institute, the meeting was attended by Friedrich Eppelein, Helmut Kern, Wilhelm Koller and Johann Stössel. Eppelein emphasized in his opening speech: "Our home mission wants to serve nothing but the German people in its own way. Since we have the belief that the NSDAP will also serve the German people, we asked for this meeting. We expect much from the NSDAP. With no other party we have so far set up in a similar way to communicate and discuss." Also "concerns and inquires" were uttered, e.g. in regard to the absoluteness of the German race. However, Kern pointed out: "The main thing is the struggle against Bolshevism." A record of this "highly confidential discussion" was sent to Hans Meiser, who informed the Supreme Church Council. In July 1931, the working group for home mission, together with the Bavarian Association for Home Missions, hosted a conference on "National Socialism and the Protestant church" in Neuendettelsau. Among the more than one hundred participants, controversy and riots between supporters and opponents of National Socialism arose. A meeting of pastors with Hitler was planned and was agreed to in principle but never took place. In 1934, Eppelein visited Hans Schemm in his Ministry of Culture in Munich. Schemm later died in 1935 in a plane crash near Bayreuth.

Under the pictures of the founding fathers Friedrich Bauer, Johannes Deinzer, and Martin Deinzer, classes were held in the Mission Seminary. (Archive Mission One World)

The terminology of the home mission statements of the Lutheran church showed striking similarities with the ideology and martial language of National Socialism. Thus, the description of the Neuendettelsau home mission by Helmut Kern under the heading "The Struggle Continues!" began with the words: "The struggle for every city, every village, for the people, the congregation, the church—the struggle of God around the world for you and for me, the struggle of God for the German nation and all nations." Further he speaks of the men of home mission as "frontier troops in the front line . . . behind the enemy barbed wire . . . in the scuffle with the enemy." Bolshevism and godlessness are named as enemies. No wonder that many Christians looked at National Socialism as allies.

The Position of the Neuendettelsau Mission under the Leadership of Friedrich Eppelein

Rev. Dr. Friedrich Eppelein (1887–1969) worked since 1926 as inspector of home mission in the Mission Institute and was appointed in 1928 as its director. Due to his proximity to National Socialism, he was forced to resign in 1945 and went as a pastor to Zirndorf near Nuremberg. (Archive Mission One World)

For Ruf's successor, in 1928 Rev. Dr. Friedrich Eppelein (1887–1969) was appointed. He was originally from Nuremberg and in 1912 he went to work as a pastor in Bayreuth. He started many activities there with the founding of a brass band, church choir, and a diaconical association, as well as the construction of a congregation center. In addition, he received his PhD in 1919 from the University of Erlangen with a thesis on "Housing and Morality." He was especially engaged in home mission; through its activities he wanted to win the working-class people for the church. In 1926, he was appointed by the Society for Inner and Outer Mission as inspector for home mission, and in 1928 he was elected to succeed Rev. Rudolf Ruf as director. His work in home mission was continued by Rev. Helmut Kern (1892–1941), who, since 1933, acted as the special representative for home mission of ELCB and organized the support for Bishop Meiser. In 1935, Kern founded the Office for Parish Services (Amt für Gemeindedienst) in Nuremberg. During his administration in 1930, the conference center in Neuendettelsau was built which is now called House Luther Rose (Haus Lutherrose). Kern was killed in action in 1941.

From 1929 to 1930 director Eppelein and mission inspector Adam Schuster (1886–1968) went on a long trip to Africa, Palestine, Australia, and New Guinea. Officially, the work of Neuendettelsau Mission in New Guinea was still managed as Finschhafen Lutheran Mission by the United

Evangelical Lutheran Church of Australia. At a conference in May 1930 in Brisbane (Australia) the Neuendettelsau Mission was permitted by the Australian and American churches to not only continue to cooperate, but also to co-chair the conference. In 1932, Eppelein attended a conference in Columbus, Ohio, where he achieved the complete restoration of the work of the Neuendettelsau Mission in New Guinea which began on January 1, 1933. In this he was supported in particular by Australian mission director Otto Theile, who for years had fought with the Australian government for the work of Neuendettelsau Mission.

From 1935 to 1946 Eppelein was also a lecturer for missiology at Erlangen University and from 1940 to 1945 deputy chairman of the Society for Inner and Outer Mission. From 1931 to 1945 he served as chairman of the Martin Luther Association and the Brazil relief organization of the Martin Luther Federation. From 1943 to 1945 he replaced Pastor Wilhelm Forstmeyer in St. Nikolai parish, who had to serve in the army. Eppelein, after the end of his service in the Mission Institute, worked from 1946 to 1957 as pastor of the congregation in Zirndorf. He died in 1969 and was buried in St. John's Cemetery in Nuremberg.

During his inspection tour on December 30, 1929, Mission Director Dr. Friedrich Eppelein (right) with Mission Senior Johann Flierl (left) visit the mango tree in Simbang, where a plaque remembers the foundation of the first Neuendettelsau mission station in New Guinea on October 8, 1886. (Archive Mission One World)

In 1934, Eppelein succeeded to buy a Junkers engine (F-13) with the name Papua and sent it as the world-wide first mission aircraft to New Guinea to support the highlands mission, which was strongly advocated by him. The aircraft came to New Guinea in 1935 and in 1939 was kidnapped by pilot Werner Garms and his flight engineer Paul Rabe to the Dutch colony of West Papua.

In 1936, the fiftieth anniversary of the New Guinea mission was celebrated in Gunzenhausen, where Bischop Meiser declared: "The Neuendettelsau Mission in New Guinea is our mission, the mission of the Bavarian church." Greetings were expressed by Mission Director Theile from Australia, President Johannes Haefner from America, and Pastor Karl Müller from Brazil.

In 1936, Bishop Hans Meiser preached at the occasion of the fiftieth anniversary of the New Guinea mission during the traditional mission festival at Gunzenhausen. To the solemn assembly came Mission Director Otto Theile from Australia, Pastor Johannes Haefner from America, and Pastor Karl Müller from Brazil representing the Lutheran churches associated with the Neuendettelsau Mission. (From left) (Archive Mission One World)

Dr. Eppelein continued to concentrate Bauer's house rules following his predecessor Ruf. In 1933, a section on political education was added: "Measures are taken to ensure that the seminarians join the Hitler Youth and the Storm Troopers (SA) and participate in their events."

Students of the Mission and Diaspora Seminary formed a "mission squad" of the Storm Troopers (SA) during the Third Reich, which marched up in uniform to show patriotic spirit. (Archive Mission One World)

From 1933 to 1955 the Russia-born Rev. Johann Langholf (1891–1955) worked in the Mission Institute as a teacher and inspector for Brazil. He also began relationships with the Lutheran congregations in Ukraine. Already beginning in 1930 young Ukrainians studied at the Seminary, and in 1936 Palestinians from Schneller School in Jerusalem also came for studies to Neuendettelsau. Gradually, therefore, the name Mission and Diaspora Seminary (MDS) came into use. Langholf's successor was Rev. Gotthard Grottke (1906–1979).

After 1933, the government restricted the collection activities of the mission considerably. Only under mission friends could the missionary societies collect donations. The association Mission Help encouraged the congregations' members to subscribe to lists in order to make mission donations. Since 1936, a church mission collection of Epiphany was raised throughout the church.

Although Eppelein had pleaded in 1932 for a distance towards any party politics, he joined the NSDAP in 1933. In the *Free Mouth* journal he stated on April 27, 1933:

> I have already written on April 12, 1933 to the local group leader of NSDAP in Neuendettelsau, Mr. Traunfelder, the following letter: 'I hereby ask you to accept my membership in the National Socialist Party. Let people think of me what they want, they may think of me as an opportunist! Since I have read the life story of Hermann Göring, I come no longer to inner peace, but feel innermost driven to put my weak force into the service of the great patriotic movement.... I know well that in the great movement of NSDAP are also personalities who can be an inner distress to Christians. I do not belong to the harmless that have no serious concerns toward this movement. But I have no doubt that these worries and concerns also press the God-given leader of this movement (i.e. Adolf Hitler) and his followers.... For my part I consider myself obliged in my conscience to thank God for the sake of our people and our church for this movement and want to serve it with the gift that God has entrusted to me.

On May 19, 1933, Eppelein wrote to Rev. Friedrich Klein, a member of the Society for Inner and Outer Mission: "On April 11, I signed up as a member of the local NSDAP. I ask to be included in the Association of National Socialist Pastors." Klein was one of the leaders of the so-called German Christians in Bavaria and later went to Berlin-Brandenburg.

In a "Word of the Editor for Today's Situation" in the *Free Mouth* journal, Eppelein warned both of overrating or underestimating the Nazi enthusiasm:

> We need to thank God on our knees for those men in spite of their stains and actual sins, because God's causeless mercy has used these men as tools. It is contempt of the lord of history, if we are not ready to learn from the guidance of God in the past, but also in the present! Hindenburg, Adolf Hitler, and the other men of the government are and will remain, like all people of the world ... error enabled, sinful men.

Eppelein advocated "constructive, forgiving, and giving criticism" and thanked God that now Bolshevism and ungodly associations are pushed back, and the dictation of Versailles is eliminated as a "herd of all evil."

The statement that Hitler was a sinner and that there are mistakes and sins even among the leaders of the Nazi Party was criticized in the Nazi paper *Franconian People* (*Fränkisches Volk*) on April 21, 1933 as an "outrageous derailment of a Bavarian Protestant mission director." Nevertheless, Eppelein appealed in the *Free Mouth* journal to "work in close communion with our God-given leader Adolf Hitler for the rescue of the

German people and fatherland." On the mission compound he planted a so-called Hitler oak.

On May 1, 1933, Eppelein and Keysser joined the Nazi-oriented movement of so-called German Christians, what they later called "a loose connection" or "purely ideal relationship" without registered membership or payment of fees. They saw in particular in the goals of their home mission a match with National Socialism. They justified their joining in an editorial in the *Free Mouth* journal of September 14, 1933 under the headline: "Why We Joined the Movement of the German Christians." They listed the following reasons:

> 1. The curse of extreme individualism has had disastrous consequences. Faith became a private matter. This has caused untold damage in the church.
>
> 2. In New Guinea Christianity and folk character stand in a relationship very different from our nation and fatherland which is contaminated by individualism. We now should come into a much more intimate relationship between Christianity and nationality.
>
> 3. The movement of the German Christians sees home and foreign missions as a matter of the church. With our membership in this movement we perform a "missionary emergency service" and prevent that the German Christians go astray and become "the platform for false prophets and a temple of pagan devotion."
>
> 4. The NSDAP represents the viewpoint of a positive Christianity. There is a danger that the mission to the Gentiles is destroyed and a neo-pagan Germanic religion is introduced. However, the German Christians will fight these trends as an "auspicious troop" to make clear the close relationship of Lutheranism and folk character.
>
> 5. Membership with the German Christians rises and falls with the loyalty to the Lutheran confession and the "leader of our church" (Bishop Meiser). The planned national church must be marked Lutheran.

Yet, Eppelein later expressed his outrage about the sports palace rally of the German Christians, which took place on November 13, 1933 in Berlin with 20,000 participants. Massive anti-Semitic speeches were held. A species-appropriate Christianity and the abolition of the Old Testament as a "book of cattle dealers and procurers" were demanded.

In 1934, when the German Christians, under the leadership of the national bishop Ludwig Müller, called for the inclusion of the Bavarian lutheran church into the German Evangelical Church, Eppelein turned increasingly away from the movement. After the war, he pointed to his initially critical attitude towards this movement because it surrendered its national missionary goals and the commitment of the church was trampled. Similarly, mission inspector Helmut Kern, as the one responsible for home mission, had at first regarded the home mission as "widely fighting in a front with National Socialists" and as an "indispensable pioneer of the nationalist movement." Until the sports palace rally in 1933, he was himself a member of the German Christians. Then he left the movement and organized support for Bishop Hans Meiser with the representatives for home mission of the Bavarian church.

On April 14, 1935, the state district office in Ansbach forbade the *Free Mouth* journal from publishing "further explanations of the Protestant clergy" over the church dispute, because this would be an "undesirable disturbance carried into the population." Some issues of the journal were seized. Eppelein was warned and threatened with protective custody. On December 9, 1935, Eppelein complained: "Every Protestant in Germany spends 12 Pfennigs for mission per year, but 114 German marks for alcohol and nicotine." This issue was also seized, and Eppelein was threatened again with protective custody.

On October 15, 1935, Eppelein was expelled from the NSDAP by an injunction of the district leader of NSDAP and mayor of Ansbach, Richard Hänel:

> In No. 40, 1935 of the Free Mouth journal, you as the responsible editor allowed Rev. Justus Götz to publish an article on the home of mentally ill persons of the Deaconess Institute at Bruckberg. In this article the eugenic principles and laws of the NS state are criticized in an unprecedented, albeit hidden form. The article contains further under the heading 'enthusiasm for SA (stormtroopers)' the following phrases: 'Käthel is so charmed by the SA that she thinks all men are SA-men. Was Abraham also a SA-man? she once asked.' This strange enthusiasm uttered in the mouth of a mentally ill person reflects the opinion of the author about the SA and implies a gross affront to this division of the party. . . . By this you have violated in the grossest form the obligation of a member of the NSDAP and are not worthy to continue to belong to it.

Perhaps the attack of NSDAP was actually aimed at Bishop Meiser, who had pleaded for the care of handicapped persons in his sermon at the occasion of the inauguration of St. Martin's church in Bruckberg on September 8, 1935.

Eppelein expressly emphasized in his reply that he would remain on the floor of the Third Reich, and that it is absolutely far from him to take position against the eugenic principles and laws of the state, "because I personally think they are correct." The sentence on the SA had escaped him, unfortunately, due to other workloads when reading the proofs. What was meant was not a denigration of the SA. "Just because of the mood of our people which seeks to free itself, rightfully, from the influences of the foreign race of Judaism and therefore cannot distinguish between the Jews and an excellent figure of faith in the Old Testament, it would have been better not to publish this article." His objection was, however, on May 27, 1936 definitively rejected, despite a letter to Hänel signed with "Hail Hitler" ("Heil Hitler"), in which Eppelein asked "to continue to be in all simplicity a party member" and be obedient "to the Third Reich and its leader at any time, not only because of my patriotic love, but also of my Christian conscience." It grieved him to be branded as a public enemy. After the war he confessed that he should have drawn clearer "the boundary between party political activities and church service."

Eppelein bravely defended the Gentile mission from which Germans, not only abroad but also at home, benefit and which strengthens the reputation of the German Reich. In connection with the acquisition of the mission aircraft Papua he wrote:

> Our foreign mission is not only a service to a distant nation, but also to our own people. The supply of the mission field is mainly done by shipping German goods. By this, German citizens are provided with work and income. The purchase of the aircraft Papua meant direct job creation among the German people, as is the printing of the New Testament in the Jabem language by the Bible Printing Co. Otherwise, the aircraft produced at the Junkers Works in Dessau bears witness in a remote part of the world—in spite of all the atrocity propaganda of the Jews and their allies—not only of German Protestant church life, but also of German efficiency in the field of science and technology.

He pointed out that in 1932 he used his foreign relations and visits to explain the intentions of the Nazi movement. Through his membership in the NSDAP he wanted to prove to the Germans abroad that his membership can combine the party membership with the loyalty to the Lutheran confession. He called missionaries the "SA men of the church."

The Neuendettelsau Mission in 1935 put the world's first mission aircraft into its service for the highlands mission in New Guinea. It bore the name Papua and was kidnapped at the beginning of the Second World War into Dutch West Papua. (Archive Mission One World)

Anti-Semitic tendencies are obvious in Eppelein's writings, even if they occur rather formulaic, e.g., as "atrocity propaganda of Jews and Freemasons." Eppelein declined the mixing of races, which according to his understanding is derived from the Lutheran theology of creation, and he fought for mission among Jews. He yet objected to the elimination of the Old Testament and the ethnic-racial interpretation of Christianity.

On February 23, 1937 the president of the Reich Press Chamber in Berlin wrote to Eppelein: "After a long, careful examination, I came to the conviction that from you, who were excluded from the NSDAP, a wholehearted commitment to National Socialism and the state cannot be expected at all times." He was therefore excluded from the Reich Press Chamber and lost "the right of any kind of press activity." As acting editors of the *Free Mouth* journal mission inspectors Keysser and Schuster officiated, and from May 15, 1937 up to its ban on May 29, 1941 (allegedly because of paper shortage) the Göggingen pastor and former mission inspector Wilhelm Koller functioned as editor.

On January 31, 1941, Eppelein was eventually forbidden by the president of the Reich Chamber of Writing to operate as a writer. When the parish council of St. Nikolai in Neuendettelsau in 1944 applied for Eppelein's approval to teach religious instruction at school, it was initially denied "due to political unreliability," but later approved. The famous Lutheran theologian Paul Althaus, as dean of the theological faculty of Erlangen University, confirmed on March 23, 1944 in a letter to the Bavarian Ministry of Culture that Eppelein had joined the NSDAP out of deep conviction and in the *Free Mouth* journal he had pleaded towards the churches abroad to understand the thoughts of the "leader [Hitler] and the new Germany."

The missionary children accommodated in the New Guinea Home in Neuendettelsau were also influenced by Nazi propaganda. So, Siegfried Wacke wrote to his parents Magdalene and Karl Wacke in 1937: "It is dark, the only light point for me are the Bible and the swastika." His parents agreed to his plans to join the National Socialist Motorist Corps and join the NS party. "We had only one condition: that he does preserve his religious position and must uphold it with the party, and then we had no objection. Both of us were members of the party." Siegfried died in action shortly afterwards in the beginning of the Second World War.

Although the Neuendettelsau Mission and other missionary societies behaved loyal to the Nazi regime, in 1934 public collections for mission had been banned. Only collections in church services and among members of missionary associations were allowed. These limitations meant a considerable reduction in revenues. Nevertheless, the Neuendettlesau Small Collection thanked its members with a picture showing "a missionary kid from New Guinea greets the leader."

Miſſionarskind aus Neuguinea grüßt den Führer!

With this card reading "A MissionaryKid from New Guinea Greets the Leader [Führer]" the Neuendettelsau Small Collection thanked its members for their donations. (Archive Mission One World)

There were repeated allegations of violations of the ban on collections. On November 14, 1940 the district court in Augsburg sentenced the missionary couple Gottfried and Magdalena Schmutterer with a penalty of one hundred Reich marks for violating this ban. They had won twenty-eight members for the Small Collection and received 5.05 German marks for the mission. The money was then drafted. The court took mitigating into account "that the accused have lived in Germany only since 1937 and could not make themselves familiar with the new streamlining alignment of our people. But it has to be realized that during the war the concentration of all efforts should not be disturbed by such activities." On January 21, 1941 a second hearing was held before the district court, and the legal proceedings were stopped.

After the war, Eppelein emphasized that he had never received a party book or party awards; neither occupied any offices or had drawn advantages from his membership. "I have never denied my office as a servant of the church." He had joined the NSDAP for the sake of the mission, because he feared that the Mission and Diaspora Seminary would be put under state control and hoped that he then could negotiate better as a member of the party. He had not interfered in church politics. He had been threatened with protective custody, because he had compared the small donations for the Gentile mission with the high expenditure on nicotine and alcohol. He had "rarely" attended party meetings. He also referred to Loehe, who in his "Call from Home" wrote in 1845: "A German, who is not a German, is a cursed man on earth."

"The Neuendettelsau Mission . . . was not a 'Nazi nest' . . . as is today claimed by people," Eppelein wrote in 1945. He and Keysser did not behave like "naïve children," but were guided by theological consideration. Their intention was to serve the Lutheran church and its mission "in confident despair" (Luther), because they realized God's hidden leadership in the former government. Eppelein adhered to Luther's words: "Do not argue against your lord and tyrant; rather suffer whatever may happen to you." He later began his life review with the word of St. Paul: "By the grace of God I am what I am, and his grace towards me has not been in vain" (1 Corinthians 15:10). In a letter dated April 10, 1959, to the head of the Free Mouth Publishing House, Leonhard Ritter, Eppelein emphasized that he, of course, belonged to the Confessing Church. He had experienced a "terrible conflict . . . between Lutheran commitment to the state power and state order and the horror of the anti-Christian ways brought by the Nazi regime." He felt, however, bound to his conscience (cf. Acts 5:29; Revelation 13; Romans 13:1–2). "We knew that we were committed to the Lutheran confession, but we were also committed to the mission in New Guinea. We had to be careful not to endanger this richly blessed mission work among the Gentiles by any thoughtless or unnecessary word."

Already in July 1945, a major of the American military government with the new Ansbach district head, a Mennonite, came to Neuendettelsau to get a picture of the situation. "Neuendettelsau has a bad note as a pacemaker of National Socialism," it says in a report of the governing board of the Deaconess Institute. On September 19, 1945 Eppelein, in the first session of the united committees of the Society for Inner and Outer Mission after the war, gave his report not realizing that there were already discussions about his replacement. On October 15, 1945 the chairman of the Society for Inner and Outer Mission, later regional bishop Heinrich Koch, disclosed that the district head had told him that the American military government thought that Eppelein was too politically burdened to remain director of the Mission Institute. Bishop Meiser could not stand up for him under these circumstances. The other members of the executive board, Adam Schuster, Johann Langholf, and Georg Vicedom, agreed "after much hesitation and serious internal struggles." On October

23, 1945 Eppelein announced his involuntary resignation on the following grounds:

> 1. I put the welfare of the mission over my person.
>
> 2. I obey the decisions of the mission committees . . . and the Supreme Church Council of ELCB, which in 1937 ordered all pastors, also me, to swear an oath to Adolf Hitler.
>
> 3. I do not make a decision for myself. The responsibility for my dismissal and its circumstances must be carried out completely by those who bid me to go.

On November 11, 1945, Bishop Meiser visited Eppelein and urged him to apply for a parish position. Eppelein remained bitter throughout his life about his dismissal and never attended any mission events afterwards. By a denacification court he was classified as "follower" (class IV) on September 23, 1946.

Eppelein acquired lasting merits by maneuvering the mission ship during the storms of the Third Reich, and thus made it possible to continue its work after the war. He was a fighter and his sometimes controversial management style fit well into that time. He was extremely diligent, writing many articles and letters in which he defended missionary activities. During his later work as a pastor in the vastly growing parish of Zirndorf near Nuremberg from 1946 to 1957, he fought for the Lutheran orientation of the public schools and the unity of his congregation. In an interim report of 1951, he presented a romanticized view of the life of the congregations in New Guinea as a model, where "every member of the church feels obliged to serve," which was not the case in Zirndorf. He also fought against anti-clerical tendencies among the ruling Social Democrats in Zirndorf and stated: "Zirndorf is a stronghold of Marxism."

Mission inspector Dr. Christian Keysser joined in April 1933, on the advice of Eppelein the NSDAP and the movement of the German Christians. In numerous presentations and publications, in particular in the *Neuendettelsau Mission Paper* (*Neuendettelsauer Missionsblatt*), edited by him, he explained his position. In an idealized view from the distance of a later time he described the Lutheran church in New Guinea as a unity of people and faith which he hoped to be realized in Germany in cooperation with National Socialism. He emphasized that according to Matthew 28:18–20 the gospel is directed towards the "peoples." Eppelein took up many of his thoughts. In spite of his sympathy for the Nazi movement,

Keysser was attacked by the government in several occasions. In January 1936, he was questioned by the Secret Police (Gestapo) because the government presumed a forbidden meeting in Sebastiansweiler, which he had mentioned in a letter to his son-in-law. The presentation of his Papua play was forbidden in 1936 because of the "glorification of the Papuan race." The Secret Police questioned him because of the subtitle of a picture in the *Neuendettelsau Children's Journal* (*Neuendettelsauer Kinderblatt*), "The Brown Man Stands like a Soldier of the German Army (Wehrmacht)," because "it makes a fool of the German soldier." Mayor Traunfelder gave support for him and prevented his arrest. His biblical riddle in the *Neuendettelsau Children's Journal* of December 1938 was criticized as irresponsible, because "German children do not execute orders of Jewish heroes." Keysser protested several times against articles in newspapers, but remained in the NSDAP, "because I did not want to be a swaying reed . . . and stand up for the Gentile mission. . . . As a Christian I felt responsible to raise criticisms again and again hoping that perhaps the good will triumph over the bad. . . . I wanted to make things better as far as possible." On the other hand he prevented the formation of a local group of the German Christians in Neuendettelsau. Like Eppelein, he was a member of the German Colonial Association (Deutsche Kolonialgesellschaft) and hoped for the return of the colonies, especially his beloved New Guinea.

Keysser defended the Old Testament as part of the Bible, but made very negative statements about Judaism:

> The Jewish people live in dispersal, restless and unpopular. There is no blessing on their work. . . . Presently the Jews are not the chosen, but the only people on earth burdened with the curse of God. Is Adolf Hitler not correct when he writes: 'I believe to act today on behalf of the Almighty Creator. When I fight against the Jews, I fight for the work of the Lord. . . . Many weak characters consider the treatment which presently happens to Jews as harsh and unCchristian. They may look into the Old Testament where the values and the education of the people are described! For example, according to Ezra 10 the Jews had to dismiss all their wives and children originating from a foreign people. Certainly, this was a cruel measure; but it happened for the sake of the people and the unity of its race. Our mildness towards individuals is often truly the biggest thoughtlessness, and injustice towards the people as a whole.

After the war he wrote in his request to change the decision of the denacification court: "The treatment of the Jews was unjust," without going into details. His son-in-law Wilhelm Fugmann wrote: "Keysser was not a connoisseur of human nature, he believed only in the goodness of every person." He was "marked by holy simplicity and wanted to live faithfully."

Keysser was retired by the chairman of the Society for Inner and Outer Mission, Rev. Heinrich Koch, on November 19, 1945. He was already sixty-eight years old and in poor health. In 1946, he wrote to the denacification court in Ansbach in response to the questionnaire:

> I was a Nazi out of conviction and free will. Why?
>
> 1. Because National Socialism came to power in a democratic way.
>
> 2. Because the NS government was legitimate and recognized by all states.
>
> 3. Because I had met the enemy propaganda during the First World War in Australia.
>
> 4. Because all the colonies had been taken away from Germany and for 15 years were not returned to democratic Germany.
>
> 5. I did not leave the NSDAP, because one could only protest as a party member, what I have done was done honestly, and because I did not know much of what is now known.
>
> 6. I was removed from the town council of Neuendettelsau in 1933, I was interrogated and warned by the Secret Police, a publication was confiscated, and the Papua play could not be performed anymore.

On September 25, 1946, he was classified without a hearing in the second highest level II (guilty, responsible). The judgment of the denacification court was three years of special work, confiscation of 75 percent of his property "as a contribution to reparation," permanent inability to hold public office, loss of all civil rights, and a ban for five years from working as a teacher and preacher. As reason his membership in the NSDAP and its affiliated organizations was given, because he was "out of conviction and free will a Nazi." His old age, his twenty-nine years of missionary activity, and his criticism against the party were taken into consideration.

Bishop Meiser visited Keysser on October 25, 1946 and classified the verdict as unjust. He also pointed out how the court decision affected Keysser's reputation among his children and grandchildren. He advised Keysser to file an objection which Keysser finally did after much hesitation and with the explicit support of the mission board. Schuster and Vicedom appeared in the hearing as witnesses. His lawyer called him "a religious idealist who accepted in good faith what the Nazis preached." Keysser pointed out that Nazism legally came to power and was recognized by other countries. "I cannot understand that my simple bona fide membership in the party should be a crime. Where I knew about a manifest injustice, I took courage to raise my voice." He was then classified as a "follower" (level IV) and sentenced only to a fine of one thousand German marks. The military government initially lifted this sentence, but later revised it as a "mistake," so that Keysser was finally acquitted in 1948.

Other mission employees worked in and for the NSDAP. Among them was the seminarian Friedrich Hormess (1898–1945), who was sent in 1925 to Brazil. He came back in 1931 and worked as a parish pastor in Pfäfflingen. The correspondence between him and the Mission Institute shows that he had difficulties with the administrations of church and mission. There were also problems in the field of finances, and the Bavarian Ministry of Culture had already announced that his employment could not be extended beyond 1935. Hormess sympathized with the German Christians, claiming in 1934 publicly: "Bishop Meiser in Munich received from Jews one million dollars to lead the church struggle with the government. Another million from the same source was prospected so that Meiser could fight with Jewish money." Thereupon an order of the district court in Oettingen forbade him to further establish this claim. In the court session witnesses stated that he had actually said this, and he was sentenced to three months' imprisonment. The court saw it as "the accusation that is unworthy of a German man and reminds of high treason." The sentence was later reduced by the court of Augsburg to one month. Even the New York Times reported on this affair. Since Hormess in 1934 supported the demand for the immediate voluntary resignation of Bishop Meiser, he was dismissed from the ministry after the end of the temporary arrest of Meiser on October 17, 1934. The church and mission administrations tried to help find a position for him in another church. He was then taken over by the Lutheran Church in Thuringia and was killed during the last days of the war in April 1945 in Dormagen.

Furthermore, the former New Guinea missionary Johann Stössel (1884–1972) was employed after his return in 1922 by the Mission Institute. He founded the Neuendettelsau Mission Help Association (Neuendettelsauer Missionshilfe) and carried out very successful collections. He soon joined the National Socialist movement. There were allegations of marital misconduct and financial irregularities. In 1931, he was dismissed by the Mission Institute. He then worked in the parish of Nuremberg-Eibach with Rev. Dr. Beer, who was also a member of the German Christians. In 1943, he became parish administrator in Alsace and, after returning from captivity in 1946, functioned as a pastor in the Württemberg church in Alpirsbach.

In 1924, Adolf Traunfelder (1899–1975) came as a teacher to the elementary school in Neuendettelsau; whom Eppelein already knew from his time in Bayreuth. Since 1929 he was also a teacher of pedagogy and didactics at the Mission Seminary and supervised students in their practical exercises in the school. Early he joined the NSDAP and acted from 1933 on as the leader of its local group and member of the town council in Neuendettelsau. From 1940 to 1945 he acted as mayor of Neuendettelsau. After leaving the church, Traunfelder could no longer teach at the Mission Seminary but continued to receive his salary. Keysser and Eppelein justified this in 1945 that if the seminary had been placed under state supervision, Traunfelder could have acted as state commissioner. Therefore, they tried to remain in good relations with Traunfelder. He protected Flierl and Keysser from the government when they publicly criticized certain measures of the Nazi party and hindered their arrest. However, he published on February 7, 1945 a terrible announcement to the population of Neuendettelsau about dealing with the forced labourers from Poland and the Soviet Union in the ammunition factory MUNA: "Foreign persons employed in the MUNA still get all kinds of food in the shops or beg in the households. This incredible state of affairs must finally be stopped. Who from now on donates or sells food to foreign persons of the MUNA, has to reckon with criminal charges and severe penalties." A memorial stone recalls this event, referring to Leviticus 19 34: "The alien who resides with you shall be to you as the citizen among you; you shall love the alien as yourself." Shortly before the end of the war Traunfelder interfered with the Nuremberg party leader Karl Holz in regard to the blowing up of the MUNA, by which many residents of Neuendettelsau would have been killed and houses of the mission and diakonia destroyed which were filled with hundreds of sick and wounded soldiers. Later,

Traunfelder worked as a teacher and headmaster in nearby Petersaurach and was especially honored for his ethnographic research with the Federal Cross of Merit. In the remaining houses of the MUNA after the war, the Augustana Theological College was started in 1947.

Early in 1946, the American military authorities demanded for the reopening of the seminary the "complete denacification of the institution." Consequently, some administrative staff was dismissed with the perspective to take them back after their denacification. Thus the lessons could start again in March 1946. At the same time the previous seminary teacher, a native of Poland, Dr. Woldemar Schilberg was elected as new director. Georg Vicedom succeeded Dr. Keysser as mission inspector.

In a letter dated August 17, 1945 to Bishop Meiser the two chairmen of the Society for Inner and Outer Mission, Koch and Eppelein, formulated a very general theologizing confession of guilt: "In the midst of the judgment of God under which we bow together with our German people as members of the Evangelical Lutheran Church, we realize and confess our guilt and failure. Nevertheless, we experience God's mercy which has not ended for us and our Lutheran church." The rest of the letter mainly deals with the preservation of the Lutheran confession in the foundation of the Protestant church in Germany. On October 22, 1946 the united committees of the Society for Inner and Outer Mission formulated a similarly vague confession: "The common struggle of the Lutheran churches in Germany for their commitment and their freedom can only be done in a clear recognition of the guilt that through many decisions and witness they failed in their commitment to the Lutheran confession."

On August 31, 1946, Vicedom wrote a letter to the interned missionaries in Australia. In it he complained that "few men saw through the hollowness and falsehood of the system." However, he noted that "our people have no conscience. . . . Sin and guilt of past years are like a spell on us, and do not let the people stop and repent. Without repent and forgiveness there is no new beginning. . . . Every thinking Christian should have recognized this trend even before the war. . . . For this system, no other option was given than to peter out or God would have had to renounce his claim to power." However, Vicedom laid the blame for the failure of Christians in particular to the union church of Prussia: "The church struggle had clearly put aside that each union leads to the death of Christendom." This may be seen from the fact that God has mainly destroyed the congregations of the union churches.

In 1946, Schilberg presented to the American administration an "Apology of the Neuendettelsau Mission," written in English, in which he emphasized besides the world wide missionary work "the persecutions and disadvantages which the Mission Society suffered under the rule of the Nazi party."

Ustorf, in his research on the relationship between mission and Nazism, comes to the conclusion that the other missions in Germany showed similar behavior. They had "not particularly suffered in Nazi Germany," because the restrictions affected all social groups. In contrast to the trade unions and political parties, the missions were never prohibited. "On the contrary, they enjoyed some attention by the Nazi foreign policy." Thus, the behavior of the Neuendettelsau Mission made no exception. However, the senior staff of other missionary societies usually avoided joining the NSDAP.

In October 1945, the representatives of the German missionary societies, at the insistence of the International Missionary Council, agreed on a very generalizing confession after difficult and controversial discussions in Hermannsburg: "Therefore we want to tell our brothers in the other missions that we take seriously the guilt of our people which is also our guilt, and we know that new life and new communion is only possible . . . out of the forgiveness of sins, and in a state of forgiveness."

Incidentally, it is significant that Pilhofer noted in his book on the history of the Neuendettelsau Mission: "Eppelein was rejected by the military government." No reason for this is given. One cannot avoid the impression that the mission personnel–like most other Germans–had well concealed and suppressed their own culpable involvement in the criminal Nazi regime. A real spirit of repentance and a scare about being abused by criminal rules cannot be observed. Rather, the emphasis was on self-justification, without taking responsibility for their actions. They saw themselves as victims rather than as perpetrators and referred to the many obstacles on the part of the Nazi authorities.

New Beginnings and Challenges: 1945–1972

As Eppelein's successor Rev. Dr. Woldemar Schilberg (1911–1972), originating from Poland, was appointed. He had studied theology in Greifswald and received a doctor's degree in theology in Poznan, where he later lectured. Since he came from a union church, there were objections to his appointment. He prevented the seizure of the mission house by the Americans. On New Year's Day 1946 the radio spread the news that the military government had approved the re-opening of the seminary. Then the ceremonial reopening with seven former and eight new students was held on February 3, 1946. In his homily, Schilberg said: "The war is over; the great storm that shook the world is over." Even the Free Mouth journal was allowed to resume publishing in 1948. In 1947, the Augustana Theological Seminary was established which later closely cooperated with the Mission Seminary. In 1950, Director Schilberg resigned for health reasons, became pastor in Freising, dean in Aschaffenburg, and later pastor in Oberstdorf.

Former New Guinea missionary Rev. *Hans Neumeyer* (1902–1992) was the first graduate of the seminary to be appointed as director in 1950. He had been sent to New Guinea in 1929. Because of the Second World War he could not go back after a furlough in Germany. He went through a church examination and worked as a pastor in several Bavarian congregations since 1942.

In 1950, mission inspector Georg Vicedom travelled to New Guinea to make contact with the missionaries who had returned from Australia. Then from 1951 on, the first missionaries after the war were sent from Neuendettelsau to New Guinea and Brazil. In 1956, Neumeyer travelled to attend the founding synod of the Evangelical Lutheran Church of Papua New Guinea (ELCONG) in Lae, where the American missionary John Kuder was elected as its first bishop.

In 1957, the first New Guinea Christians, Christian Gwang and Mufuano Quewai, visited Neuendettelsau. They were accompanied by the first bishop of the Lutheran Church in New Guinea, John Kuder. (Archive Mission One World)

On August 29, 1957, the first two New Guinea Christians arrived in Neuendettelsau: Christian Gwang and Mufuano Quewai. They were followed in 1963 by the first female Christian from PNG, the teacher and nurse Basano. Until then Bavarian mission friends knew Niuginis only through the reports of the missionaries. In 1961, the seventy-five-year anniversary of the New Guinea mission was celebrated in Gunzenhausen with Bishop Hermann Dietzfelbinger. The media department of the Mission Institute began with its work and has been a pioneer in introducing new media for parish work within the Bavarian church.

In the 1950s and 1960s there was a great temporary rush to the Mission and Diaspora Seminary, in which up to eighty students were taught in a total of seven years of study with four years lower course and three years upper course. Up to seventy students applied for twenty-three seminary places. In 1955, the new seminary building was inaugurated by Bishop Hermann Dietzfelbinger. The students also attended lectures at Augustana Theological Seminary and studied abroad at Wartburg Theological Seminary in Dubuque, Iowa, and the Theological College EST in Sao Leopoldo in Brazil.

In 1955, a new seminary building was opened, which is now used as a conference center. (Archive Mission One World)

At that time there were several conflicts between the students and the direction of the Mission Institute, which led to the temporary closure of the seminary operation. The students criticized the authoritarian management style and the teaching of a conservative theology. Neumeyer resigned from his office and was transferred in 1961 to Munich to work as a secretary for mission in the headquarters of ELCB.

Rev. Hagen Katterfeld (1916–1964) followed Rev. Neumeyer in 1962 but died suddenly in 1964 after a trip to New Guinea. He was followed by Rev. Dr. Wolfram von Krause (1914–1989). The theologian had taught at the Mission and Diaspora Seminary in Neuendettelsau since 1946 and went from 1957 to 1964 as General Superintendent of the Hermannsburg Mission to South Africa. From 1964 to 1972 he worked as director of the

Mission Institute, and then, like his predecessor Hans Neumeyer, became secretary for mission in the headquarters of ELCB in Munich.

In 1961, the Mission and Diaspora Seminary was separated from the mission administration due to reorganization and received its own rector. The seminary became an independent organ of the Society for Inner and Outer Mission with its own board of trustees, headed by church official Kurt Horn. Rector and mission director sat on the other's board. Since 1962, the final exam for the seminarians was chaired by a member of the Supreme Council of the ELCB. The church financed the seminary. A supplementary study at a theological faculty was made possible. The seminary took now "an intermediate position between the mission institute old-style and a theological college." (Pilhofer) From a Bible school the seminary differed by its scholarly orientation, from a theological faculty by its orientation to the profession of a missionary. The new rector, Dr. Oswald Henke (1961–1975), emphasized that the Holy Spirit is not bound to a high school diploma. The goal was a theological education in the horizon of world mission on the basis of the Lutheran confession.

"With this reorganization of the seminary, an important step was taken on the road to the integration of church and mission," wrote Pilhofer. The Lutheran church proved, through increasing subsidies, its responsibility for mission. Since 1968, the service of seminarians overseas was no longer mandatory, but the graduates were able to go directly into the church service. Certainly, the lack of pastors played a role for this decision. Some graduates also attended an additional course to receive a high school diploma.

The house rules with the so-called engagement paragraphs were gradually liberalized. While it was once forbidden to begin or maintain relationships with girls, since 1963 only "reluctance to girls" was expected. "Frivolous and early bonds were to be avoided." Engagements required the approval of the rector and the marriage was allowed the earliest at the end of the vicariate. Under the penultimate rector Rev. Ernst Lippold (1975–1980), students of the upper courses were allowed to live outside the seminary, even if they were not married. A one-year visiting study at a theological facility now was also permitted. The last rector was Rev. Dr. Hermann Reiner, who officiated until the closure of the seminary in 1985.

In 1965, ELCB enacted the first Church Law on World Mission and Ecumenical Work and founded the Committee on World Mission and Ecumenical Work. Thus, the Bavarian church increasingly took over the responsibility for mission and saw it as a necessary expression of church life.

The Department for World Mission within an Ecumenical Network: 1972–2007

So far, the Mission Institute was a legally independent institution that was working in and for the Bavarian church, but no organizational part of it. Loehe understood the foundation of the Society for Inner Mission in 1849 as temporary in time "until the church as the society of societies unites in itself all right societies."

In 1961, during its General Assembly in New Delhi, the World Council of Churches merged with the International Missionary Council. This represented an important step towards the integration of church and mission at an international level. This initiative was taken up in Germany. The term "young churches" became more than obsolete. The churches in the South wanted to establish church to church relations. Mission was now understood not only as a matter of mission friends and action groups, but as an indispensable expression of the life and nature of the whole church and of all its congregations. In 1963, the Protestant Liaison Board for World Mission was created as a national liaison committee between the German Protestant Mission Council and the Evangelical Church in Germany (EKD). From both institutions in 1975 the Association of Protestant Churches and Missions in Germany (EMW) was constituted with its headquarter in Hamburg.

In Germany from 1970 onwards, regional mission departments emerged in Wuppertal, Hamburg, Stuttgart, Berlin, Bremen, and Hermannsburg, in which the regional churches cooperated with the former missionary societies. The now independent partner churches in the South reached by this direct access to the decision-makers of the churches in the North. It was a lengthy process with critical stages. The regional churches saw some danger in the mission departments becoming independent. The grass-roots groups and ecumenical networks with their commitment to disarmament, justice, peace and integrity of creation warned against the clericalization of the mission by the church. Evangelicals feared a petrifaction or absorption of mission. In addition, concern was raised that the mission circles subsided in their support through prayer and money.

In Bavaria, the integration of church and mission was also driven forward. After two years of negotiations, the General Synod of the ELCB in

Bayreuth unanimously adopted on October 21, 1971 the revised Church Law on World Mission and Ecumenical Work. By this law effectiveApril 1, 1972, the Department for World Mission of the Evangelical Lutheran Church in Bavaria (Missionswerk der Evangelisch-Lutherischen Kirche in Bayern) was established. In this institution the missionary work of Neuendettelsau Mission was united with the missionary work of Leipzig Mission and ELCB, after the signing of contracts of ELCB with Leipzig Mission and the Society for Inner and Outer Mission. By the contract signed by Bishop Hermann Dietzfelbinger and the representatives of the Society Rev. Werner Ost and Rev. Konrad Kressel the Society transferred to ELCB "its New Guinea work and the home missionary evangelizing and information service." The Bavarian church commissioned these services to the Department for World Mission which was "to maintain the legacy of Neuendettelsau Mission." The Society handed over the administrative buildings to the new mission department. It kept the evangelistic work based on the Lutheran confession, most of the other buildings and houses for missionaries on furlough, House Luther Rose, and Free Mouth publishing house and bookstore.

The new law determined that the Department for World Mission (DWM) would get "the freedom and mobility necessary for its service" and work under the supervision of the ELCB Supreme Church Council. By that, a certain conflict was already created. Church lawyer Dr. Theodor Köberlin explained before the synod that the new institution has a "structure with extensive organizational independence," however unincorporated. It should receive "greater autonomy in the organization than all other institutions of ELCB." The Supreme Church Council provides only supervision "according to the church order."

The new institution was accompanied by a governing board with representatives from the Supreme Council, General Synod, Leipzig Mission, and the Society for Inner and Outer Mission. The ELCB governing bodies decide on finances and personnel, the Supreme Church Council appoints pastors and staff of the higher service of DWM.

For coordinating all ecumenical missionary work the Committee for World Mission and Ecumenics (Landesausschuss für Weltmission und Ökumene) was founded. It was presided over by a "representative of the Supreme Church Council," usually the executive (Oberkirchenrat) in charge of mission and ecumenism. Other members are designated by the Supreme Church Council, General Synod, Leipzig Mission, and the Mission Society. The committee should inform the church governing bodies, discuss issues, give suggestions, and work to ensure that the use of funds will be matched. It has to approve the adoption of the statutes of DWM and the appointment of its director.

New Guinea and Tanzania were stated as working fields. "Further, stable long-term partnerships require the consent of the General Synod," it says in the law. Brazil was excluded and assigned to the newly formed Association of Diaspora Services (Arbeitsgemeinschaft der Diasporadienste). It is clear that the law was still governed by thinking in terms of mission fields.

The executive board of DWM should work differently than other church bodies, in which a director is solely responsible. For DWM, not a board of directors but a staff executive board (Kollegium) was established, chaired by the director as a primus inter pares. He is—as in the Supreme Church Council of ELCB—bound by its decisions. However, he performs the administrative supervision over the secretaries and all other employees and represents the department—legally and otherwise—to the outside. The secretaries operate largely autonomously. Quorum meetings serve the exchange of experiences and ideas, consulting, coordination of work and decision-making.

Following the adoption of the new law on mission and ecumenism by the General Synod, Bishop Hermann Dietzfelbinger gave a final statement. He pointed out "that the word mission is no longer used today in many parts of ecumenism," but the Bavarian church "continues to venture the word mission." He finished his speech with a greeting to the churches overseas. "Let them take the hand that is extended to them here." The chairman of the Society for Inner and Outer Mission, Rev. Werner Ost, who had mainly handled the negotiations, emphasized: "We dare to believe that the Spirit of God can rekindle missionary action, thought, prayer, faith, and sacrifice again and again."

The law had significant effects on the structure of missionary work and the status of missionaries. The missionaries previously sent to New Guinea received as employees of the Mission Institute, only pocket money and were provided by the Lutheran Mission New Guinea with all necessary goods. With the establishment of DWM they were directly employed by ELCB, while those working in Brazil were still remunerated by the local church and the congregations. In 1976, an adopted overseas order regulated the legal and financial aspects of the service of missionaries and other employees overseas. It was later revised several times and adapted to current developments.

In 1972, the Evangelical Lutheran Church in Bavaria made an agreement with the Society for Inner and Outer Mission to take over the responsibility in relation to the Evangelical Church of the Lutheran Confession in Brazil (IECLB). The Brazil desk of the Society was not given to the newly established Department for World Mission but taken over by the church directly. At the same time, the Asssociation of Diaspora Services (Arbeitsgemeinschaft der Diasporadienste) was founded as a joint diaspora work of the Gustavus Adolphus Work and Martin Luther Association. Its first secretary was the former Brazilian pastor Ulrich Fischer, who also served as secretary for Latin America. After his departure in 1986, this function was transferred to the church headquarters in Munich and returned to Neuendettelsau in 2006.

In 1853, after the separation from Missouri Synod, Loehe's followers founded Wartburg Theological Seminary, which was relocated in 1889 to Dubuque, Iowa. In 1916, the current building was inaugurated, which was modelled after the Wartburg castle in Eisenach. Students celebrate their devotions in the Loehe Chapel. Since the 1950s, intensive relations between the Neuendettelsau Mission and Diaspora Seminary and Wartburg Theological Seminary developed. The students from Neuendettelsau could now study there for one semester. Numerous graduates of Wartburg Theological Seminary worked in PNG. Therefore, there is also a New Guinea museum.

In the new building of Wartburg Theological Seminary in Dubuque, Iowa, erected in 1916, in the Loehe Chapel a plaque commemorates of the founder of this seminary, where many Neuendettelsau seminarians studied. (Privately owned)

Since the 1970s, negotiations on the future of the Mission and Diaspora Seminary took place repeatedly. The number of seminarians varied between thirty-five and eighty. There were occasional recruitment stops, and the costs of one million Deutschmarks per year played a role. The ELCB General Synod finally decided on April 30, 1979 by a large majority that no new applicants be taken, but the current students should finish their education. The possibility of a continuation of the MDS has been kept open.

The following reasons were given in the proceedings of the General Synod:

> 1. School education opportunities have improved and the number of high school graduates has risen. There are now few applicants for a non-academic education.
>
> 2. The newly founded seminary for later called young men (Pfarrverwalterseminar) can receive candidates.
>
> 3. Many of the graduates do not go overseas or often return after only one period of work.
>
> 4. The Institute for Mission Studies (Missionskolleg) began its work and offers courses in the field of mission and ecumenism.

5. The number of students of theology at the universities has risen considerably.

6. The ELCB can no longer hold the moral obligation to provide a pastoral position for the graduates.

7. The model of a lifelong missionary is obsolete. The service in a partner church is now only a temporary missionary task. Also, there is ambiguity in the partner churches on future requirements for overseas employees.

8. The last courses consisted mainly of high school or middle school students, not of young men who had completed their vocational training as was originally intended.

DWM informed the Supreme Church Council that, due to the changed situation in the partner churches, all-round missionaries are no longer needed. Rather, DWM seeks primarily academically trained theologians for special tasks. A role was also played by the moratorium demand of the World Missionary Conference in Bangkok in 1972, so that it was uncertain how long missionaries could be sent.

In 1985, therefore, the mission seminary which was founded by Friedrich Bauer in 1846 ended after 138 years of blessed work. Nearly nine hundred young men had successfully completed the seminary and went into the service of the Lutheran churches in America, Brazil, Australia, New Guinea, Ukraine, Palestine, Austria, and other countries. They formed the core of the missionary work. Later theologians and non-theologians who were in the service of the mission had not experienced, like the seminarians had, a missionary embossed living and learning community. They were prepared for their work in courses of only some weeks. Other mission seminaries in Germany also closed; the last being the seminary in Hermannsburg. The building of the Mission and Diaspora Seminary was converted into a conference center in which from 1986 on, courses and seminars on topics of mission and ecumenism were held.

In a joint statement the Society for Inner and Outer Mission and the ELCB Supreme Church Council on the occasion of the closure of the Mission and Diaspora Seminary (MDS) expressed "their common thanks to those who worked in the MDS and to all who worked in the mission of our overseas partner churches and in our church and still do." Both declared at the same time their willingness "to enter into a re-examination of the matter, if a situation should arise in which a resumption of this work will be in the interest of ELCB and its mission tasks." Rector Oswald

Henke said in his speech at the occasion of the closure of the MDS on September 28, 1985: "As a result of an attempt to bring together the visible fruits of their labor, it can only be stated: Men from this seminary are responsible, and often instrumental in the development and growth of a number of Lutheran churches around the world."

Rev. Horst Becker, DD (born 1926), worked from 1972 to 1991 as the first director of the newly established Department for World Mission (Missionswerk) and promoted cooperation with Lutheran churches in Africa and Asia. (Archive Mission One World)

Rev. Horst Becker, DD, (born 1926) began working in 1972 as the first director of the Department for World Mission. He was sent in 1958 by Leipzig Mission to Tanzania, where he worked as a missionary and later deputy bishop in the ELCT Northern Diocese. In 1965, he was appointed secretary for mission (Oberkirchenrat) of the Evangelical Lutheran Church of Germany. He was installed in his office as director on July 12, 1972 at the mission festival in Gunzenhausen by Bishop Hermann Dietzfelbinger. He first had to achieve the task of fitting the previously independent missionary institution into the structures of ELCB. He also saw the negative consequences of the integration of church and mission. "Integration should not be the keyword for domestication, uncomfortable missionary activity or for bureaucratization of relations with partner churches." He demanded that the identification of congregation members, pastors and church leaders with the missionary work could be improved. He saw the danger of a "bureaucratization of the mission," in which the tension cannot be bared "between an unconventional working style of people with a heart for mission and the normal procedures within the church."

The discussions in Germany in the 1970s were especially marked by two conflicts. On the one hand the evangelical and ecumenical groups were hostile towards one another. In 1970, the Confessing Movement "No Other Gospel" adopted the Frankfurt Declaration Concerning the Fundamental Crisis in Mission which emphasized preaching and conversion as the essence of missionary work. In Lausanne in 1974 the International Congress on World Evangelization was held. Also within DWM discussions took place about the right allocation of evangelization and development-related work. The request of the Ethiopian Evangelical Church Mekane Yesus on the relationship between gospel and development played a role. The LWF responded in 1974 pointing out the holistic nature of the mission.

On the other hand, the World Missionary Conference in Bangkok in 1972 demanded a moratorium on human resources and finances. The churches in the South should thus express their independence by temporarily waiving away missionaries and money from the North. In discussions with partners, DWM won the conviction that these are still dependent on professionals and grants from the North for their numerous projects, and therefore continue to ask for employees from overseas.

In most church districts in Bavaria, partnership programs were founded which cultivated relations with districts and congregations particularly in Tanzania and Papua New Guinea. The result was an extended network which was accompanied by the DWM secretariat for parish work and regional offices. These were established in Bayreuth (1975), Munich (1980), Würzburg (1986), and Altdorf (1991) and later concentrated into the regions of north (Bayreuth) and south (Munich). The secretariat for parish work also organized a yearly mission festival, which took place at various locations in Bavaria until 1992.

Already since 1922, there was a mission museum in Neuendettelsau which was visited by many congregation groups and confirmation classes. Due to the modified missionary situation it needed redesigning. Thus ‚the permanent exhibition "World Mission Today" was opened in 1974, which took the place of the former mission museum. Its purpose was "to make visible and clear for congregations and confirmation classes, as well as individual visitors . . . what is at stake in world mission, why its service just today and tomorrow is so urgently needed, and why Christianity is committed to such a service."

In the 1980s, there were negotiations with the Evangelical Lutheran Church of Papua New Guinea (ELCPNG) for whether ethnographic objects, brought by missionaries and previously shown in the mission museum, should be returned to the church. The Bavarian church agreed to provide funds for the establishment of a museum in Lae. All over the world the UNESCO demanded the former colonial powers to return the objects brought from the colonies to Europe, to their home countries. Australia did that and presented objects and funds for the National Museum in Port Moresby. The present state of this museum can, however, doubt the sense of such a return. Negotiations between DWM and ELCPNG ended in 1987 without result. The ethnological collection will now form the basis for a new exhibition which is a project pursued by the Association for Culture of New Guinea, which was founded in 2006.

In the 1970s, all over Germany, the concept of two-way traffic developed. "World Mission—Today we are Partners" could be read on many posters. Mission takes place no longer alone from North to South, but also from South to North. Therefore in 1978, Rev. Zephaniah Mgeyekwa (1938–2012) came as the first African exchange pastor to Bavaria and worked from 1979 to 1982 in Coburg. On his return to Tanzania, he officiated from 1991 to 2003 as bishop of ELCT Southern Diocese. The first New Guinea exchange pastor came only twenty years later, Rev. Baafecke Bamiringnu, who from 1998 to 2002 worked in the parish of Dietenhofen near Neuendettelsau. Regularly, guest lecturers from the partner churches were invited for one year by the Institute for Mission Studies. Already from 1975 to 1978 the Korean theologian Dr. Won Yong Ji worked as the first ecumenical staff in the director's office of DWM. In 1989, a native of Lebanon, Dr. Wanis Semaan, began his service as a lecturer in the Institute for Mission Studies with a focus on Christian-Islamic dialogue.

Bishop Zephaniah Mgeyekwa (1938–2012) worked, starting in 1979, as the first African exchange pastor in Bavaria. After his return, he served from 1991 to 2003 as bishop in southern Tanzania. (Archive Mission One World)

The youth desk, established in 1976, reached many students with the ecumenical cooperation of the Catholic organization Missio Munich. The executive board of DWM coordinated the work of the secretaries and developed common concepts, e.g. guidelines for missionary service. In these guidelines, the mission statement of LWF (1983) was taken up and reference made to the conciliar process. Witness and service belong together; ecumenical learning is to be done in dialogue with partner churches.

The funds of DWM were split three ways, the thirds going to Africa, PNG, and to the local administration. Director Becker repeatedly pointed out that the budget of DWM compared to the general budget of ELCB had not increased but had dropped from 2.8 percent to 2.2 percent. Collections and donations contributed about 20 percent to the budget. They, however, did not increase as much as the church tax revenue. Becker emphasized in this regard that mission was a mandatory task of the church. Although the subsidies to the partner churches are not a legal obligation, they have nevertheless an ethical quality.

In the 1970s and 1980s, the scope of DWM expanded greatly beyond its previous priorities in New Guinea and Tanzania. Becker brought with him, from his previous position at the Lutheran church headquarters in Hanover, many contacts with Lutheran churches in Asia. These churches looked for connections with a church in the land of Luther, which DMW facilitated and invited them for East Asia seminars. In 1988, DWM developed the first long-range planning for Asia / Pacific, which was updated in 1997. In the budget of DWM, an amount for innovative missionary projects in Asia was set. In Africa, DWM followed in the footsteps of the missionary activities of the Tanzanian church in Kenya, Congo / Zaire, and Mozambique. LWF asked the Bavarian church to support the work of the Lutheran Church in Liberia. The cooperation with LWF was intensified. DWM developed more and more into an international missionary center which took part in the world mission on behalf of the Bavarian church.

DWM intensified the cooperation with the Leipzig Mission. Since 1908, it owned a house in Erlangen, from where coworkers toured the Bavarian congregations. Due to the division of Germany after the Second World War, the Lutheran Mission (Leipzig Mission) Erlangen was established. Because missionaries could no longer be sent from the German Democratic Republic beginning in 1960, they were sent by the office in Erlangen to India, Tanzania, New Guinea, and Brazil. Mission candidates from Leipzig Mission were also trained at the seminary in Neuendettelsau. The Publishing House of the Evangelical Lutheran Mission (Verlag der Ev.-Luth. Mission), which was reestablished in 1950 in Erlangen, developed since 1965 a broad journalistic activity, especially under the leadership of Rev. Christoph Jahn. It was acquired in 1995 by DWM and purchased for the symbolic sum of one German mark. Under the name "Erlangen Publishing Company for Missions and Ecumenics" (Erlanger Verlag für Mission und Ökumene) it is today one of the leading mission publishers in Germany.

In the German Democratic Republic, the mission has long been considered as a relic of the colonial past. Therefore, the Leipzig Mission had difficulties in its operations. In 1951 an agreement was signed, according to which the offices in Erlangen and Hildesheim should be self-reliant in their congregational work, but the unity of the Leipzig Mission should be maintained. Although these were economically independent and subordinate to the executive board in Leipzig, the East German government forbade any financial connection with West Germany. Among the missionaries circulated the saying: "From Erlangen we receive our contract and our money, but the Leipzig Mission is our home." Bavaria was the largest field of work for the Leipzig Mission in West Germany. The United Evangelical Lutheran Church of Germany in the time of the division of Germany considered the Leipzig Mission in continuation of its founding concept as "a direct expression of the life of the Lutheran church," which extends to all Lutheran churches. It facilitated contacts and transferred financial resources from West to East, in which the Bavarian mission participated intensively. Regular contacts took place especially during trade fairs in Leipzig.

The regionalization of the mission societies ended the universal outreach of the Leipzig Mission and its importance for Bavaria in the 1970s. Many Leipzig missionaries were taken into the service of the Bavarian mission and retired in Bavaria after their return from overseas. For a long time, the Leipzig Mission was represented in the Evangelical Lutheran Central Association for Foreign Mission, the ELCB Committee for World Mission and Ecumenics, and the governing board of the Department for World Mission. Until 1995, it had to be consulted at the appointment of a director. It influenced, thereby, the missionary work in Bavaria. After the reunification of Germany in 1990, the Leipzig Mission has been reconstituted as Leipzig Mission Society (Leipziger Mission e.V.). It took back the direct responsibility for missionary work in India, Tanzania, and

New Guinea. It lost, however, its Lutheran universality and became the regional missionary institute of the churches in Saxony, Thuringia, and Mecklenburg.

The political changes in Germany beginning in 1989 also influenced the mission scene. The Association of Churches and Missions in Germany (EMW) was redesigned. The partner churches feared that the Germans would now only deal with themselves and all funds would go into the reconstruction of the new federal states. But these fears were dispelled.

Director Becker criticized the fact that the Bavarian church did not do enough with the missionary challenges that arose from the presence of Muslims in Germany. Not only were social activities needed, but also a spiritual testimony. Therefore in 1989, he invited three missionaries from the Finnish Evangelical Lutheran Mission (FELM) to Bavaria, who were prepared for their task in Neuendettelsau. In 1992, the negotiations between FELM and DWM led to the formation of the Center for Christian-Muslim Encounter "Bridge-Koprü" in Nuremberg.

At the end of Becker's time Helmut Winter described in the Bavarian Lutheran Sunday Journal the present state of mission work: DWM currently has eighty employees overseas, forty-six in PNG, twenty-six in Tanzania, five in Zaire, and three in Kenya. They come from many professions such as doctors, teachers, financial and administrative specialists, engineers, etc. Only one third are theologians. Sixty-five employees work in the administration in Neuendettelsau. "We will have to make sure that soon not more mission personnel work in our own country than overseas."

On January 31, 1992, Bishop Johannes Hanselmann installed Rev. Dr. Hermann Vorländer (born 1942) from Munich as mission director. Vorländer had received a doctorate in theology from the University of Erlangen in 1971 and taught from 1972 to 1976 as professor of Old Testament at the Near East School of Theology in Beirut (Lebanon). Later he worked as a pastor in Kaufbeuren, and as church executive and dean in Munich. He was, according to press reports, considered as a "surprise candidate" because he had not gone through a classical missionary career. During his installation service in St. Nikolai Church, he preached on Romans 1:16f. and called for a joyful missionary testimony, which shares the power of God becoming manifest in Christ.

In Vorländer's early months there was some turbulence. With the support of DWM the Starnberg Institute for the Survival Conditions of the Twenty-First Century had written, on behalf of the Papua New

Guinea Council of Churches, the study *Development and Environment— Economic-Ecological Development in Papua New Guinea*. The study showed drastically the contamination of the rivers Ok Tedi and Fly River that are caused by the daily breakdown of 150,000 tons of scree at Mt. Fubilan for extracting gold and copper. An originally planned retention dam was never built. The study was published in 1991 by the church-owned magazine *PNG Times*.

Based on this study, the government of Papua New Guinea (PNG) issued, at the end of 1991, a decree according to which all individuals and institutions associated with the Starnberg study should be set on a blacklist and deported from the country. It felt offended in its honor as a sovereign, democratic state. Also, financial aspects played a role, since 50 percent of the exports of PNG come from the mine, and provide considerable revenue to the state through taxes and government shares. The German Federal Government reacted angrily, since it feared diplomatic complications. Through the German Development Company (DEG) the government was a shareholder of the Ok Tedi Mining Ltd. (OTML) in cooperation with the German companies Degussa and Metal Society (Metallgesellschaft). The news of the expulsion of the Bavarian missionaries struck in Neuendettelsau like a bomb. Was this the end of the hundred-year close relationship between Bavaria and PNG? This news was followed by multiple negotiations with the governments in Bonn and Port Moresby, with firms and organizations. The PNG secretary Rev. Gernot Fugmann entered PNG on January 21, 1992, although simultaneously the instruction had been given to the PNG embassy in Bonn not to issue a visa for him. This obviously had been threaded by OTML since he was planning a visit to the mine.

In the context of the debate over the Ok Tedi Mine in PNG, German Development Minister Carl-Dieter Spranger visited the Mission Institute and met with (from the left) Bishop Ronald Diggs (Liberia), Bishop Samson Mushemba (Tanzania), Bishop Sir Getacke Gam (PNG), MP Bart Philemon (PNG), and Director Hermann Vorländer. (Archive Mission One World)

In the Protestant Academy Tutzing in April 1992, a conference was held on "Papua New Guinea at the Focal Point of the South Pacific," which was attended by PNG Minister of Justice Bernard Narakobi (1936–2010) and Ambassador Peter Donigi. In personal conversations, misunderstandings could be clarified. The visit of the Federal Minister for Economic Cooperation and Development, Carl-Dieter Spranger, on April 22, 1992 in Neuendettelsau brought some clarifications and relaxation of the conflict situation. The matter of Ok Tedi was discussed in the Committee on Economic Cooperation and Development of the German Federal Parliament (Bundestag). The party Alliance 90 / The Greens formulated a resolution that was adopted on January 14, 1993 in a modified form by the plenary. In it, the federal government had been asked to put pressure on the German shareholders on OTML that it reduces the negative impact of mining operations on the environment according to internationally valid standards and that the affected people are more compensated. Because of the fierce public debate, Germany withdrew from its shares in the mine. Later the mine was mainly acquired by the Australian group Broken Hills Pty (BHP), which sold its shares in 2001 to a welfare fund.

Its income mainly went into structural development measures in the villages along the areas affected by the toxic clearing from the mine, until the PNG government completely took over the mine into its possession. In January 1993, Vorländer and Fugmann visited the mine in order to get a clear picture of the site. For the first time DWM has been involved in an important development debate, which had far-reaching consequences not only in Germany, but particularly in PNG and Australia.

At an evening of encounter in March 1992, the establishment of DWM twenty years earlier was commemorated. In this context, contacts were made with ELCB governing bodies and the Committee for World Mission and Ecumenics to take up again the stalled negotiations on an amendment of the mission and ecumenism law of 1971. The law was still determined by an outdated bilateral mission field thinking and too little took into account the current multilateral cooperation of churches and missions in the context of ecumenical networks. Mission can no longer be understood geographically-regional, but theologically-functional as a manifestation of the global nature of churches in every continent.

On 12 July 1992, the farewell of the first two missioners, Adam Ernst and Georg Burger, sent by Wilhelm Loehe to North America on July 12, 1842, was remembered with a special service and assembly under the slogan "150 Years of Missioners Sent from Neuendettelsau." From this event the annual feast of the worldwide church was developed, which attracts many people to a colorful festival with music, reports, and information booths. On January 1, 1993 the dean of Nuremberg district, Dr. Johannes Friedrich, inaugurated the Christian Muslim Center of Encounter "Bridge-Köprü" in Nuremberg. In the beginning, the Finnish Evangelical Lutheran Mission (FELM) made available personnel and finances for this unique project. As "a testimony service among Muslims in mutual respect," this project should encourage encounters between Christians and Muslims and inform the congregations about Islam.

In July 1994, a consultation with representatives of partner churches in Neuendettelsau was held in preparation for the meeting of the General Synod in Regensburg on "Global Responsibility in Dialogue with Partner Churches." The final declaration highlighted the unjust consequences of the international economic order for developing countries. A solution for the high indebtedness of the so-called Third World must be found so that more funds can be made available for education, health, agriculture, drinking water, etc. After the consultation, the participants took part in the installation of the new ELCB bishop, Hermann von Loewenich in Nuremberg.

As a follow-up of the East Asia seminars, the new concept of a summer school was developed, to which all Lutheran churches were invited. It dealt with aspects of the overall theme "Lutheran Theology in the Land of Martin Luther." Also, women and youth leader consultations were carried out regularly.

In 1995, a financial scandal shook DWM, which led to the dismissal of the secretary for finance and administration. DWM had partly invested donated funds in shares in the 1980s, which led to substantial losses in 1987. This had now been uncovered and provoked quite a media response. All shares were sold. Vorländer emphasized in an interview: "As long as I am director, no single share will be bought." An official investigation found no unjust enrichment or embezzlement. However, losses could have been avoided if the money would have been conservatively invested in fixed income securities. The headlines about the unfortunate share transactions did not significantly affect the income through donations.

The meeting of the General Synod in Regensburg in November 1995 was opened with a service in which the bishop of the Lutheran Church in Congo and former DWM scholarship holder, Ngoy Kasukuti, delivered the sermon. The final declaration of the synod included demands on politics, society and church in sustainable production, sustainable agriculture and rural development, partnerships, statements against deforestation and nuclear tests in the Pacific, demands for the promotion of women's work, strengthening the democratization process in Africa, debt relief, etc. The initiative to promote alternative energy sources in Africa was welcomed by the synod. It decided that subsidies for partner churches should not be shortened, although the church budget was reduced by 8 percent.

At the same time, the amended Church Law on Mission and Ecumenism was adopted. The new law differed between mission and ecumenism as areas of work, for which DWM and the church headquarters are respectively responsible. While the primary goal of the church law of 1971 was the establishment of DWM, this new church law now also describes the activities of the church headquarters in the fields of ecumenism, conciliar process, interreligious dialogue, study and education work.

Under the new law, DWM was to develop and strengthen the understanding and responsibility for ecumenical-missionary and developmental work, especially through publicity, study work, and accompanying of partnerships. It was important that its "freedom and mobility necessary for the performance of its duties" was retained. Also, the scope has been expanded: DWM performs tasks, "arising from the historically grown connections to the partner churches in Africa, Asia, and the Pacific. Other time-limited tasks in international cooperation can be adopted as far as the necessary funding can be made available. Only "new stable, long-term partnerships with other churches must be approved by the synod."

A missionary conference was installed as an instrument of the basis. In recent decades, an almost countrywide network of district and congregation partnerships had arisen that came together to annual consultations. In the new form of a missionary conference it received a solid structure and is composed of the district mission pastors and lay mission representatives. They send their representatives into the ELCB Committee for Mission and Ecumenics and the governing board of DWM.

On July 11, 1997 the Department for World Mission celebrated its twenty-fifth anniversary. During the service at St.Nikolai Church Bishop Hermann von Loewenich (right) held the sermon. (Archive Mission One World)

During a festive service on the occasion of the twenty-fifth anniversary of DWM on July 11, 1997, Bishop Dr Hermann von Loewenich held the sermon. He emphasized the unity of inner and outer mission, calling Neuendettelsau the "gateway to the world" of the Bavarian church. "The globalization of the gospel will prove to be more viable than the globalization of capital."

At the feast of the worldwide church in July 2000, von Loewenich's successor Bishop Dr. Johannes Friedrich stated: "I say yes to mission as the task of our church and therefore I say yes to the Department for World Mission of our church." He continued by saying that Germany is not the center of the world, and mission is no longer a one-way street. "The globalization of the gospel must take precedence over the global economy." The idea of tolerance does not mean the renunciation of mission, because the only way of salvation with God goes through Christ. In 2001, the bishop made a visitation in DWM and won a positive impression, especially of the partnership relations in the congregations and districts. He expressed the wish to hold talks with returnees regularly, and his willingness to encourage Bavarian pastors to work in overseas churches. He suggested a better link of DWM with other institutions of the church.

Initiated by ELCB synod member Fritz Schroth, a consultation process in various forms was carried out for several years to clarify how the entire field of ecumenism, mission, development, and partnership work was to be reorganized. Some considered DWM as too big, powerful, independent, and non-transparent. The church governing bodies demanded more influence. The new mission center should be organized more like other church institutions. Its independence should be preserved, but the church headquarters should be more involved in the ongoing decision-making process.

A long and arduous journey had to be followed. Vorländer indicated in the numerous meetings that ELCB still needs a missionary institution as a service center with a global missionary dimension. As a big and rich Lutheran church, ELCB carries responsibility for the dissemination of the gospel throughout the world. It has considerable importance as a global player within the Lutheran churches worldwide and in Germany.

As a result of these discussions, the General Synod unanimously decided the new Church Law on Ecumenics, Mission, Development Service, and Partnership at its meeting in Rummelsberg on November 30, 2006. The Department for World Mission became Mission One World—Center for Partnership, Development and Mission of the Evangelical

Lutheran Church in Bavaria (Mission EineWelt—Centrum für Partnerschaft, Entwicklung und Mission der Evangelisch-Lutherischen Kirche in Bayern—MEW). After a long discussion the word "mission" could be kept and a useful name was finally found in which are included both mission as the holistic proclamation of the faith as well as development work as a commitment to the One World.

The current law is much shorter than its predecessors. In the deliberations, reference was made to paragraph 38 of the church constitution: "ELCB is firmly committed to the participation in world mission and worldwide ecumenical partnership. It calls persons into missionary work, trains them and sends them . . . This happens through worship, congregation events, fundraising activities. . . . The missionary institutions within the church order have the right to organize their work as it corresponds to their mission." The church headquarters is responsible for the operational management of the entire field of ecumenism, mission, development service, and partnership. The Center Mission One World carries out on behalf of ELCB, partnership relations with churches in Africa, Pacific, East Asia, and Latin America. It should continue to accomplish this in "self-responsibility and freedom." It is designed to work through staff exchange and financial assistance with other churches. It should promote the understanding of mission and development by publicity and educational work, lobbying, and advocacy.

With the establishment of the new organization, the responsibility for the Latin American churches returned to Neuendettelsau. Already in connection with the General Synod of 1995 DWM tried to convince the church governing bodies that relations with Latin America should be treated as equal with the relations to Africa or PNG and bundled in one center. This request was then rejected, but now realized. On January 1, 2006 the secretary for Latin America, Rev. Wolfgang Döbrich, moved his desk to Neuendettelsau and prepared the inclusion of its operating range into the new center. Also, the Bavarian Church Development Service, which formerly was attached to the Diaconic Services in Nuremberg, was now integrated into the new center as department for development and politics.

The director and the seven department heads form the executive board (Kollegium). Its meetings are attended by the mission secretary of ELCB church headquarters in an advisory capacity. The conference of mission, ecumenics, development, and partnership accompanies and coordinates cooperation in the whole field of action. The church headquarters exerts the operational and strategic management of the area of action and transmits most operational tasks to the new center. The governing board (Kuratorium) is made up of the chairpersons of the six advisory committees to supervise the work. It also decides on the appointment of the director and the department heads.

The former Institute for Mission Studies was renamed the Department for Mission and Intercultural Studies. In conferences, seminars, and international study weeks current themes from intercultural and missionary theology are addressed dealing with the world's growing neo-Pentecostal churches and the theology of prosperity, the relationship and dialogue between Christianity and Islam world-wide, new approaches to liberation theology, mission theology, theology and spirituality of migrant congregations in Germany, etc. The department is also responsible for the Evangelical Lutheran Central Association for Foreign Mission.

By integrating the responsibilities for Latin America and Church Development Service, new issues came into foreground such as global justice and the causes of global injustice, impacts of globalization, fair trade, etc.

With a worship and ceremony, the new Center Mission One World was opened on January 14, 2007. The sermon was held by Bishop Dr. Johannes Friedrich. On behalf of the partner churches Bishop Medardo Gómez from El Salvador pleaded: "Let us not alone."

The General Synod in Rummelsberg also approved a declaration of principles: "The External Relations of the ELCB—a Contribution to the Worldwide Communion." It describes partnership in mission as a common path and emphasizes the communication between equal partners.

On November 20–23, 2007, the first consultation of the Bavarian church with its overseas partners was held in Neuendettelsau. (Archive Mission One World)

The completion of the reorganization of the field of action was marked by a consultation of the Bavarian church with its sixteen overseas partners November 20–23, 2007. In its final declaration, the participants emphasized that they wanted to fulfill, as missionary churches, a common mission in partnership responsibility. They called for regular multilateral consultations of ELCB with its partners and advocated mutual visits in both directions. The networking and cooperation between the southern partners was to be encouraged. The participants also attended the farewell ceremonies for Dr. Vorländer.

As Vorländer`s successor, Rev. Peter Weigand (born 1949) was appointed and took over his office on January 1, 2008. As a graduate of the Neuendettelsau Mission and Diaspora Seminary he had worked from 1977 to 1985 in Lutheran churches in Brazil and Chile. He then headed the Collegium Oecumenicum in Munich which was erected by the Martin Luther Association as an ecumenical center for students. From 1993 to 2007, he worked as secretary for the Americas in the EKD headquarters in Hannover. He retired in 2015.

In 2008, the Evangelical Lutheran Church in Bavaria celebrated the two-hundredth birthday of Wilhelm Loehe. During the festival a replica of the bell that Loehe in 1845 gave to the emigrants for the settlement in Frankenmuth was displayed in front of the Loehe Era Museum (Löhe-Zeit-Museum) in Neuendettelsau.

During 2008 the ELCB celebrated the two-hundredth birthday of Wilhelm Loehe as one of the most influcential persons of the church. A festive assembly was held in Neuendettelsau in front of the Loehe Era Museum. A replica of the bell that Loehe gave to the emigrants in 1845 is displayed and Judy Zehnder from Frankenmuth, Michigan, gives a word of greeting. (Privately owned)

In 2012, the town of Neuendettelsau and the Center Mission One World celebrated the two-hundredth birthday of Friedrich Bauer. During the festive service the Bavarian Bishop Dr. Heinrich Bedford-Strohm held his sermon simultaneously in German and English. A memorial for Bauer was erected by the town of Neuendettelsau. Bauer's descendants James, John, and Levi Bauer came from America and took part in the celebration.

In July 2012 the two-hundredth birthday of Friedrich Bauer was celebrated in Neuendettelsau. Bauer's descendants James, John, and Levi Bauer (from left) stand in front of the memorial for their ancestor. (Privately owned)

The governing board of Mission One World elected in 2014 the missionary couple Dr. Gabriele Hoerschelmann (born 1968) and Hanns Hoerschelmann (born 1965) as new directors. They were installed during the festival of the worldwide church on July 18, 2015 by church official Michael Martin. The Hoerschelmanns were sent in 2004 by DWM to Hong Kong. Dr. Gabriele Hoerschelmann worked as a lecturer and assistant dean at the Lutheran Theological Seminary, Hanns Hoerschelmann worked as secretary of the Mekong Mission Forum and pastor of the German-speaking congregation. They practice job sharing in dividing their responsibilities.

Rev. Dr. Gabriele and Hanns Hoerschelmann have shared the director's position of the Center Mission One World since 2015.

2

The History of Cooperation of the Bavarian Lutheran Mission with Overseas Churches

Pacific and East Asia

Australia and New Guinea came to the attention of the Neuendettelsau Mission in the nineteenth century. The connections with the East Asian Lutheran churches arose only in the 1980s. In 1977, Director Horst Becker enabled a Taiwanese delegation to enter Bavaria after they had been refused by the Tanzanian government to attend the LWF Assembly in Dar es Salaam. From this developed the East Asia seminars, which were organized by the DWM Institute for Mission Studies since 1979, to present "the church of the Reformation in the land of the Reformation." The mostly small Lutheran churches sought contact with the country of origin of the Reformation. DWM responded to such requests only if those churches had not yet had any direct relations with Germany.

The Korean theologian Dr. Won Yong Ji worked from 1975 to 1978 as assistant to the director of DWM. He encouraged DWM to expand its relations with Asia. He called Asia a "sleeping giant," to which world Christianity should pay special attention.

In 1991, a LWF mission consultation was held in Malacca (Malaysia), where in the nineteenth century the German missionary Karl Gützlaff (1803–1851) had started his missionary work in China. Countries were distinguished according to their eating habits, namely chopstick (China, Japan, Korea), satay (Indonesia, Philippines, PNG), curry (India, Bangladesh, Malaysia), potato (Europe, USA). The participants agreed on more intensive cooperation in terms of missionary projects, theological education, promotion of theological literature, etc.

Christianity exerts in Asia a high attraction, far beyond the numerically often small churches. The Bible contains outstanding ethics; Christian faith is combined with Western culture, music, and art. The congregations share in worship, pastoral care, and the recognition of the individual. Except in Korea and the Philippines, there are small churches which develop an amazing missionary power in the diaspora. Twice as many people as church members consider themselves Christians but shy away from baptism for various reasons.

Australia

General

Australia is a huge country with more than seven million square kilometers and about 23 million inhabitants. It is a parliamentary monarchy, with Queen Elisabeth II as head of state, who is represented by a governor general. Its capital is Canberra. The indigenous population, called Aborigines, has lived here for more than 50,000 years. Since the eighteenth century their lives have been constantly cut back by the settlers invading from Europe. In 1770, James Cook conquered the country for the British crown.

The Cooperation with the Lutheran Church

In 1838, the first German immigrants came to Australia, since they had been expelled because of their Lutheran faith from Silesia (Prussia). They settled in the Barossa Valley near Adelaide in South Australia. From 1860, Queensland was the main settlement area of the Germans in the north. The Lutherans were split early into several synods.

In 1838, two Dresden and several Gossner missionaries began to work among the original population, the Aborigines. In 1860, the Africa missionary Johann Meischel, originating from Bavaria, was sent by the Neuendettelsau Mission to the Evangelical Lutheran Synod of Australia. On his initiative, the Australian Lutherans in 1863 began with the missionary work among the Aborigines. In 1874, the Hermannsburg Mission started a mission station in Central Australia, which bears the name of Hermannsburg to this day. However, the Hermannsburg Mission withdrew in 1891 and handed over its missionary work to the Immanuel Synod.

Since 1873, the Immanuel Synod put forth several requests for missioners from the Mission Institute in Neuendettelsau. Finally, in 1875 Johann Stolz was sent as the first graduate of the seminary. He was followed up to 1933 by fifty-seven missioners, among them Johann Flierl, who was sent to Australia in 1878 and worked there until 1885 among the Aborigines.

Carl F. Strehlow (1871–1922) came as a Neuendettelsau missioner to Australia and worked especially among the Aborigines in Central Australia. He gained great merits both in ethnological research and in defending the rights of indigenous people. The picture shows him with his wife, Frieda, sister of Christian Keysser. (Privately owned)

Another important missioner was Carl F. Strehlow (1871–1922), who since 1892 worked among the Aborigines in the Finke River Mission in Hermannsburg. He was married to Frieda, a sister of Christian Keysser who vigorously supported him in his work. Both campaigned for the rights of the Aborigines and defended them against the widespread abuses by farmers and policemen. The local population was suffering from syphilis, high infant mortality, lack of educational opportunities, and arbitrary executions. Strehlow also rendered great services in the study of language, religion, and culture of the Aranda and Luritja peoples. He translated parts of the Bible in the Aranda language. Strehlow influenced, by his research, European ethnological and linguistic research, for example, Sigmund Freud (*Totem and Taboo*), Claude Lévi-Strauss, and Mircea Eliade.

Because of their links to Germany, the German language in the Lutheran churches and schools was banned during the First World War. The government suspected the parishioners of espionage and imprisoned some of them. After the war, New Guinea became an Australian mandated territory. According to the Treaty of Versailles, the German missionaries were to be expelled and their work assigned to another Protestant denomination. In particular, mission director Otto Theile, who had studied in Neuendettelsau, vigorously represented the interests of the Neuendettelsau Mission. He intervened with the Australian government against the impending expulsion of the missionaries and prevented the work falling to the Australian Anglicans. The United Evangelical Lutheran Church of Australia set up a trust company that took over the legal ownership of the former German mission bodies in New Guinea.

After the United Evangelical Lutheran Church of Australia took over the sponsorship for the Neuendettelsau Mission, it reinforced the missionary work in New Guinea by sending personnel. Many intense, even family relationships developed between the Neuendettelsau missionaries and the Lutheran Christians in Australia. When the Neuendettelsau missionaries were interned during the Second World War in Australia, the local Lutherans took care of their families. The children of the missionaries were able to visit, since 1945, St. Peter's College with boarding school in Brisbane. Missionary families went repeatedly to recreation or medical treatment to Australia.

Seven synods formed the Evangelical Lutheran Church in Australia in 1921, which cooperated with the Lutheran Church–Missouri Synod (LCMS) and the United Evangelical Lutheran Church of Australia, which cooperated with the Neuendettelsau Mission and later the LWF. They joined together in 1967 to form the Lutheran Church of Australia (LCA) based in Adelaide. They agreed that they would not maintain closer relations with the LCMS or with the LWF. Later the LCA joined the LWF as an associate member. As its first president, Rev. Max Loehe was elected, whose father Paul, a grandnephew of Loehe, had been sent in 1889 from Neuendettelsau. The church has about 80,000 members in five districts, including New Zealand, who are looked after by four hundred pastors in three hundred congregations. The church had almost three hundred schools with approximately 23,000 pupils. In Adelaide, the church runs a theological college, founded in 1923 by Paul Loehe, to which it also invites scholars from abroad, as well as a teacher college. On the introduction of women's ordination, the church has not yet made a decision. Lately it is strongly committed to protecting the Aborigines and the reconciliation between black and white. Six thousand Aborigines belong to the church under the leadership of ordained indigenous pastors.

Australian Lutherans seconded from 1902 to 1990 a total of 175 missionaries to New Guinea, and later to Malaysia. They worked closely with the Neuendettelsau missionaries. In the church headquarters in Adelaide the financial grants of overseas partners for ELCPNG were handled for many years. From the work of the mission in Australia, the Neuendettelsau missionary work in New Guinea developed since 1886. Many PNG missionaries from Bavaria completed their language and orientation program with the help of the LCA in Australia or stay there for medical treatments.

Since 1992, the LCA more and more pulled out from New Guinea. Financial constraints and the concentration on the home mission are given as reasons. Also, the church wishes to operate more in the Asia region by sending counselors and teachers to Sumatra, Thailand and Malaysia. It is also a member of the Mekong Mission Forum.

New Guinea

General

New Guinea is one of the oldest cultures in the world. Already, over 40,000 years ago, people lived there. In no other country in the world are there so many languages, namely eight hundred of about five thousand known languages. In the 1920s thousands of adventurers flocked into the country under a huge gold rush. At that time also began the gradual development of the highlands, which continued in the 1950s. New Guinea is a rugged land where the transport links are difficult. Many places can be reached, especially in the rainy season, only by plane. Earlier, the fear of vendetta prevented people leaving their tribal territory. In addition to the original inhabitants, who are related to the Australian Aborigines, Melanesians later arrived, who settled particularly on the coast. In the tribes there is no hereditary chief, as in Africa, but a so-called big man, whose exercise of power is temporary. Just as long as he is able to hand out gifts to his tribesmen and to lead successful wars, he is able to exercise his office. Frequent change of power and power struggles are the result. This principle of rule affects the state, society, and the church in New Guinea until today.

Until about six thousand years ago, there was a land connection with Australia at today's Torres Street, which was then interrupted by a storm surge. The name papua is derived from the Portuguese word for curly-head because of the appearance of its inhabitants.

The Berlin banker Adolph von Hansemann was the first major German banker who stood up for the acquisition of colonies. He observed the other major European powers structure a huge colonial empire and demanded the government to do likewise. Certainly, economic aspects played a role. In 1882, von Hansemann founded the New Guinea Company. Following the Berlin Conference of 1884, Germany acquired colonies in eastern, western, and southern Africa. Since von Hansemann had already established business relations with Samoa in the South Pacific, he suggested to the imperial government to acquire the northeast of New Guinea as the last "white spot" on the colonial map. The southeast of the island was occupied by Great Britain and the western part by Holland, which is now part of Indonesia. The German government sent a warship to New Guinea in 1884 which raised the imperial flag at various points of the island and the archipelago. On behalf of New Guinea Company, Dr. Otto Finsch explored the island and landed in the area which is now called Finschhafen. In 1885, the New Guinea Company received an imperial letter of protection with the right to exercise sovereignty in the territory now called Emperor William Land. The company issued its own New Guinea money and maintained a small security force.

The Berlin banker Adolph von Hansemann as chairman of the New Guinea Company allowed the Neuendettelsau missionaries to work in New Guinea. (Privately owned)

The business of the company did not go well. Due to imminent insolvency the German government, in 1899, bought back the sovereignty from the New Guinea Company. The company retained, until the First World War, vast estates which they partly sold to the Neuendettelsau Mission. The administration gave rules for the employment of local workers and left the medical care and education mainly to the missions.

In 1920, the German colony was combined with the British colony of Papua as an Australian mandated territory with the capital Port Moresby. During the Second World War in 1941, the Japanese occupied the north of the country. In 1943, the Allies drove off the Japanese and used Finschhafen as the largest base in the Pacific, where hundreds of thousands of soldiers were stationed and huge military equipment was stored. In 1946, the two parts Papua and New Guinea were united under the name Territory of Papua and New Guinea under Australian administration and supervised by the United Nations. The western part of New Guinea was annexed under the name Irian Jaya by Indonesia.

In 1975, the country received its independence as the State of Papua New Guinea (PNG). Prince Charles represented the British crown at the ceremony as "pikinini bilong mama kwin" ("son of Ms. Queen"). The leader of the Pangu Party (Progress Party), Sir Michael Somare, was elected the first prime minister and is considered the father of independence. The state belongs to the British Commonwealth. Head of state is Queen Elizabeth II as the Queen of New Guinea, who is represented by a governor general elected by the parliament in Port Moresby. Its population is about seven million, half of it consists of young people. Pidgin, a mixture of English and Melanesian written in German phonetics, is in use as a lingua franca and English is the official language.

Unfortunately, corruption, mismanagement, and crime hinder the development of the country. Loyalty to the tribe is widely more important than loyalty to the state. For years, a civil war smoldered on the island of Bougainville because of dispute over the local mine, which is now settled. The country considers itself a Christian country because almost all inhabitants at least formally belong to a church. According to its constitution, it is based on Christianity and the "noble traditions" of the ancestors.

The contrast between town and countryside is huge. Today most people still live in rural areas of their farms in the form of subsistence economy. Only 10 percent exercise a paid activity. The illiteracy rate is still high. In the villages, people still live almost like in the Stone Age, while in the cities the computer age started. In particular, many young people are out of work and often try to gain access to the blessings of modern civilization as criminals.

The History of the Bavarian Mission in New Guinea

Rev. Johann Flierl (1858–1947) landed in New Guinea on July 12, 1886 and founded in Simbang the first Lutheran mission station. When he left New Guinea in 1930, there were 50,000 Lutheran Christians. He died in 1947 in Neuendettelsau. (Archive Mission One World)

Since 1860, and intensively since 1875, Neuendettelsau missionaries worked in the Lutheran congregations in Australia. Among them was *Johann Flierl*. He was born in 1858 in the hamlet Buchhof near Nuremberg and entered the Mission Seminary at the age of seventeen. After completing his training, he was sent in 1878 to Australia to serve in the Immanuel Synod. For a few years he worked in the Hermannsburg mission among the Aborigines. There he heard the news that part of New Guinea had been placed under German protection. "Flierl heard from this message the call of the Macedonian 'Come over and help us' (Acts 16:9)!" Later he wrote: "The thought and desire to go to New Guinea, came over me like a force majeure . . . I did not conceal from myself the dangers of a tropical country, but I could easily disregard all doubts similar to queen Esther who said: If I perish, I perish."

Flierl asked mission inspector Johannes Deinzer for permission to go to New Guinea because he wanted to save the inhabitants of New Guinea from the fate he experienced among the Aborigines:

> What will happen with the relatively more numerous indigenes there, when soon enough merchants, growers, besides solid people probably droves of adventurers will enter there, to seek mostly at the expense of the original inhabitants their fortune. Rush is urgently needed on the part of the missionary church, lest culture as after-culture in those areas make disappear the poor race of the Papua from the ground. . . . As an advocate of the Papua I might also remind that the German Empire has annexed with the land in New Guinea also tens of thousands of poor blacks, and that therefore it is the high honor of all true Christians of Germany, to help bring the treasures of the blessed gospel to those far away living Gentile fellow citizens.

After lengthy deliberations and the agreement with the Immanuel Synod, Deinzer gave his consent, and he hoped that through this new mission field also "mission interest" and "missionary zeal" are stimulated and "supported by the now prevailing enthusiasm in Germany for colonization. . . . Why should we hesitate and other . . . missionary societies come first? My advice is: In God's name forward to New Guinea. But quickly and quietly! The area should be already occupied before the news reach Germany that you deal with the plan to occupy it." This correspondence was also published in the mission journal.

Now it was Deinzer's task to contact Adolph von Hansemann as the chairman of the directorate of the New Guinea Company in Berlin to obtain an entry permit for Flierl. Deinzer wrote on January 13, 1886: "Certainly you are also convinced that the Protestant Christians in Germany owe the gospel to the newly acquired countries and their population and look at the mission not as an opponent, but an ally of the present colonizing efforts." Von Hansemann replied on January 18 "that we are not only not averse to the Christian missionary activity in the German protectorates in the Pacific but ready to promote it." He held, however, the time not yet appropriate, because the New Guinea Company must first gain a foothold in the country.

In the meantime, Flierl had been solemnly commissioned by the Immanuel Synod and went to Cooktown in northern Australia, in the immediate vicinity of New Guinea. There he built the Elim mission station and waited eagerly for an entry permit. By the local representatives of the company he was repeatedly put off or dismissed. Then Deinzer put a fait accompli to von Hansemann and wrote on January 21, 1886 that the plan for the mission in New Guinea had already been announced in the church papers. "Nor can I imagine that before the whole Christian world you would like to take the responsibility to have scuppered by your refusal a Christian, in its execution a so far advanced enterprise." Shortly thereafter, on February 2, 1886 the positive answer came that the company gives to Flierl "free passage in the first cabin" to Finschhafen and also takes over the handling of the mail until the establishment of a regular postal connection. However, the company cannot accept any responsibility for Flierl's security. Mission stations should be established only in agreement with the company.

This confirmation, however, Fierl did not receive at first so that his departure was delayed by further months. On July 12, 1886 Flierl finally arrived in Finschhafen on the company's freighter Ottilie, named after von Hansemann's wife. The ship, by the way, sank a few years later (1891). In a letter dated July 7, 1886, the company explained the delay with a specious argument: "The rejection of the missionary Flierl in Cooktown has had its reason, to our regret, that in our telegram the name of Mr. Flierl, which we assumed to be known in Cooktown due to his longer stay, was not understood."

In his early days Flierl received strong support from the New Guinea Company and its governor, retired Vice Admiral Baron Georg von Schleinitz, who resided in Finschhafen. Flierl was invited to hold church services on Sundays for the officials of the company. A room was made available for him and he could dine with the officers. The directorate in Berlin had given orders "to support the missionaries and to give them food and goods to the prices applicable to officials." Unlike some local representatives of the company, von Schleinitz was friendly towards missionary work and expressed the belief that the New Guineans could not be won otherwise for the culture than through a commitment to Christianity. In 1887, his forty-year-old wife, Margot, was swept away by an infectious disease, after which he returned to Germany. In 1891, one third of whites died in Finschhafen of the so-called black water fever—probably malaria tropica—which led to death from one day to the other. Then the company moved its headquarters to Madang and later to Rabaul on New Pomerania, now East New Britain.

The New Guinea Company, in 1887, also allowed the Rhenish Mission to begin missionary activities in the Astrolabe Bay, located north of Finschhafen. At a missionary conference in Bremen in 1885, where the Neuendettelsau Mission did not participate, it was actually agreed that the Rhenish Mission should work in the Emperor William Land. However, it sent only a few missionaries, many of whom died of disease and two were killed by the locals. Their missionary work had little success and was connected with the riots in the Madang region in 1904 and 1912. Not until 1903 could the first baptism be celebrated. The Rhenish Mission also ran into competition with the Catholic mission, which operated from Alexishafen.

Johann Flierl contributed more than forty years of pioneering work among the New Guineans. (Archive Mission One World)

Von Hansemann supported the missionary work, but his local staff frequently disagreed. From an officer of the company, the statement has been handed down: "Hopefully we remain spared of priests and missionaries that would spoil everything." If the natives are raised by the mission, educated and lifted to the state of Europeans, they would oppose the acquisition of land and its exploitation. Otto Finsch took the view that "guns to shoot down the blacks are better than missionaries." Where the English missions came, the natives would do no work on Sundays. They come to colonial officials saying: "Hallelujah, Jesus. We are Christians now."

Adolph von Hansemann, who never visited New Guinea, had decisively contributed to the development of New Guinea and thus created the conditions for the blessed and successful work of the Neuendettelsau

Mission. Its starting point was Finschhafen because here the company originally had its headquarters. After its departure, the Neuendettelsau missionaries could freely operate there. Martin Deinzer therefore, on the obituary notice for von Hansemann in 1901, noted down: "grateful remembrance for friendly obligingness."

On October 6, 1886, Flierl founded the first mission station in Simbang near Finschhafen, which was followed by Tami in 1889, Sattelberg in1892, Deinzerhill in 1899 and Heldsbach in 1903. Plots were acquired from the New Guinea Company, where large plantations were established. They served to finance the missionary work, especially when the connections with Germany during the world wars were interrupted or the Mission Institute could not make money or foreign currency available. The plantations were later transferred to the Lutheran church, for which it generates revenue still today.

After thirteen years, the first Lutheran baptism took place on August 20, 1899. The people in Neuendettelsau had been waiting anxiously. It was no overnight success. The Mission Institute told its friends that it took hard work "until the stupidity, arrogance, and superstition of the people could be overcome." All the greater was the joy when the two mission students Kaboing and Kamunsang publicly refused ancestor worship, witchcraft, and the cult of questioning the dead. Missionary Georg Pfalzer led the christening following Loehe's liturgy in the pouring rain in Simbang and said in his homily: The missionaries came here, "because God loves you, every village and every tribe. . . . Do not think that Kaboing and Kumungsang are to become whites. You have your way, we have our way. But the evil you shall give up." Here already the later hotly debated issue of contextualization of the gospel is addressed.

Kaboing received the baptismal name Tobias, Kamunsang Silas. The two returned to their villages in order to "act as salt and shine as light in their pagan environment." But the two "first-fruits" did not make a lot of joy. Kaboing died three years later. The New Guineans understood this as a revenge of the ancestral spirits. Kamungsang repudiated his wife, looked for another and was ruled out for five years from the congregation. He was "a wavering tube, does not know what he wants, roams around, wants to be popular everywhere, chatters a lot of nonsense," wrote missionary Konrad Vetter. Gradually, more and more young men who had nothing to say in their tribes came. As Christians, they were thus double outsiders. "Since the young people are baptized, they behave like chiefs," says Vetter. The breakthrough happened only by Christian Keysser, when whole villages and tribal groups, led by their chiefs, accepted the new faith. The first two women were baptized in 1903 on Tami Island.

On August 24, 1902, the first Lutheran Communion service was celebrated by the missionaries Karl Tremel and Heinrich Zahn in Obasega near Finschhafen. Kaboing, as the first person to be baptized, had recently died. According to the report in the mission journal, in the preceding night mice had eaten the wafers. Then the missionary's wife baked new wafers. For the one hundredth anniversary in 2002 Bishop Johannes Friedrich came to Obasega and celebrated a Communion service there.

As the first female "mission helper" from 1889 to 1897, the Bavarian pastor's daughter Frieda Götz (died 1905) worked as a nurse in the area of Finschhafen and Sattelberg. She had come into the country with her brother, an employee of the New Guinea Company, and was then hired by the Neuendettelsau Mission. As the first directly sent woman from Neuendettelsau in 1902, the teacher Emilie Heumann came to New Guinea. As a successor to her future husband, Christian Keysser, she taught the missionary children on the Sattelberg mountain. Other nurses and midwives followed. The first missionary after the First World War was the missionary nurse and midwife Helene Moll, who from 1927 to 1961 worked in New Guinea. In 1932, the physician Dr. Martha Koller was sent.

In 1908, the first native missionaries from Sattelberg were sent into Hube area. Missionary work expanded into the hinterland and along the coast. In 1911, Ampo was founded in Lae, in 1918 Kaiapit as a starting point for the highlands mission.

Because the mission did not want to introduce the Bavarian understanding of the office of a pastor, there were until the Second World War only indigenous elders, teachers, and evangelists. The administration of the sacraments was initially in the hands of the missionaries, with some exceptions. In 1939, a missionary conference in Malolo decided to start a pastor's course. The war interrupted these efforts. Only in 1950 the first course finished, and the graduates could be ordained. The ordination of women has not yet been introduced in the church.

As Farnbacher observed properly, mission was initially understood "as the founding of a church in the European style of the Bavarian Lutheran church, as it had been suggested by Wilhelm Loehe: sermons according to the sermon series, liturgy according to the Bavarian agenda with German melodies and translations of German hymns." Later influences were added from America and Australia. The service is still celebrated according to the general liturgy of the Lutheran churches; now many indigenous songs have been developed. In the seminary, the missionaries had yet met no explicit mission theology but followed the textbooks about Lutheran dogmatics and ethics published by the Deinzer brothers on the basis of Friedrich Bauer.

In 1899, Christian Keysser came to New Guinea, first as a teacher of missionary children on the Sattelberg mountain. He was of the opinion that one can convert and baptize individuals only with the consent of their tribe. He won the confidence of big-man Zake and exposed sorcerers with his help in 1903 in a famous dance festival in Bore. He then went on to the Sattelberg mountain and started his so-called helper mission, which was operated in the responsibility of a congregation and not of the missionary. In 1910, he designed a congregation and people's order for the Sattelberg congregations, where he set up rules for everyday life in the villages. Among them were penalties for offenses up to the exclusion from the congregation. Keysser wanted to link together "Christian community" and "civil community."

In 1914, Mission inspector Karl Steck travelled from Neuendettelsau to New Guinea. In 1915, at the main conference in Heldsbach, a heated debate took place about the right mission strategy. Steck had visited for several months all mission stations and criticized at the conference the transfer of European ideas to the local people, the lack of independence of the congregations, and their dependency on the missionary. In his report he wrote: "If here in New Guinea, a brown-skinned Bavarian Lutheran church is to be built, then my report is completed with three lines." To his assessment the missionaries simply transfer German or Franconian church forms to New Guinea. He saw it as a fundamentally wrong method and welcomed Keysser's contextual approach in his congregation work on the Sattelberg mountain. This was contradicted by Flierl as field director, looking at the approach of Steck as gross interference of the home office in his rights as field director. Nevertheless, most missionaries agreed with Steck and followed, in the future, the methods of Keysser which were oriented towards the local structures of the clans and elders, and fundamentally focusing on the kingdom of God.

According to Keysser's conviction, the word of the cross must be placed in the background and God as father and creator in the foreground. He described his missionary method, by which he later became one of the most influential mission writers and one of the most popular mission speakers, in a letter as follows:

> The first task is to bring close to these people the living God as their God. Only when God according to their experience really was their God, then they were obliged to him and were able to recognize their guilt and get to know Jesus. If I emphasized the necessity of a personal faith, the people refused pointing to their duty towards ancestors and gods. Through this experience I felt I have to appeal to the people as a whole. So I did not start from theological considerations, but from practical experience. This reminded me of Paul who has gone new ways due to his experience.

The number of baptized Christians grew significantly, new mission stations were established, and the missionary activities widened throughout the Huon Gulf region. Native missionaries, called barefoot evangelists, went into the hinterland and later in the newly developed highlands. The Neuendettelsau Mission benefited from the fact that the colonial administration was far away and remained the only functioning institution in the region. The infrastructure was improved and schools, plantations, sawmills etc. were built. In 1914, there were sixteen mission stations with thirty-one substations that were administered by twenty-eight missionaries and twelve lay missionaries. The missionaries contributed significantly to the opening up and development of the country, for example, by expeditions into previously untapped areas. Important was in particular the training of mission helpers begun by Keysser in 1910 who carried the gospel to the villages. In 1936, over eight hundred mission helpers worked alongside thirty missionaries. They also brought Kotte and Jabim as church languages from the coast into the whole region. Until 1933, 184 schools were established, where 595 teachers taught thousands of students. Furthermore, the mission ran a shipping company, which until recently under the name Lutheran Shipping often provided the only connections between places on the coast. This was important for the development of trade.

The gospel, in the Jabim language called "miti" (literally: "everything which is good and nicely done or spoken") contributed significantly to the pacification of the tribes that previously feuded constantly. The vendetta was dammed and people could move freely. The mission took over the task of an advocate of the native population towards the German, later the Australian colonial administration and the many other Europeans who looked at the country and its people as objects of exploitation and took advantage of their helplessness to use them as cheap laborers for plantations or as porters.

Johann Flierl with his grandson Helmut and a New Guinea child. (Archive Mission One World)

In particular, in the Madang region, the so-called cargo cult developed that is also found in other parts of Melanesia. It goes back to the encounter between Melanesians and Europeans. Through symbolic acts of compensation, the return of the ancestors is to be brought about by those who bring with them Western goods (cargo). Such cultic practices can be observed today in New Guinea and provide a challenge for the proclamation of the church.

After the outbreak of the First World War, the Australians conquered the seat of the colonial government in Rabaul in September 1914. The missionaries were required to swear an oath of neutrality. Karl Steck, as a German reserve officer, refused and was therefore interned in Australia together with Wilhelm Flierl and Hans Raum and expelled after the war. The other missionaries were allowed to continue to work, as far as they swore the neutrality oath. In 1919, the Emperor William Land was handed over to the Australians for administration. In 1920, according to the Treaty of Versailles, all German missionaries should leave the former colonies and pass on their work to denominational related missions. This concerned also the Neuendettelsau missionaries in New Guinea. In Australia Otto Theile, as mission director of the Lutheran church, spoke up for the Neuendettelsau Mission. He was closely associated with Neuendettelsau because he had been trained there, even though he had been born in Australia. He was able to continually push back the date for the expulsion of the missionaries. On June 20, 1925 the Australian government informed him, "that the government has now decided that the missionaries should be allowed to stay in the colony, on the condition that their attitude and leadership is not hostile to the administrative authority and to the maintenance of public order." After the Treaty of Locarno in 1925 and the admission of Germany to the League of Nations in 1926, the corresponding provision of the Versailles Treaty was finally overridden at the insistence of the International Missionary Council.

The United Evangelical Lutheran Church of Australia (UELCA) and the Iowa Synod had taken over the mission fields of the Neuendettelsau and Rhenish missions. They founded the Lutheran missions in Finschhafen and Madang. From the beginning the Iowa Synod, due to its close connection to Neuendettelsau, supported missionary work in New Guinea and since 1921 it also sent missionaries. Between the graduates of the Neuendettelsau Seminary and the American and Australian missionaries many personal relationships developed. In 1926, the assets of the missionary societies were entrusted to a board of trustees of UELCA. At a conference in Brisbane (Australia) in 1929 the two missions were given back their independence. Since the Rhenish Mission, because of its union character and probably also for financial reasons, did not want to participate in missionary work dominated by Lutherans in the long run, it handed over its work to the newly founded American Lutheran Church during another conference in Columbus (USA) in 1932. At this conference, also attended by Dr. Eppelein, the return of the missionary work to Neuendettelsau was agreed to take effect on January 1, 1933.

The Neuendettelsau missionaries could not make friends with the new Australian mandate government. They complained that Australians hindered their work and paved the way for a modern spirit; they destroyed the village and community life. The Australians promoted the English language and wanted to introduce it in schools, while the Neuendettelsau missionaries taught in the native languages. Conversely, the Australians were suspicious of the missionaries since, due to their knowledge of the native languages and culture, they were much closer to the people. They suspected a "Lutheran theocracy" in much of the country. Their suspicions were intensified after Hitler publicly demanded the return of the German colonies in 1937. The field director Georg Pilhofer wrote to Dr. Eppelein in 1939: "We are all waiting with pain on the solution of the colonial question. Perseverance is more and more difficult because one thing is certain, that our destruction is wanted. Urgent requests remain unanswered for months." In 1926, as a result of the gold rush, thousands of white adventurers flooded into the country, in particular to Wau and

Bulolo. With them also modern civilization came with all its concomitants. The young men flocked from the villages in the emerging cities. This meant that the young women in the villages remained without men, while their men enjoyed modern life in the cities. The village life, including the church's life, was destroyed. Also, sects came into the country, for example the Seven-Day Adventists, who competed with the Neuendettelsau missionaries. Johann Flierl complained to officials about the negative consequences of policies supported by the Australian recruitment of workers, e.g. for the goldfields in Wau.

In 1930, Johann Flierl left after forty-five years of missionary work New Guinea and lived in retirement, at first in Australia with his wife Louise's family in Tanunda. When he left New Guinea, there were already 50,000 Lutheran Christians. After his wife's death in 1934, he returned in 1937 with his daughter Dora to Germany and died in 1947 in Neuendettelsau.

For the hundredth anniversary of the New Guinea mission in 1986 the state of Papua New Guinea dedicated a stamp to Johann Flierl. (Archive Mission One World)

Already in the 1920s, contacts had been made to the highlands, since in 1926 mission helpers were sent there. As the first station in the highlands in 1931 Kambaidam was founded; followed by Onerunka, Raipinka, Asaroka, Ega and Ogelbeng. In 1934, an extended mission expedition was held with the participation of Stephan Lehner, Wilhelm Bergmann, and Jakob Herrlinger. They were amazed at how many people lived there who had never seen the ocean; they farmed and led their own lives. The Australian government restricted the missionary work more and more. Since 1936, after the murder of two Catholic missionaries, indigenous evangelists were not allowed to live alone in the mission stations. Also, certain areas were closed to them, because the development of the highlands should preferably be done by the government. In 1935, the mission aircraft Papua was used in the highlands. It marked the beginning of aviation in New Guinea, to which on the occasion of the fiftieth anniversary even a postage stamp was dedicated. After the Second World War the airline Luther Air was founded, which later joined with the Missionary Aviation Fellowship (MAF). Many mission stations were established. There was a race against the also-expanding Catholic mission.

Nazism radiated to New Guinea. In the 1930s, many young missionaries went to New Guinea. They brought with them the general enthusiasm for Nazism, which they had experienced in Germany and at the Mission Institute. Between the Australian government and the missionaries there were many tensions. The missionaries hoped for the return of the German administration, especially after Hitler reclaimed German colonies in 1937. Their hope was supported by the diverse activities that the NSDAP unfolded in Australia and the Pacific.

In 1936, in the Pacific Islands Monthly, an article appeared which was published in 1937 in a major Australian weekly. "Nazi agents, in the guise of Lutheran missionaries, are deliberately fostering among natives contempt of British rule, disloyalty to the government, and the campaign of fear and intimidation are developing pro-German sympathy among the natives." The Lutheran mission director Otto Theile defended the missionaries to the Australian government by emphasizing that they only want to preach the gospel. He prevented a sharp retort planned by Georg Pilhofer.

In 1936, the German Consul Walter Hellenthal came from Sydney. He visited New Guinea and was pleased that a conch choir played the Horst-Wessel Hymn on his arrival in Finschhafen, and everywhere swastika flags were flying. He found an "excellent spirit of National Socialism" and said: "Especially the Germans abroad are now required, not just with words to affirm the leader [Adolf Hitler], but also to become party members." Accordingly, almost all missionaries applied for membership and founded in 1937, with the approval of the acting field director Georg Pilhofer, a stronghold of the NSDAP in Finschhafen which was supported by the lay missionary and holder of the golden party badge Hubert Stürzenhofecker (1906–1974). Wilhelm Fugmann acted as treasurer. The stronghold comprised 16 missionaries, including three women missionaries. However, the recording forms remained hanging with the party representatives in Rabaul and fell after the outbreak of the war in the hands of the Australians. They also found in many missionary homes Hitler pictures and Nazi emblems, which confirmed their distrust of the missionaries.

Hellenthal had promised, during his visit to Finschhafen, to urge the government in Berlin for the relaxation of the ban on collection in Germany, which was then not mentioned in his report to the Foreign Office in Berlin.

Professor Paul Althaus, as dean of the faculty of theology, dealt in a letter to the rector of the University of Erlangen with the question of whether Eppelein could continue to be active as a lecturer in the faculty: The young missionaries trained by Eppelein went "under his influence and according to his example overseas as champions of the new Germany . . . They are presently detained for the sake of their loyalty to the leader (Hitler) and their party affiliation in enemy camps." The mission leadership in Neuendettelsau, however, did not promote these activities, because "Nazism is not an export product," said Keysser after the war, who was otherwise quite inclined toward Nazism. Cooperation with the Nazis should be maintained only in the field of inner mission, not of Gentile mission.

After the outbreak of Second World War, the first 16 missionaries were arrested and deported to Australia in September 1939. They were mainly party members or applicants while other missionaries were allowed to remain. The weeping women said goodbye to their husbands with the Hitler salute and the national anthem. In 1940, more missionaries were deported, mostly those who had come to the port in 1939 to say goodbye to the first group with the German salute and national anthem. Only three remained, namely the anti-Nazi Stephan Lehner and Johann Decker, who had to leave the country in 1943, and Adolf Wagner, who was hiding in the jungle and was killed on November 9, 1943 by the Japanese. Later some missionaries made the excuse that their applications had not yet been approved for membership of the party. But the Australians made no distinction, especially since most missionaries openly declared to be supporters of the Nazi movement.

Missionary Adolf Wagner was a staunch opponent of National Socialism and remained after the deportation of most missionaries in the country. He was assassinated in 1943 by the Japanese, making him the second martyr of the Neuendettelsau Mission. (Archive Mission One World)

Most Catholic missionaries remained in the country, though a lot of them later had to pay with their lives. When the Japanese deported them in 1943, their ship was bombed by Americans and many died. So the party membership and deportation had, so-to-say, saved the lives of many Neuendettelsau missionaries. As justification for the deportation, the Australians argued that they were afraid that German missionaries could incite the natives against them and become a Fifth Column. They could also help the Japanese allied with Germany, after they had occupied the north of New Guinea in 1942. The kidnapping of the mission aircraft Papua to Dutch New Guinea in 1939 aroused additional distrust among the Australians, since military purposes for the aircraft were previously suspected by the Australians.

After some time, the missionaries were interned in the camp Tatura I in the state of Victoria. It was considered a "Nazi camp," where a lot of persons loyal to the Nazi regime were housed. There was a court of honor, in which Georg Pilhofer temporarily acted as chairman. It was appointed according to the proposal of the NSDAP and could impose disciplinary penalties, which were then enforced by the camp service of order (Lagerordnungsdienst). Since there were among the interned Germans both Nazi friends as well as opponents, including Jews, these groups were distributed to various camps. The missionaries' wives came with their children at the end of 1941 to Australia and were initially housed with

Lutheran families. Then they voluntarily joined their husbands in 1942 in the family camp Tatura.

In the camp the German national festivals were celebrated in which the party members wore their party badges, and swastikas and pictures of Hitler were hung. Party meetings, so-called comradeship evenings, were held, and Hitler Youth and BDM girl groups marched at ceremonies in uniform. When, at the end of April 1945, Hitler's alleged heroic death was announced, the camp community celebrated a memorial service in which the song of the good comrade was sung. The pastor, probably Rev. Hermann Schneller from Jerusalem, preached on John 15:13, "No one has greater love than this that he lay down his life for his friends." Wilhelm Fugmann concluded his report with the words "What an aberration!"

The missionaries were able to live a reasonably normal life with their families. In the camp there were sports and game events, home and lecture evenings. The children went to school. Theater performances of classical pieces offered an enjoyable change to the gray camp environments. After the capitulation of 1945, the missionaries were allowed to gradually leave the camp. Judging by their membership in the NSDAP or by their attitude, it was decided whether they were sent back to Germany or whether they were allowed to return to New Guinea. So, the "long arm of the Third Reich" (Winter) reached beyond the end of Nazi Germany to Australia and New Guinea. Some missionaries were also offered the opportunity to become Australian citizens, but most of them rejected the offer.

At the end of 1943, the allied forces pushed back the Japanese more and more in PNG. Finschhafen was expanded to the largest military base of the allies in the Pacific. There, more than 100,000 US soldiers stayed temporarily; at the same time, at least one million soldiers were transported from there to other battlefields. One can only imagine how the military machinery of the Japanese and Americans, which also caused a large amount of destruction, affected the local Christians.

In late 1945, a delegation from the Lutheran church of America visited New Guinea to make an assessment. Participants expected nothing and experienced "the miracle of New Guinea" and wrote about it: "The mission has gone, but the church has remained." With the return of the first Neuendettelsau missionaries from Australia in 1947 they found congregations, almost all of them were organizationally and spiritually intact.

The Lutheran churches in Australia and America founded in 1953, on the suggestion of the LWF, the Lutheran Mission New Guinea in which the American Lutheran Mission Madang and the German-Australian Lutheran Mission Finschhafen were combined. It was considered the largest Lutheran mission organization in the world. It had numerous economic enterprises, including the purchase and sale cooperative Namasu (Native Marketing and Supply), which was founded in 1959 by the Neuendettelsau business-missionary Wilhelm Fugmann and managed by him for many years. Since 1953, missionaries could be sent directly from Neuendettelsau. In 1959, the pastors' seminaries were founded in Logaweng on the coast and Ogelbeng in the highlands. They were followed in 1968 by the Martin Luther Seminary in Lae, which teaches in English at the university level. In the 1960s, there were numerous mass baptisms especially in the highlands.

Since 1936, the more conservative Evangelical Lutheran Church in Australia worked together with the Lutheran Church—Missouri-Synod in New Guinea, especially in the highlands and on the island of Siassi. While Siassi joined the ELCONG, in 1948, the Gutnius Lutheran Church was founded in the highlands. It belongs to both the Lutheran World Federation and the International Lutheran Council which is dominated by the Missourians. A good working relationship exists with ELCPNG, for example, in running the Martin Luther Seminary in Lae.

In 1956, in the presence of the Neuendettelsau mission director Hans Neumeyer, the Evangelical Lutheran Church of New Guinea (ELCONG) was established at the synod meeting in Simbang. Dr. John Kuder of the American Lutheran Church was elected as its first bishop. He was followed in 1973 by Sir Zurewe Zurenuo, the first indigenous bishop, who was installed in his office by ELCB Bishop Hermann Dietzfelbinger. After the independence of the country in 1975, the Evangelical Lutheran Church of Papua New Guinea (ELCPNG) was established in 1976. At their foundation ceremony, seventy years after the arrival of Johann Flierl in Finschhafen, Bishop Zurewe emphasized the autonomy of the church on the basis of the three-self principles: "We Christians in the ELCPNG fulfill our task to give witness to Christ to those who do not know him, to administer our church ourselves, to support our church ourselves, to lead the church work in our own responsibility and practice it." His successor in 1982 was Bishop Sir Getacke Gam. He was succeeded in 1998 by Bishop Dr Wesley Kigasung, who was installed by Bishop Hermann von Loewenich, but unfortunately died in 2008. His successors were Giegere Wenge (2010–2016) and Jack Urame 2016.

Founded in 1945 by World War II pilots, the international airline Mission Aviation Fellowship (MAF) is the most important link to the outside world for many remote villages of New Guinea. During his visit to New Guinea in 2005, Rev. Michael Martin from the ELCB headquarters speaks with the missionary chief pilot, Volkher Jacobsen. Next to him are an employee of the MAF and Rev. Dr. Traugott Farnbacher from Neuendettelsau. (Privately owned)

Since the 1950s, the government of the church went increasingly into indigenous hands. As the supreme body the church council was formed, consisting of representatives of the districts. They were headed by the district president, which may be ordained or non-ordained. The seat of administration is in Ampo near Lae. Since the turn of the millennium no missionaries from overseas work in senior positions of the church.

In 1973, the Lutheran Mission New Guinea was dissolved and the New Guinea Coordination Committee (NGCC) was founded as a successor institution to organize the affairs of the missionaries. It included, besides the Bavarian Department for World Mission, the Northelbian Mission Center, Leipzig Mission, and the Lutheran churches in Australia, America and Canada. The local church was not represented but was involved in the negotiations. In Kainantu in 1997 a consultation of the church with its overseas partners was held. The demand for participation of the church in the decisions on the financial grants and project support was raised. Bishop Gam mediated by pointing out that the church is still in need of money and personnel from outside. The church stands in tension between autonomy and interdependence. Then after lengthy negotiations, a new approach to cooperation with the overseas partners of ELCPNG was developed. On the day after the installation of the third indigenous bishop in 1998, the ELCPNG Partners Forum was established in which the ELCPNG and its partners have the same number of seats. It is chaired by a representative of the ELCPNG and his deputy is to be provided by the partner churches. For the purposes of the Lutheran missionaries, the Lutheran Overseas Partners Committee (LOPC) was established. It began with its work on January 1, 1999. In the church headquarters, an office for ecumenical affairs was opened.

The year 1992 was dominated by the debate on the Ok Tedi mine. Even later, the Department for World Mission cooperated with ELCPNG in criticizing the violent felling of trees, whose products go mainly to China and Malaysia. "All the Trees Are Gone Away and All the Game Has Disappeared" was the title of a study. The Malaysian timber company Rimbunan Hijau launched a new daily newspaper *National* and brought the church magazine *PNG Times* with dumping prices for advertisments in economic difficulties. This paper was published by Word Publishing, which is funded by DWM and other mission and development organizations. Meanwhile Word Publishing had stopped *PNG Times* and its successor, *Independent*. It publishes the only Pidgin newspaper *Wantok*, which is jokingly referred to as "the most smoked newspaper in the world." It is particularly important, as it can be read by most people in PNG, who often do not know English.

Most church services and official duties in the villages are held by elders. They only partly receive a salary, most of them just a Christmas bonus called "belgut mani" ("good belly money"). Most church members live in rural areas and benefit little from the national church. ELCPNG is financed almost exclusively by grants from overseas, and the income from land and property ownership, investment, and Lutheran Shipping under the umbrella of Kambang Holding Inc.

At the synod meeting in Wasu, the Lutheran Church of Papua New Guinea on January 11, 2006 celebrated its fiftieth anniversary. The picture shows from left Bishop Dr. Wesley Kigasung, Governor Luther Wenge, and Governor-General Palias Matiane, the representative of Queen Elizabeth II as Queen of Papua New Guinea. (Privately owned)

ELCPNG is definitely a lay church where the ordained ministry must still find its role. In the villages the local leaders lead the congregations. Its country-wide structure was essentially conceived by the missionaries with a church headquarters in Ampo / Lae as the central authority, under which districts and circuits operate. There is a danger that the number of districts increase according to the diverse ethnic groups. On the basis of the big-man principle leaders are often quickly replaced, as the ecclesiastical and theological qualifications play a less important role than tribal affiliation. The unity of the church is threatened by the contrast between highlands and coast. In the highlands, a split in Hagen district led to the forming of the Melpa Lutheran Church.

Charismatic movements from the inside and sects from the outside threaten the congregations. The church members are turning back to the ancestor worship because the church offers too little orientation. Bishop Kigasung in 2000 reached reconciliation with the Lutheran revival movement, the so-called Nupela Luteren.

The church maintains numerous hospitals and health centers as part of the Lutheran Health Service. The medical care in the country is poor, often for 50,000 people there is only one doctor. The indigenous doctors, who have often received scholarships for their education from the church, do not want to work in rural hospitals, so the church hospitals have to rely on doctors sent from overseas. Magical thinking is still in people's minds, so many patients are accustomed to thinking that disease is caused by death spells and often resort to magical means before they are brought to the hospital at the last minute. Numerous development projects are managed by the Lutheran Development Service. This includes the support of small loans.

The Lutheran church comprises, with about one million members, about 20 percent of the country's population. Its share of the total population, however, declined slightly in recent decades. It counted in 2007 six thousand congregations, eight hundred pastors, three thousand evangelists, two hundred primary and secondary schools, five high schools, schools for evangelists and women in Amron and Baitabag, the Madang Lutheran School of Nursing as a department of the Catholic Divine Word University, and the Balob Teachers College in Lae. In the Lutheran Church College Banz, young people are trained in theology, agriculture, administration, technical skills, and home economics to become youth leaders and women workers in the congregations. The National Women's Training Centre is also located in Banz.

The Lutheran Church–Missouri Synod began mission work in the highlands after the Second World War and established in 1948 the Gutnius (English: Good News) Lutheran Church. It comprises about 100,000 members and belongs to the Lutheran World Federation as well as the International Lutheran Council. It runs the Balob Teachers College and the Martin Luther Seminary in Lae together with ELCPNG.

From Bavaria since 1886 about four hundred missionaries were sent. They worked in particular in the field of theological education and training, religious education, health service, administration, and rural development. The total number of missionaries has been greatly reduced in recent decades. While in 1975 about 250 missionaries worked in the church, in 2007 there were only a maximum of fifty, most of them from Bavaria. The Americans and Australians have largely withdrawn. For the missionaries it became more and more difficult to find their place in the church. "We are strangers but not foreigners," missionaries complained at a conference. Lack of concept and cooperation, lack of job descriptions, unclear leadership and decision-making structures complicate their work. Bishop Kigasung emphasized the independence of the church, but also, the need for cooperation. Due to the drop of missionary families, the Katharine Lehmann School in Wau as a boarding school for missionary children was closed.

The Melanesian Institute in Goroka was founded in 1968 by the Catholic Church and in 1971 opened to all churches. Courses for introduction to the culture of New Guinea are held, which are important for the Neuendettelsau missionaries. Its publications help to understand the country and its people.

Trumpet playing is very popular in New Guinea. Bavarian missionaries help in training. (Privately owned)

Pacific

The Pacific is called the "liquid continent" and consists of countless islands and many states. As the largest ocean it covers more than one third of the earth's surface, but has only 11 million inhabitants, including New Guinea. The churches that date back mainly to the missionary work of Anglo-American missionary societies in the nineteenth century play a major role in social and political life. They mostly have a conservative character and are closely linked with the traditional power structures. Lately they are challenged by the "Winds of Change" (Ernst) to deal with the activity of new churches and sects in the Pacific.

Since the 1990s, ELCPNG built its relationships in the Pacific and joined the Pacific Council of Churches (PCC). In Suva (Fiji) there is the *Pacific Theological College* (PTC), to which in 1991 the former PNG missionary Dr. Wolfgang Krüger was sent by DMW. In this leading Protestant school in the Pacific, a contextual "coconut theology" is taught. The seminary also offers theological correspondence courses.

In 1988, the Pacific Network was founded in Neuendettelsau which, in collaboration with DWM and other mission agencies, established the Pacific Information Center based in Neuendettelsau. Through developmental education it informs about social, cultural, environmental, and economic issues of the twenty-six island countries in the region. It draws the public attention to the consequences of climate change for the many small and low islands of the Pacific, marine pollution by wasteand pollution due to nuclear tests.

China

General

Already in the eighth century, the Nestorian Church sent missionaries to China. Later, the Jesuits arrived. In 1724, the Emperor prohibited Christian mission. After the Opium War (1835–1842) China was forced by Britain to open some ports for trade. The Treaty of Nanjing in 1841 is still regarded as the humiliation of China in living memory. In 1831, the first Lutheran missionary, Karl Gützlaff, came to the country. He was followed by numerous other Western missionaries. But the mission was able to achieve only limited success in spite of great efforts until the communist revolution in 1949 under Mao Zedong. At that time there were only about two million Christians in China.

Traditionally in China, in addition to the indigenous Taoism, religions which were imported from abroad prevail, like Islam and Buddhism. Religion has never played an independent role in China compared with Europe. It consists mainly of attending festivals, visiting temples, and practicing ancestor worship. People sometimes go to a temple and light incense. Houses, tombs, and gardens must be built according to certain rules to achieve blessing for the living. While Taoism is geared to practical life, Buddhism focuses on the afterlife.

The teachings of Confucius determine the lives of Chinese people everywhere in Asia, and shape their self-confidence still to this day.

Actually, it is really agnostic ethics. Tolerance plays an important role. Therefore, the absoluteness of Christianity does not fit into Chinese culture. The Chinese mentality is geared towards harmony between man, nature, and society. For the sake of harmony, the opposites must be repealed and a peaceful coexistence in the search for long life, happiness, and wealth must be found. In particular Confucianism teaches an authoritarian state ethics with respect for the elderly. Prestige and prosperity are important, which can be achieved through obedience, diligence, and discipline. The loyalty within the family is fundamental.

The Chinese communist government tried from the beginning to enforce a one-child policy to curb population growth. Only minorities and farmers were allowed to have more children, especially if the first child is a girl. Otherwise, families will be subject to sanctions if they have several children. Abortion is not only permitted but is even encouraged or arranged. In such a society lone children grow up who do not have siblings, uncles, aunts, and cousins. The society is characterized by isolation and loneliness. Under the high pressure many break down and commit suicide, for example because of school failure.

Under Christian influence Hong Yin erected in the mid-nineteenth century his heavenly kingdom in the area of Nanjing. He called himself "brother of Jesus," demanded land reform and general justice. The uprising in 1864 was bloodily suppressed by the imperial government with Western assistance.

The missions established institutions in the areas reserved for Westerners in Beijing, Shanghai, Nanjing, and Ghounzhou (Canton). During the Boxer Rebellion in 1902, many missionaries were killed because they were considered "white devils" and stooges of the colonial powers. Their religion was considered as the religion of the oppressors of the Chinese people. Nevertheless, education and modern society models came with the missions to the country. The revolution of 1911 started under Christian influence. Its leader Sun Yat Sen belonged to a Protestant family and had attended a mission school in Macau.

The Cooperation with the Christian Church

After the communist revolution of 1949 under Mao Zedong, the Christians were increasingly harassed. Their faith was regarded as un-Chinese and foreign. "Win a Christian and lose a good Chinese" was the slogan.

In 1952, the last missionaries left China. The number of church-goers diminished more and more and approached zero during the Cultural Revolution and the rule of the so-called red guards between 1966 and 1976. Many pastors have been sent for the re-education to the country side or were forced to work in factories. Churches, temples, and mosques were closed. The government was based on the phrase of Karl Marx, according to whom religion is the opium of the people, and therefore must die.

The turning point came in 1979 when Deng Xao Ping propagated a new open-door policy and the socialist market economy. Shortly before Christmas of 1979, the news spread like wildfire among the remaining Christians in Shanghai that the largest Protestant church would reopen. And really here and in four other cities, the first public worships in years were held. Also, Buddhist temples and Islamic mosques were opened.

In the following decades, more and more people joined the church and were baptized. Christianity exerts a huge attraction still today. Within the brutal achievement-oriented society people look for consolation by the gospel. The often lonely people find support and security in a congregation. Many come to faith because of healing experiences and ask for blessing. Lately intellectuals turn to the Christian faith. Christianity is closely linked with Western culture; its music, literature, and art attract young people. Christianity teaches the appreciation of the individual and provides answers to the question of the origin and purpose of life and world.

A curiosity for Europe may be observed among Chinese: How is it that Europe has overtaken China, although the Chinese culture was superior to the European civilization until 1500? Does this have to do with Christianity? What did the Reformation of Martin Luther achieve and how is it related to the communist revolution? The Institute of Social Sciences in Beijing is concerned with these issues.

The government watches over the religion by an office called the State Administration for Religious Affairs (SARA). It is housed in the palace of the last Chinese emperor Puyi. Its director, Vice Minister Wang, visited Neuendettelsau in 2004. At a reception, the Deputy Bavarian Prime Minister Dr. Günther Beckstein spoke about the relationship between Christianity and politics. The Chinese visitors were surprised to note that in Germany a person can be both a politician and a Christian. In 2007, Vice Minister Wang received a delegation of the Bavarian church headed by Bishop Johannes Friedrich at his official residence.

In the palace of the last emperor, Puyi, the State Administration for Religious Affairs (SARA) is housed. In 2007, its director, Vice-Minister Wang, received a Bavarian delegation headed by Bishop Dr. Johannes Friedrich and Synod President Heidi Schülke. (Privately owned)

A distinction is made between Catholics and Protestants, who are also called Christians. They are considered as two religions because they came to China at different times; they use different names of God and Bible translations. So there are five officially recognized religions: Protestantism, Catholicism, Buddhism, Islam, and Taoism. They may practice their faith within certain limits but cannot interfere in politics. There are registered and non-registered Christian congregations. The latter are also known as house or underground churches; they celebrate their services but by no means only in secret. They often have thousands of members and are tolerated by the local authorities in many cases. For the official registration they have to prove the possession of a building, membership records, statutes, and regular finances. Many congregations shy away from registering because they want to escape state control.

Officially, there are 16,000,000 Protestants who are cared for by three thousand pastors in 60,000 congregations. In addition, supporters and so-called culture Christians, who shy away from baptism and membership, attend services. Especially in rural areas, the number of Christians is growing. Some estimate up to 100,000,000 Christians.

After the communist revolution, the government organized the Christians in the Three Self Patriotic Movement (TSPM). It was based on the principles the three-selves, namely, self-proclaiming, self-governing, and self-financing. All foreign interference was banned.

Festive groundbreaking of the new building of the Amity Printing Press in Nanjing in 2005 with its founder Bishop K.H. Ting, one of the great figures of Protestantism in the twentieth century. (Privately owned)

In 1980, the China Christian Council (CCC) was established. It sent the message to world Christianity: "Come to China and see what happens here. Leave us not alone. We are guided by the principle of the three-selves, but do not want to live in self-isolation." CCC is responsible for external relations, TSPM for internal affairs. Lately they work together in the new center in Shanghai, which is located next to the former Anglican cathedral that was used for many years as a cinema and recently was returned to the church.

The pastors of the Protestant church are trained in eighteen seminaries, which have more applicants than places to offer. Because of decades of persecutions and restrictions, there are fewer young pastors. The older pastors dominate and point out that they could not exercise their profession before 1980. The church considers itself as a post-denominational union church, because the traditional denominations are assigned to the era of colonialism. The grand old man was the former Anglican Bishop K. H. Ting (1915–2012), on whom reportedly Prime Minister Chou En Lai held his protective hand. The church may be characterized as conservative-patriarchal. Elements of an independent Chinese theology are just beginning to develop.

Services are often held multiple times in a congregation; on Sundays in the cities they are usually crowded. One has to be there in time to get a seat. Many non-baptized come to church. However, they may not partake of the Holy Communion. In former times only at least eighteen-year-old persons were allowed to be baptized, after a longer baptismal instruction. Now younger persons may be baptized, but no infants. The government allows the churches to care for old, sick, and handicapped persons. Church-run kindergartens were also recently admitted.

In June 2007, a Bible exhibition designed by the Chinese church was opened in Neuendettelsau by the chairperson of the China Christian Council Rev. Dr. Cao Shengjie and the director of Amity Foundation Qin Zhongui. Dr. Cao formulated the basic principle of Christians in China: "We want to love our country and our church, in order to glorify God." Redemption and satisfaction of earthly needs must go together.

In 2007, for the first time a lecturer from Germany, Dr. Sigurd Kaiser, was sent by DWM to the Theological Seminary in Nanjing. In the suburbs of Nanjing, the government built a new building for five hundred students.

In 1985, Bishop K.H. Ting founded the Chinese diaconic institution Amity Foundation, headquartered in Nanjing. Its name is made up of the two Chinese characters for love and virtue. It wants to contribute to building a harmonious society. It was initially financed mainly by Western development organizations; the German Church Development Service was the largest donor. Amity mainly supports projects in rural areas, for example the training of village doctors in the context of rural health services, water projects, and micro-credit programs, particularly for women. Given the large differences between urban and rural, rich and poor, east and west, the fight against poverty in the countryside is in the foreground. Amity has also developed a big teacher's program. For this it has recruited teachers for German and English from abroad. DWM contacted Amity already in 1987 and sent a teacher to China.

Since 1987, Amity runs a Bible printing company as a joint venture with the United Bible Societies (London), which also provide the paper. It has already printed more than 40 million Bibles. New buildings were opened in Nanjing. The Bibles are distributed via centers to the parishes throughout the country. They can be purchased only in churches and not in public bookstores. One must therefore not smuggle Bibles into China, as some evangelical groups claim. They may be acquired after each Sunday service. Even so-called house churches get Bibles.

During his visit in 2007, Bishop Dr. Johannes Friedrich preached in the church in Nanjing. Left, a woman pastor of the church can be seen. (Privately owned)

While in former times religion was devalued as superstition, now on formal occasions the representatives of the state emphasize the importance of the churches for society. They should contribute to the development of a harmonious society. In the constitution, human rights and religious freedom are officially guaranteed. However, this does not always affect the local level. China is a big country with a huge population which only can be ruled by strict laws, as it is claimed. Western individualism is rejected, and the Chinese community model preferred.

Since the 1990s, ethnic Chinese churches in Southeast Asia, USA, and Canada established contacts with congregations in China. The Lutheran churches in Hong Kong, Malaysia, and Singapore organize Bible courses and provide training in church growth.

The number of Catholics is estimated at six million. There are registered congregations which are grouped together in the Patriotic Association with 115 dioceses and are cared for by about one thousand priests. Because of the one-child policy, it is difficult to attract young celibate priests, since there will be no male heir for the family who might care for the worship of ancestors. The bishops are elected by the priests' councils. An intervention of the Vatican is not permitted. Many bishops are however subsequently legitimized by Rome. Male religious orders are prohibited, though some female convents are allowed. The Catholic Church maintains hospitals, outpatient clinics, nursing homes, kindergartens, homes for the disabled, etc. Their motto is "Praising charity and witnessing faith."

In order to intensify and coordinate contacts between German churches and missions with China, in 1996, the China Information Agency was founded in Hamburg as a cooperation of mission agencies, including DWM.

Hong Kong

General

In 1897, China leased the then deserted coastal areas near Hong Kong to Great Britain, which after one hundred years in 1997 returned its crown colony to China. Before that event for many years on Tiananmen Square in Beijing a huge clock ran, which indicated how many years, months, days, hours, and seconds, remain until Hong Kong is returned to China. Even before 1997, China expanded its economic relations with Hong Kong. Symbol of this was the skyscraper of the Bank of China in the Hong Kong Island district. In the 1990s, many Christians were afraid of the magic date: July 1, 1997. In particular, wealthy families left the city and were gladly taken up with their capital in Australia or Canada. After the Second World War, a lot of money was earned thanks to low taxes and wages.

The handover to China was sealed with a contract. It guaranteed for the next fifty years the status of Hong Kong as Special Administrative

Region (SAR). Democracy and human rights are guaranteed. Even the status of denominational churches should be retained in contrast to the post-denominational church in China. Fifty percent of schools and 20 percent of hospitals are run by the churches.

The Cooperation with the Lutheran Churches

There are seven small Lutheran churches in Hong Kong, which work together under the umbrella of LWF and the Hong Kong Christian Council. The *Rhenisch Church* goes back to the Rhenish Mission, the *Tsung Tsin Mission* to the Basel Mission, where the services are held in various Chinese languages.

Partnership relations have developed between DWM and *the Evangelical Lutheran Church in Hong Kong (ELCHK)*. In 1996, DWM joined the China Area Coordination Committee of ELCHK. The church was founded in 1954 by American Lutherans in connection with the aid actions to refugees of LWF. It includes about 16,000 church members; half of them attend a church service on Sundays. Sixty pastors and fifty evangelists take care of 120 congregations. In 2004, the fiftieth anniversary was celebrated in a huge arena. At that time the former DWM scholarship holder Dr. Nicholas Tai, who received his doctor's degree from Munich University, was elected bishop. ELCHK also operates the Taosheng Publishing House which publishes general religious and theological literature, which is urgently needed in China. The church operates educational work in its numerous kindergartens and schools. It supports missionary work in China, Thailand, and Fiji.

In 1992, the new building of the Lutheran Theological Seminary (LTS) was inaugurated on the premises of the Norwegian Areopagus Foundation. At the celebration, the Chinese Bishop K. H. Ting marked the building as a sign of hope for China. President Dr. Hasiao had put the building under the prophetic word: "Behold, I am starting anew" (Isaiah 43:18), which has now been fulfilled. The seminary looks back on a hundred years of history that began in China's Hubei province in 1913 and was continued in Hong Kong after the communist revolution in 1949. Since 1977, LTS is supported by several churches and represents a broad ecumenical spectrum based on a clearly Lutheran profile. Today, LTS is one of most important Protestant institutions throughout Asia. Approximately five hundred students from seventy denominations and twenty countries are trained in the seminary to become pastors and church leaders, only 10 percent of them Lutherans. The Institute for Luther Studies is associated with LTS, which received the Weimar edition of the works of Martin Luther by the United Evangelical Lutheran Church of Germany. Since 1993, lecturers were sent by DWM to teach at the seminary. In addition, DWM awards scholarships for students from the Mekong countries and China and supports study programs to strengthen Lutheran identity in Asia. LTS sends its lecturers to courses in the churches of Southeast Asia. Recently there is a partnership agreement with the University of Erlangen-Nuremberg.

In 1992, the new building of the Lutheran Theological Seminary was inaugurated in Hong Kong. The seminary is one of the most important theological institutions in Asia, where theologians from Bavaria lecture since 1993. (Privately owned)

Under the theme "In Christ Called to Witness," in July 1997 the Ninth General Assembly of LWF met in Hong Kong. The newly appointed Chief Executive Tung Chee Hwah made a speech, emphasizing that the status of Hong Kong is also retained for the churches. In the General Assembly, a resolution was introduced which called for democracy and human rights in China. But the decision was abandoned because of possible political complications. It was pointed out that the understanding of human rights is based on Western individualism which is alien to Asians.

Korea

General

The "Land of Morning Calm" looks back on three thousand years of cultural history between the great powers China and Japan. After the Russo-Japanese War in 1905, the country was occupied by Japan. The Japanese oppressed the Koreans in a brutal manner and banned their language. Some bombastic buildings in Seoul still remember the time of the Japanese occupation, which ended with the end of the Second World War. From 1950 to 1953 a bloody civil war was fought, many people fled from the communist north to the south. Seoul had been destroyed twice. Still today the truce has not been replaced by a peace treaty, so that there is the constant risk of a re-erupting war. The ceasefire is monitored by UN troops. The consequences for the division are far worse for the people than in the previously divided Germany. There are no possibilities of visits or exchange of letters or telephone calls, apart from exceptional actions. Because of this, suffering plays a big role for Koreans.

After the end of the civil war, South Korea experienced an astonishing economic growth although the country has no raw materials. The Koreans are very hard-working, disciplined, and eager for education. Many people flocked from the countryside into the cities. The Seoul metropolitan area now has more than 10 million inhabitants.

The traditional religion is a mixture of Confucianism, Buddhism, and Shamanism. In the nineteenth century Catholic and Protestant missionaries came into the country. Their work had an amazing resonance, so that today about one third of Koreans belong to a Christian church. Unlike China, Christianity in Korea is not intertwined with the colonial history. Protestant personalities led the resistance against Japan.

Korea has, besides the Philippines, the largest number of Christians in Asia, namely, about 10 million Protestants and five million Catholics. The classic denominations Methodists and Presbyterians decrease recently against the Pentecostal-charismatic churches. In large megachurches several services are held on Sundays with thousands of visitors. People like to belong to a congregation because they find friends there and come into contact with others.

After the Second World War, there was a big growth of the churches that has recently come to a standstill. Calvinism, with its success thinking, applies well to Koreans in the sense of a "success gospel." In the background of Shamanism there is access to personal piety with prayer and meditation. Famous, in particular, is the early morning prayer which is practiced in many churches. Often the churches require tithe from their faithful.

The Cooperation with the Lutheran Church

Amid this multiplicity of churches and religions, there is the small Lutheran Church in Korea (LCK). Although in 1832 Karl August Gützlaff, as the first German Lutheran missionary to China, stepped on Korean soil, the Lutheran mission began very late. As the Korean theologian Wong Yong Ji (1924–2013) received his PhD in the USA, he suggested to the Missouri Synod in 1958 to start Lutheran missionary work in Korea. The first three missionaries were officially sent out as military chaplains for the American soldiers stationed in Korea and founded the Lutheran Mission in Korea. They devoted themselves at first mainly to supporting the preaching work done by the Protestant churches. They founded the Concordia Publishing House and started the production of the Christian radio program called Lutheran Hour Korea. With the Bethel Bible seminars in the form of learning by extension, they offered a theological training to lay coworkers. In 1959, the first Lutheran congregation was founded. The church got its independence in 1971. It became a member of the International Lutheran Council founded by the Missouri Synod, and in 1972 also joined the Lutheran World Federation. Approximately five thousand church members in fifty congregations are cared for by fifty pastors. In spring and autumn all families are visited. In 1965, Wong Yong Ji founded the Lutheran Theological Seminary and served until 1968 as its first rector. Today the Luther University trains theologians, lawyers and social workers. The Luther Study Institute is affiliated with it. Dr. Malte Rhinow came in 2002 as the first Bavarian pastor to LCK, where he initially managed an institute for church planting and then taught at the Luther University. 1975 to 1978 Dr. Won Yong Ji worked in the directorate of DWM after he had previously been the Asia secretary of LWF. He also oversaw the translation of Luther's works into Korean. The church is committed to a missionary work in China and Siberia.

After the service in the central Lutheran church in Seoul, in which Bishop Dr. Johannes Friedrich preached the sermon, representatives of the Lutheran Church in Korea stand with their guests from Bavaria for photographers. (Privately owned)

The church is small compared to the major Protestant churches in the country. Nevertheless, it brings important fundamental insights of the Reformation into Korean Protestantism. Recently, criticism arose because some mega-churches are behaving like large business enterprises. Many promises of success are being recognized as unfounded and people turn away from them, frustrated and disoriented. It is all the more important that the Lutheran church raises its voice and points to Luther's theology of the cross.

Malaysia

General

The country which until after the Second World War was under British rule, consists of West and East Malaysia. East Malaysia is the northern part of the island of Borneo with the states of Sabbah and Sarawak. Natives, called Katazan, who live there partially converted to Christianity, not least because of the consumption of pork and rice wine which is allowed by Christians in contrast to Muslims.

Nine states of West Malaysia are ruled by sultans, who today are only in charge of religion and culture and choosing a common king on time. The majority of the population consists of Malays, who as bumi putra (sons of the country) have special privileges. Ten percent of the population is Chinese, who exert a dominant position in the economy. Ten percent are of Indian origin and were brought by the British to work in the huge rubber plantations. The official language is Bahasa Malay.

Mission among Muslims is forbidden. Some states have introduced sharia law which, strictly speaking, applies only to Muslims. A Christian woman who, through marriage, converted to Islam cannot go back to Christianity after the death of her husband. The religion is visible through a chip in the passport. The government maneuvers between the demands of sharia and the requirements of modernity. Once the government wanted to ban the use of the word Allah in the Bible, but the Supreme Court refused. Since then, the preface to the Bible points out that Allah in the Bible means the God of the Christians. The religious police monitor the compliance of Islamic law, for example the food ban during Ramadan. For Muslims, the visiting of temples and churches is prohibited. If a Muslim for some reason gets into a church service, the pastor has to stop with the sermon so that the Muslim will not be exposed to the Christian proclamation. The morning greeting at school says: "Greetings to all my Muslim brothers and sisters and our brothers and sisters who are still not Muslims."

The activities of churches are sometimes limited by the state bureaucracy, for example regarding permits for buildings and cemeteries. Christian mission is only permitted among Chinese and Indians. As an umbrella organization the Christian Fellowship of Malaysia negotiates with authorities and intensifies the community of churches and Christians.

The Cooperation with the Lutheran Church in Malaysia

After the Second World War, a state of emergency prevailed in Malaysia because of the threat of communist China. Half a milllion Chinese were interned because they were suspected of collaborating with China. They were settled in the so-called new villages as a bulwark against communism.

Only in 1961, the state of emergency was lifted, with its strict controls. In 1952, American missionaries began missionary work in the new villages and founded the Lutheran Church in Malaysia and Singapore (LCMS). In 1997, the Lutheran Church in Singapore separated from the Lutheran Church in Malaysia. The reasons for the separation lie in the political, economic, and cultural differences between the two states.

LCMS has about 10,000 members in sixty congregations with about fifty pastors and evangelists. It gains new members from the ethnic Chinese population, making use of new missionary opportunities. So, it operates in Ipoh the project Xin Yi Dai (new generation), which aims at "mission through culture." The center offers low-threshold services for young people, e.g., by computer and language classes or music events. Some young people are then baptized. In some supermarkets the church maintains bookstores called "Glad Sounds" in which religious and other literature and CDs are offered. In the north of the country the church operates missionary work among the indigenous people, the Oran Asli in the Cameron Mountains. Since the opening of China and other countries in Southeast Asia, the churches in China, Myanmar, Madagascar, and Vietnam are supported in particular through Bible and theological courses. Rev. Wolfgang Grieninger, sent by DWM, came in 2002 as a theological adviser in Lutheran theology to LCMS, where he prepares candidates for the ministry who come from other churches.

The Lutheran church operates very successful missionary work among the Malaysian indigenous people, the so-called Oran Asli. In 1997, along with Bishop Gideon Chang and his wife, a delegation of the Bavarian church visited the congregation located in the Cameron Mountains. (Privately owned)

DWM also developed contacts with other churches in Malaysia, especially with the Basel Christian Church of Malaysia. The Basel Christian Church of Malaysia (BCCM) is made up of immigrants from China who came to Sabah in the north of the island of Borneo in the nineteenth century. They derived the name from the Basel Mission which in 1882 founded their church in China. They built their new church independently, without missionaries from Basel. The church has about 50,000 members in 150 congregations. Lately, it operates mission among the indigenous people. Its headquarters is located in Kota Kinabalu, and is connected with the Sabah Theological Seminary, founded in 1988, which was developed under the leadership of Dr. Thu En Yu into an international training center.

Furthermore, there is the *Evangelical Lutheran Church in Malaysia (ELCM)*. It goes back to the missionary work of Swedish missionaries and has about three thousand members. Its members are mainly people of Indian descent who were brought by the British from Tamil Nadu to work in the rubber plantations. Anyone who has experienced the different eating habits of ethnic Indian and Chinese Lutherans in Malaysia can guess why the churches can not merge. The church is particularly active in the diaconic field and maintains orphanages, homes for unwed mothers, etc.

Singapore

Singapore seceded from Malaysia in the 1960s as a city-state with its immense port. Seventy percent of the population is Chinese, 20 percent is Malay, and 10 percent is of Indian origin. Politics was determined for many years by Senior Statesman Lee, who held the view that democracy is harmful for development, as it was imported from the West. Successful development, he believed, needed clear conditions and an authoritarian government. Everything has to be avoided which disrupts the balance of religions, harmony, and threatens the economic stability. The Asians must go their own way on the basis of Chinese virtues. Approximately 14 percent of the inhabitants are Christians.

The Lutheran Church in Singapore (LCS) in 1997 seceded from the LCMS. It has about three thousand members. Its pastors are trained either at Singapore Bible College or the Anglican Trinity Theological College. The first Bavarian staff was missionary Werner Strauss, who previously worked in Papua New Guinea, and was sent in 1992 by DWM in cooperation with the ELCPNG to work at the Seafarers' Mission in Singapore. In the multireligious city state, the church invites people to the Christian faith through numerous missionary and evangelistic programs. It is particularly active among Thai migrant workers and seamen in one of the largest ports in the world. Moreover, it sponsors missionary activities in China, Cambodia, Thailand, Myanmar, and Mongolia.

Relations with Other Churches and Organizations in Southeast Asia

As a result of the 1991 LWF Mission Consultation in Malacca, LWF founded, at its General Assembly in 1997 in Hong Kong, the Mekong Mission Forum as a platform for cooperation between churches in the five Mekong countries Thailand, Vietnam, Laos, Cambodia, and Myanmar, where DWM was involved from the start. The promotion of theological education and training, congregation building, scholarships, seminars, and publications are in the foreground. The secretariat is affiliated with the Lutheran Theological Seminary in Hong Kong.

Furthermore, DWM maintains relations with the Lutheran Church in the Philippines (LCP). The LCP was founded by American missionaries of the Missouri Synod in 1957. In 1973 the LCP joined the LWF and annoyed its mother church in America with its social activities. Two factions arose: one based on the Missouri Synod, the other on the Lutheran World Federation. They argued in court not least over buildings and assets. Recently, there is hope for a reunification. The church began special relations with ELCPNG and sends theology students and faculty there.

Africa

General

Africa still suffers to this day from the consequences of colonialism. In the Berlin Conference in 1884, the continent was divided like a cake among the major European powers of Great Britain, France, Germany, Belgium, and Portugal. The borders were drawn arbitrarily. Nations were torn apart and others forcibly united in colonial boundaries. The colonial powers encouraged certain groups, e.g., the Tutsis in Rwanda, or the Muslim coastal tribes of the Swahili on the Tanzanian coast. They also imported their European law and forced the people to their economic interests. On the other hand, the colonial powers brought Western civilization, technology, and education to the people of Africa. On this basis, they could gradually participate in the global economy and work for the future of their countries.

Following the end of colonialism, the Western powers in Africa continued to interfere and use ethnic and religious tensions for their goals. They pursued their own political, strategic, and economic interests. The Cold War was raging in Africa as a hot war, in which millions of people died. So the East-West conflict was often fought at the expense of Africans. The international arms trade provides big business in Africa, by which the continent still suffers. Former LWF General Secretary Dr. Ishmael Noko, a native of Zimbabwe, expressed regret that there are more guns than loaves of bread in Africa. Africa is regarded as a continent of civil wars, refugees, overpopulation, unemployment, droughts, and natural disasters. But it is also a continent full of faith, life, music, and community spirit.

Since the sixteenth century through the so-called slave trade triangle, millions of West Africans were deported to the Americas. From Europe weapons were sold to Africa for slaves, shipped to America and from there, cotton delivered to Europe. The slave trade flourished even in the nineteenth century in East Africa until the British government banned the slave trade in 1880 at last under the influence of the missionary and Africa explorer David Livingstone. This bloodletting leaves its tracks until today.

Religion has traditionally played a major role in Africa. It is described as an inclusive religion that combines various deities and traditions peacefully. From outside, religions came with a claim to absoluteness, namely Christianity and Islam, which do not actually fit into African thinking and attitude towards life. Islam spread from the north and Christianity came from Europe and America. Both religions struggle for supremacy in many areas, for example, in Nigeria. Many observers thought that with the end of colonial rule, the end of Christianity would come. However, the opposite is the case. The number of Christians is growing, and many Africans are attracted to the churches because of their teaching, the church service, the Western-influenced music, and the sense of community. In their services the Christians combine African with European-American elements. The missionary work of the Muslims is heavily supported by the rich oil states. Fundamentalist tendencies increase and mix with political interests. But despite all efforts, the Muslim missionaries are far less successful than the Christian churches.

Most Africans assess the history of the Christian mission as positive, because with the missionaries came schools and health facilities. For them, the word "mission" has a good sound. The first generation of African leaders had received their education in missionary schools and learned Western values such as freedom, democracy, and individuality. The colonial governments left the educational system widely to the missionary societies. However, there were also negative effects, often unintentionally on the part of the missionaries, as the founding father of Kenya Jomo Kenyatta once remarked: "When the missionaries arrived, the Africans had the land and the missionaries the Bible. They taught us to pray with our eyes closed. When we opened them, they had the land and we the Bible."

The history of the Lutheran churches in Africa is closely linked to its political, economic, and cultural development in the second half of the twentieth century. During this time, most states gained independence, but continued to suffer from the unequal terms of trade between North and South. Imports from Europe, such as clothing, harmed the local economy. Many billions of dollars flowed into Africa as development aid, but much money went into the pockets of the rich. Corruption and mismanagement grew more and more.

In 1972, the Department for World Mission took over the missionary work of the Bavarian church and the Leipzig Mission. From 1977 to 1999, the Africa secretary and former missionary Rev. Friedrich Durst particularly promoted the development of Lutheran churches in Africa, starting with Tanzania. Under his leadership DWM designed several perspective plans for the use of human resources and finances.

Tanzania

General

Since 1884, the adventurer and pastor's son Carl Peters (1856–1918) acquired, often by unfair sales and contracts on behalf of the Society for German Colonization, parts of the East Africa. In 1891, the German Empire took over the administration of the Protectorate German East Africa. In 1890, Zanzibar, by the exchange with the island of Helgoland, became a British protectorate where the Sultan of Oman ruled. After the

First World War, most of the former German colony of East Africa became a British mandate, called Tanganyika, while the western part was taken over by Belgium. In 1961, Tanganyika gained its independence under the leadership of Julius Nyerere, who was elected the first president. In 1964, Tanganyika united with Zanzibar to form the United Republic of Tanzania after the local sultan had been expelled. The Arabs excelled particularly in the slave trade, which was channeled through Bagamoyo and Zanzibar. Within the union, almost 100 percent of Muslims living in Zanzibar retained certain independence with a separate government, which always leads to political tensions.

The Catholic Julius Nyerere (1922–1999) was originally a teacher and led the country in 1961 as chairman of his "Party of the Revolution" (Chama Cha Mapinduzi—CCM) into independence, which the United Kingdom granted relatively quickly. Since 1960, he served as prime minister, and in 1962 was elected president. Throughout his life he was called by the honorary title mwalimu (teacher). His lasting merit is that he procured the unity of the country and a long period of peace. For the unification of about 120 ethnic groups a common language was necessary. Therefore, he promoted the Kiswahili language, which was originally spoken only by a small ethnic group on the coast and spread inland beginning with the German colonial era.

To unite the ethnic groups, he built so-called ujamaa (community) villages, where people from different tribes lived together. Unfortunately, they often lacked the financial and organizational prerequisites for this relocation, which was not popular with the people. Nyerere wanted by all means to forge the Tanzanians into a national community (ujamaa). His concept was referred to as African Socialism, which was, however, understood as non-atheistic. Nyerere promoted more general education than the secondary education. This meant that in Tanzania a huge shortage of skilled workers was created, which was resolved only recently by the increased opening of secondary schools and universities.

In Tanzania, Christians, Muslims, and adherents of indigenous religions traditionally lived peacefully together. Since the 1990s, Islamic fundamentalists repeatedly disturbed religious peace, mostly directed from the outside. Also, aggressive Christians contribute to tensions. Since the Christians inherited many schools and hospitals from the missions, Nyerere nationalized them to establish the equality with the Muslims. So, until the end of Nyerere's tenure, the Lutheran church could run only the Morogoro Lutheran Junior Seminary, because it was considered as the preparation for the ministerial formation. It was rated for many years as one of the best high schools in Tanzania.

Officially, there are one-third Muslims, Christians, and adherents of traditional religions. But these are political figures. Many experts assume, however, that up to 50 percent of the population is Christian. Of course, figures should be dealt with caution in Africa. The government attaches great importance to a peaceful coexistence of religions. It intervenes in armed conflicts or aggressive events immediately; for example, when in 1993 church buildings and Christian butchers who sold pork were attacked on Easter Sunday in Dar es Salaam by Muslims. The state recognizes the religions as an important basis of society but prohibits them from any direct involvement in politics. It promotes the balancing aspirations of the Islamic umbrella organization Bakwata and advocates also towards Muslims for the neutrality of the state and a tolerant religious policy.

In the 1980s, more and more pressure came from the outside, to introduce a multiparty political system and to liberalize the economy. Nyerere focused on rural development and brought, despite huge sums of development aid from both East and West, the country to the brink of national bankruptcy. Hospitals lacked essential medicines and instruments. Initially, Nyerere did not accept a multi-party government because he was of the opinion that the people were not yet ripe. In 1985, he resigned after 25 years as the first African statesman from his post as president but remained initially chairman of the CCM party. Until his death, as a gray eminence, he exerted major influence on the political development. As his successor, the Muslim Ali Hassan Mwinyi was elected.

World Bank and International Monetary Fund demanded the depreciation of the Tanzanian Shilling, the reduction of tariffs and the introduction of a free market economy. State enterprises were privatized, and the economy flourished. Suddenly one could buy in shops things that were previously only available on the black market. In particular, the Indians play a major role in the economy. Simultaneously, however, the gap between rich and poor increased. In 1992, under international pressure and with Nyerere's consent, a multiparty democracy was introduced. In 1995 Benjamin Mkapa was elected president; he was Catholic and his wife Lutheran. He was followed in 2005 by the former foreign minister and Muslim Jakaya Kikwete. In 2015 the Catholic John Magufuli was elected.

The state now allowed the establishment of schools and universities, which were urgently needed to train professionals for the country.

Hospitals and schools were returned to the churches. With the help of the German Ministry for Economic Cooperation and Development, the Churches Social Services Commission (CSSC) was established, which provides drugs and devices for hospitals as well as books and materials for schools.

Nevertheless, Tanzania is still one of the poorest countries on earth. It has certain natural resources and lives mainly from tourism. The north around Kilimanjaro is much better off than the south. However, the economy is growing significantly, sometimes in double digits. But inflation eats up incomes, in particular of the poor. The living situation is gradually improving, and the young people have more opportunities for education. However, unemployment particularly among young people remains high. Western companies buy more and more land to use for their production.

The AIDS pandemic, in particular, leaves behind many orphans. The deaconess community Ushirika wa Neema in Moshi takes care of them. The picture shows Mother Superior Agnes Lema with an orphan. (Diaconess Institute Augsburg)

The immunodeficiency AIDS is a huge problem in Tanzania, which spread particularly in the wake of the Uganda war. AIDS mainly affects younger persons between ages twenty and forty. Disproportionately, teachers and police officers are affected. In the church hospitals 50 percent of patients and 25 percent of pregnant women are infected with AIDS. The rate in the total population is at about 10 percent, which does not significantly reduce the population growth, because the people are dying of AIDS after they have produced children. Many women are affected by it and can not defend themselves against their husbands. For a number of years there have been, in all regions of the country, free medicines available that allow a reasonably normal life for the sick. The churches have initially, largely, ignored the AIDS problem. They urged for abstinence and preached against immorality. After AIDS occurred even in the families of church leaders, the Lutheran bishops have become milder. In particular, they have recognized that they must take care of the many AIDS orphans. Polygamy and the tendency to promiscuity are still deep in the minds of men. Women must be subordinate to the men's sexual desires, eg. to teachers and classmates. When a girl gets pregnant, she has to leave the school.

The state budget is funded up to 40 percent of development funds and has to spend one third of its revenue on debt servicing. Its high debt burden comes from the 1970s as some states offered Tanzania new loans from their oil revenues that must now be repaid. As part of the campaign Jubilee 2000 debt relief was partially adopted in order to invest more resources in hospitals and schools.

The Cooperation with the Evangelical Lutheran Church in Tanzania

From 1886 to 1892, the Hersbruck Mission sent graduates of the Neuendettelsau Seminary to Africa until it dissolved and handed over its work to Leipzig Mission. In 1891 the Berlin Mission began to work in southern Tanganyika, followed in 1892 by the Leipzig Mission with its missionary work among the Chaggas in Kilimanjaro region. Since 1880, besides the Berlin Mission, the Evangelical Mission Society of German East Africa (later Bethel Mission) worked in present-day Tanzania, especially on the coast, in the Usambara Mountains and west of Lake Victoria. In 1970, it joined with the Rhenish Mission to form the United Evangelical Mission.

In 1962, the Bavarian Lutheran church became a member of the Joint Executive Commission of the Lutheran Church in Southern Tanganyika. For the first time, a church and not a mission began missionary work in Tanzania. In 1964, Rev. Hans-Gernot Kleefeld was sent as the first Bavarian missionary to Tanzania. Congregations in southern Tanganyika were founded by Berlin missionaries who came up the Rift Valley from South Africa and built their first mission stations on Lake Nyassa. Since 1891, also the Moravian mission operated in southern and central

Tanzania. The Moravians have their worldwide biggest church province here and cooperate with the Lutherans.

The Evangelical Lutheran Church in Tanzania (ELCT) comprises about six million members and is the second largest church in the country after the Roman Catholic Church. It was founded on June 19, 1963 as a merger of seven Lutheran churches that emerged from the work of various missionary organizations. The signatories also include the Neuendettelsau mission director Horst Becker. In addition to Swedes, Norwegians, Finns, Danes, and Americans, the missions of Bavaria, Berlin, Bethel, Hamburg, and Leipzig joined ELCT.

The establishment of the ELCT was closely linked to the independence of Tanzania. It pursued the objective of strengthening the country's unity. From the beginning it put emphasis on making its decisions independently. However, it invited missionary societies to continue sending coworkers on request. These coworkers, however, had to submit to the local church. As the umbrella organization for most Protestants, the Christian Council of Tanganyika (CCT) was founded.

Dr. Stefano Moshi from the Northern Diocese was elected as the first presiding bishop of ELCT. After the LWF Assembly in Dar es Salaam, Bishop Josiah Kibira officiated from 1977 to 1984 as president of the LWF. To coordinate the cooperation of ELCT with its overseas partners, the Lutheran Coordination Service East Africa (LCS) was established in 1973. It had its first headquarters in Hamburg-Bergedorf, and later in Helsinki (Finland). It was followed by the Lutheran Mission Cooperation Tanzania (LMC), which was solemnly constituted in 1998 in Bukoba. The most important change was that now ELCT had as many voting members as its fifteen overseas partners and could thus participate on an equal footing in all decisions.

ELCT comprises twenty-two dioceses where about 1,300 pastors and three thousand evangelists work. Some dioceses had presidents originally but now all have bishops, some with and some without apostolic succession. There was and is always a tendency to establish new dioceses. But ELCT has agreed to set up new dioceses only in mission territories in order to preserve its unity. Sizes of the dioceses vary from 20,000 to 300,000 members. The church as a whole is growing faster than the total population. Even Muslims convert to Christianity occasionally and are baptized.

Lately, many Massai join the Lutheran church because some dioceses allow that a man may keep his previous wives even after baptism.

This had long been impossible, so that many men were not baptized. The services are held in their own language or bilingual. In addition, the Massai are hoping to get help from the church for problems in the question of land ownership.

Evangelical and charismatic groups unsettle Christians and break into congregations. They preach the supposedly true faith and demand re-baptism. They also often promise the people prosperity and healing. The church has responded by encouraging the congregations to hold prayer services on Sunday afternoon. It is important to strengthen the identity of the Lutheran church members, who in many cases still belong to the first generation of Christians.

The pastors of the church are called mchungaji (shepherd) and generally have a high reputation. They are paid by their congregations but have to add to their low salaries by cultivating their own fields. The first seminary for local teachers was built in Marangu in 1926 in the Kilimanjaro area. In 1934, the first graduates were ordained after thorough theological training. At present, pastors are trained in Makumira (founded in 1954), Mwika, and Iringa within the Tumaini University founded in 1997. Since 1990, the ordination of women was introduced.

The congregations are financially self-sufficient and give a percentage of their collections to the diocese and the national church. About 40 Bavarian districts maintain partnership relations with districts and dioceses in Tanzania. In this way, a lot of support comes to the congregations. The funds channeled through LMC are mainly earmarked for the common institutions, for the budgets of the dioceses, and for the national church. For many years a process for financial consolidation was carried out. Most dioceses run hospitals, schools, guesthouses, women's centers, etc. which can mostly only be financed with foreign aid.

In 1993, the arrival of the first missionaries from Leipzig on the Kilimanjaro one hundred years ago was celebrated under the motto "Unto us a Beautiful Heritage is given" (Psalm 16:6). Thousands of Christians celebrated a big service in Machame. Even the Muslim president Mwinyi came and thanked the church and its overseas partners for its services to the society. The northern dioceses gave thanks for the gift of the gospel and adopted a commitment to further joint proclamation of the gospel.

Recently, many Massai have joined the Lutheran church. Left: The Massai bishop Thomas Laiser is talking to a church member. Middle: A car wheel replaces the bell and calls for worship. Right: An evangelist is preaching at a church service in the open air in the Massai Plains. (Privately owned)

African theology is still in its beginning. The church is based theologically on the traditions taken over from the missions. In ethical terms, however, the church goes its own way, for example in the strong condemnation of homosexuality in the Bukoba Declaration of 2004. Church workers who divorce are dismissed. Church discipline is practiced, especially in marital transgressions. In a special ceremony a Christian is readmitted to the congregation. Alcohol is forbidden for church workers.

ELCT has strongly supported the policy of Nyerere, despite some drawbacks, and exercised loyalty to the state. Many were concerned that, under the new Muslim president Mwinyi, difficulties for the churches would arise. The new president dispelled the fears and called for the cooperation of the churches in the building of the country and the new economic policy. During the Meru crisis the church realized that it must exercise its rights in relation to the government now led by a Muslim. In the first multiparty elections in 1995, leading circles of ELCT showed sympathy with the opposition party. In 2004 within ELCT there was tension with General Secretary Amani Mwenegoha, who had undiplomatically interfered in politics and was finally dismissed. Currently the relationship of ELCT to the government can be described as good, although ELCT expressed repeated criticism on issues of corruption and mismanagement. As a platform for Christian-Islamic dialogue TUWWAMUTA was founded in 1999, however it has long played no discernible role.

The statutes of Lutheran Mission Cooperation have installed a conference of bishops and mission directors alongside the meeting of its members. It took place twice in 1999 and 2003 and dealt, e.g., with the coexistence of Christians and Muslims. DWM contributes half of the budget of LMC, while the other half comes from the fourteen other partners. The idea of a "common basket," into which all parties pay and together distribute the funds, has not really worked well. The bilateral support and partnership programs continue and should be linked multilaterally.

In ELCT there are a number of educational and diaconal institutions: The diaconess community Ushirika wa Neema (community of grace) in Moshi was built with the support of the Augsburg Diaconess Institute and recently opened a second deaconess congregation Ushirika wa Upendo (community of love) in the Southern Diocese. The Faraja Diaconic Centre was established with the assistance of Rummelsberg Deacon's Institute and trains deacons. Tumaini University with faculties of theology, law, and human sciences teaches students at various locations around the country. Recently Masoka Training Centre was incorporated. The health worker Georg Kamm sent from Neuendettelsau founded the Infusion Unit in Moshi, which was converted into St. Luke's Foundation. The neighboring Kilimanjaro Christian Medical Centre (KCMC) had been expropriated under Nyerere and was returned to the church in order to redevelop it with the help of development funds. The Good Samaritan Foundation was established as its umbrella organization. The hospital now acts as the medical faculty of Tumaini University and is one of the best hospitals in the country.

In addition to numerous high schools, there are vocational schools in Hai (Hai Vocational Training Centre), Usa River (Usa River Rehabilitation Centre), and Mafinga (Mafinga Lutheran Vocational Training Centre) where young people are trained as bricklayers, electricians, mechanics, bakers, carpenters, etc. Handicapped may attend special schools in Mwanga and Njombe. In Kidugala and other places Bible schools train evangelists.

Almost every diocese maintains a hospital that was mostly founded by missionary doctors. In women's centers like Angaza Women Centre in Northern Diocese, the church strengthens the self-confidence of women and equips them for their work in the congregations. Missionaries from Bavaria have decisively contributed to the establishment of many of these institutions.

Following in the footsteps of the radio station Voice of the Gospel, established in 1963 by LWF in Addis Ababa, the church maintains the Radio Voice of the Gospel in Moshi. The programs are broadcasted via shortwave radio from Kilimanjaro or in FM from Swaziland. The programs range from the proclamation of the gospel, prayer, and worship, to daily news, social and development-related programs. This includes programs to increase awareness of the practice of circumcision of girls and women, on children's rights, food security, as well as preservation of the environment and land use. It can reach about five million people in northern and central Tanzania.

Overall, the relationship of the Tanzanian Christians to their Western partners has developed more and more towards a partnership of equals. Bishop Dr. Erasto Kweka argued that the Northern partners should not treat ELCT like a helpless patient. All partners together should strive for transparency and accountability. The number of missionaries employed from overseas has more than halved in the past twenty years. There were and are many personal contacts between leading personalities of ELCT and ELCB. Bishop Hermann Dietzfelbinger in 1977 participated in the LWF Assembly in Dar es Salaam. In 2005, Bishop Dr Johannes Friedrich visited numerous congregations and institutions of ELCT. Approximately thirty Bavarian districts and numerous other institutions and congregations maintain partnerships with the regions, especially in the north and south of the country.

ELCT goes confidently into the future. It has a rich spiritual and liturgical life in which African elements combine with the legacy of the missionaries and the impulses from world Christendom. Fifty percent of its members regularly participate in worship. The church carries out missionary activities in its own country

The church wants to send missionaries to the North. A number of its pastors and staff were already working in German congregations. The first was Rev. Zephaniah Mgeyekwa from the Southern Diocese, who worked in Bavaria as an exchange pastor from 1978 to 1982. The church observes, with restraint, efforts for Christian-Islamic dialogue in the North and refers to fanatic attacks by Islamists on Christians in its country. Nevertheless, ELCT is basically ready for a peaceful coexistence of Christians and Muslims, especially since there are members of both religions in many families.

In 2012, the General Synod of ELCB decided on a partnership treaty with ELCT which includes the areas of cooperation. Dr. Frederick Shoo, who studied at the Augustana Theological Seminary in Neuendettelsau was elected Presiding Bishop of ELCT in 2016.

The Lutheran church in Tanzania has, since the 1960s, unfolded missionary activities in neighboring Kenya, Congo, and Mozambique, which led to the formation of Lutheran churches with the help of the Bavarian and other missionary societies.

Kenya

General

Kenya was a British colony and got its independence in 1963 under the leadership of Jomo Kenyatta. He came from the large ethnic group of Kikuyu which still today exerts much influence. He was succeeded by Daniel arap Moi and Mwai Kibaki. After a dictatorial phase under the autocratic rule of KANU (Kenya African National Union), Kibaki introduced reforms and a multiparty system. During the Cold War period, Kenya received billions of development assistance as a bulwark of the West and a haven of stability in East Africa. Many international institutions for environment, economic affairs, and development chose Nairobi as their location. In the 1970s, the East African Union (EAU) was founded by the countries of Tanzania, Kenya, and Uganda. Conflicts led in 1977 to the close of the border to Tanzania, which was then reopened in 1984. Lately the EAU is to be reactivated with its headquarters in Arusha.

The development and education in Kenya is significantly better than in Tanzania. More people speak English. Nairobi is the hub for East Africa in regard to transport and communication links, business, and culture. In economic life the Indians take a leading position. 80,000 Britons live as landowners and businessmen in Kenya and have partially Kenyan citizenship. Crime and corruption are widespread. The contrast between rich and poor is increasing. Tourism is one of the main sources of income.

Eighty percent of Kenyans are Christians and about 10 percent are Muslims, who live particularly on the coast. Normally, Christians and Muslims maintain good relations. Local assaults are mostly stimulated from the outside. The headquarters of the All African Conference of Churches (AACC) is located in Nairobi, which offers many opportunities such as communication courses for African churches. The Anglican church and the National Council of Churches in Kenya are very active politically and criticize abuses in the country.

The Cooperation with the Lutheran Church

Already at the end of the nineteenth century, Neuendettelsau missionaries were working on behalf of Hersbruck Mission in southern Kenya among the Wakamba. In the 1960s, many Tanzanians went to Kenya because there were better income conditions. Among them were many Lutherans. They founded congregations especially in Nairobi, Mombasa, and Malindi. Gradually also Kenyans joined. The congregations formed the ELCT Kenya Synod, which was officially registered in Kenya in 1968. Rev. Volker Faigle was sent to Kenya and contributed significantly to the consolidation of the church as treasurer and pastor. In 1989, the synod declared its independence with the consent of ELCT. The formal foundation of the Kenya Evangelical Lutheran Church (KELC) took place in 1992. In 1997, Zachariah Kahuthu was elected the first bishop.

The Kenya Evangelical Lutheran Church comprises around 20,000 church members in fifteen congregations with 110 preaching points that are served by seventeen pastors, ten pastoral assistants, and eighteen evangelists. Outside the cities, the main area of church work is in the region of the Tana River on the coast. The church maintains guesthouses, a youth center, and in particular the Pangani Lutheran Children Centre for Girls in Nairobi. There, girls receive a lunch and are supported to attend school. Its finances come almost exclusively from the outside. The Joint Mission Committee for Kenya (JMCK) includes the Swedish Women Mission, the Northelbian Mission Center, the church district of Niederberg, ELCT, and DWM.

Bishop Kahuthu emphasizes the independence of his church and wants to reduce its dependency on partners. He focuses on Christian education, church growth, evangelism, and diakonia.

There is another Lutheran church in Kenya, namely the Evangelical Lutheran Church in Kenya (ELCK), which is located mainly in the western part of the country near Kisi. It was founded after the Second World War by the evangelically oriented Finnish mission LEAF. Despite years of negotiations, a union of the two churches did not materialize. The bishop of ELCK which is also a member of the LWF has joined groups which oppose the ordination of women in Sweden.

Congo / Zaire

General

The former Belgian colony of Congo is the largest and richest country in Africa. Its blessing and its curse are the vast natural resources that are desired by big corporations and the neighboring nations. The country got its independence in 1960 and then fell into the East-West conflict. Belgium supported the separation movements in the Katanga province which is particularly rich in copper. The CIA overthrew the leftist Lumumba and installed Mobutu Sese Seko. He was superseded in 1997 by Joseph Kabila after a bloody civil war. Mobutu pursued a policy of africanization and renamed Congo to Zaire. Since the takeover by Laurent Desiré Kabila Zaire is back to Congo, the official name being the Democratic Republic of Congo, in contrast to Congo-Brazzaville. In 2001 Joseph Kabila followed his father as president. Approximately three million people have so far been killed in the civil war. Tens of thousands have lost their homes and livelihood opportunities. Most of the 70 million inhabitants of the country belong to the Roman Catholic Church.

The Cooperation with the Evangelical Lutheran Church

Under the leadership of Mobutu all Protestant churches had to join together to Église Évangélique du Zaire (ECZ). The only exception was the Lutheran church. It emerged in the 1960s due to the programs of the Lutheran radio Voice of the Gospel broadcasted from Addis Ababa in Kiswahili. Since 1966, people met in the mining town of Manono in the north of the country to study the Bible. They called themselves "disciples of Martin Luther" and founded congregations in the east of the country at Kalemie on Lake Nyassa. They celebrated services and made contact with the adjacent ELCT. Students were sent to study theology in Makumira with the help of DWM and other missions.

In 1977, the Joint Committee for Zaire was established in Arusha, which has equal representation of all members: ELCT, Finnish Evangelical Lutheran Mission (FELM), Northelbian Mission Center, DWM, and the local Lutheran church. It was established in 1983 and registered with the government after the renaming of the country as Église Évangélique du Congo (EELCo). FELM pulled out gradually. Ngoy Kasukuti (1953–2013) became senior pastor in 1975 and in 1992 was consecrated by the ELCT Presiding Bishop Dr. Samson Mushemba as the first bishop of the church. Thereafter, the new bishop began to install four prelates and ordain eight pastors. Meanwhile, Lutheran congregations in western Zaire and Kinshasa had joined the church. Kasukuti was the first Lutheran bishop in francophone Africa who had studied in Makumira and Neuendettelsau. From 2001 to 2003 he was a member of a government committee which drew up a peace plan for the country. The headquarters of the church was transferred from Kalemie to Lubumbashi, formerly Elisabethville. In view of the erupting fighting since 1998 in the north of Congo which continues up today, it was a good decision. In 1994, the cathedral was inaugurated in Lubumbashi. The total membership is estimated at about 50,000, which is served by sixty pastors. Because of the vast distances and the bad roads, communication within the church is difficult.

In 1983, Rev. Walter Lupp was the first Bavarian missionary sent to Congo. He, in particular, intensified the congregation growth and began to edit a church calendar. In the area of Kalemie, a farm and a fishing project were established. During the war in 1991, missionaries briefly left the country; Lubumbashi was looted by government soldiers.

The church maintains numerous schools, including ten secondary schools under the name Epiphany with a total of about seven thousand students. Therefore, it has developed religious educational material, partly with the help of Bavaria. In Kimbeimbe, a theological college was built on the site of a former Belgian farm in 1998. It was called Institut de Formation Théologique Académique et d'Apprentissage (IAFTA) and recently formed the Lutheran University. Here pastors of the Lutheran church are trained in four years. Also, women are allowed for one year and can attend a three-month course at the Centre des Femmes. They receive instruction on Luther's life, pastoral care, domestic violence, peace work, family planning, and home economics. In 1998, the first female pastor of the church was ordained. The church leads evangelism programs among the Pygmies (Basimbi) in the north of the country. It also participates in the fight against HIV / AIDS and the reintegration of former combatants.

After long negotiations, the church decided to restructure in 2002 into five dioceses in order to achieve the decentralization of decision-making and grassroots administration in this huge country with its difficult communications. Daniel Kabamba Mukala was elected as the new presiding bishop. He was succeeded in 2010 by Bishop Mwamba Sumaili, who presides over now eight dioceses. The cooperation in respect to personnel and finances has become difficult.

Since 1998, at the theological college in Kimbeimbe, now Lutheran University, almost one hundred pastors were trained. (Privately owned)

Mozambique

General

The country comprises about 800,000 square kilometers and has 30 million inhabitants. Until the end of the Salazar regime in 1975, it was a Portuguese colony. At the time of independence, overnight hundreds of thousands of Portuguese left the country. The Portuguese were particularly active as small traders on the coast and in the cities. The colonial government did little for the country's development. Ninety-five percent of people at this time were illiterate.

Since 1964, a war for independence raged. It calmed down initially after independence, but then broke off again. With the support of South Africa, the Resistance Nationale de Mocambique (RENAMO) fought against the socialist-oriented Fronte Libertação de Mocambique (FRELIMO). The FRELIMO operated from Tanzania, where many Mozambicans had fled. There they were looked after by LWF and Tanganyika Christian Refugee Service. Therefore, since 1975, LWF maintained an office in Dar es Salaam. The leader of FRELIMO, Dr. Edmondo Mondliane, was the son of an evangelist and had visited the Swiss Reformed school in Ricatla. He was killed in a bombing in Dar es Salaam.

For a long time, only the Roman Catholic Church was allowed in the country. Since the nineteenth century Protestant missionaries from Rhodesia came despite a ban into the north of the country. Today, about 25 percent are Catholic, 10 percent Protestant, and 15 percent Muslim; the rest are allocated to traditional religions. FRELIMO initially pursued an anti-church policy. Churches were closed and expropriated. Lately it shows more openness to the churches. From 1990 to 1992 the Catholic community of San Egidio mediated a peace treaty. In the first free elections FRELIMO achieved 45 percent and RENAMO 40 percent of the votes. Poverty, especially in rural areas, is widespread. There is high unemployment and crime.

The Cooperation with the Evangelical Lutheran Church

In the mid-1960s, the Lutheran World Federation supported Tanganyika Christian Refugee Service which took care of the refugees in Tanzania who had fled from Mozambique. This humanitarian work caused the Marxist government of Mozambique to ask LWF, after their independence in 1975, to assist in the repatriation and resettlement of refugees. With this task the Lutheran Tanzanian police officer Geofrey Sawaya was commissioned. In 1984, a consultation of Lutheran churches of Tanzania and Zimbabwe was held to negotiate with the government, the Christian Council of Mozambique, and the Anglican church on the formation of a Lutheran church. It was designed as a spiritual center for Lutherans from Tanzania, East Germany, Denmark, and Sweden. In 1997, during a consultation of LWF in Arusha, the Joint Mission Board for Mozambique (JMBM) was founded. The United Evangelical Lutheran Church of Germany delegated its membership to DWM. JMBM includes representatives from ELCT, LWF, the Brazilian Lutheran church IECLB, ELCA, and the Evangelical Lutheran Church in Zimbabwe (ELCZ). In 1990, the state gave to the church a plot near the center of Maputo, a land on which a stately church and a congregation center were built. In 1994, the government registered the Evangelical Lutheran Church in Mozambique, which comprises about five thousand members. It includes also congregations in the north, e.g. in Gaza, Beira, and Chimmoio. In 1998, Horst Seeger was sent as the first pastor from the Bavarian church. In the 1990s, there was a lot of tension between Brazilian, Tanzanian, German, and local church workers. There were allegations of embezzlement which led to mistrust between the church and the Lutheran World Service. In the conflict itself, elements of religion, ethics, money, politics, power, and ethnic differences mingled. The activities of the church were temporarily paralyzed. In 2004, the Brazilian deaconess Doraci Edinger was murdered in her home in the north of the country. This murder, which must have been committed by a person close to the church, has not been cleared up. Gradually peace returned. In 2006, Rev. José Mabasso was elected senior pastor and later became bishop.

Liberia

General

In 1822, Liberia was founded by former black slaves from the United States. The name is derived from Latin libertas (freedom) and includes a vision for the foundation of the state. Liberia is a wealthy country on the west coast of Africa and has rich natural resources. Monrovia is considered the wettest capital in the world. Extensive rain forests were cut down in the 1920s by the American tire company Firestone to get rubber for tire production. The ore deposits in Bong and Nimba County were exploited by Germany and Sweden. The country has about four million inhabitants. They are mostly Christians and 20 percent Muslims. Lebanese and Indians partially dominate business activities. Today, the country achieves high revenue as a FOC country.

Liberia has long been regarded as a model country in Africa. This changed abruptly in 1980. That year, Samuel Doe murdered President William Tolbert. The Africa secretary of DWM Rev. Friedrich Durst experienced the change of power because he was attending a conference in Monrovia, where Tolbert was supposed to speak a word of greeting. It is suspected that the CIA helped, because Tolbert had fallen in disgrace during the period of the Cold War since he flirted with China and USSR. Tolbert's assassination marked the end of the rule of the descendants of slaves, the so-called Americo-Liberians. Doe publicly shot ministers on the beach. Then, however, he lost the confidence of the United States and was assassinated on December 24, 1990 by Prince Johnson. Charles Taylor, who was jailed in the US, escaped in a strange way from a maximum -security prison and avenged the murder of Tolbert with American aid operating from Ivory Coast. The struggle had been widely performed with child soldiers. Taylor took the country, except the capital, Monrovia, where the task force of West African countries was stationed. After everything, he was elected president in 1997. In 2001, the rebel group LURD interfered in the fight from Guinea, murdered and plundered, also using child soldiers, and was supported by USA.

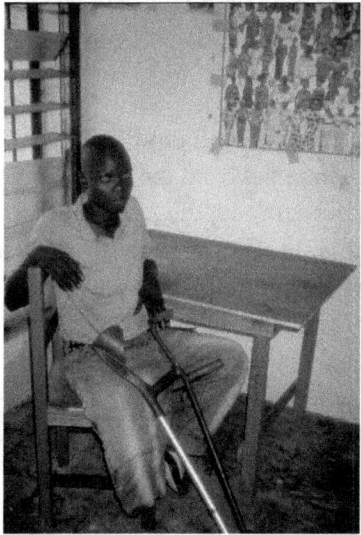

Many young people have suffered permanent injuries as child soldiers during the civil war in Liberia. DWM participated together with Missio Munich in the campaign "No War with Children." (Privately owned)

The use of child soldiers was only possible because the modern industry manufactures small arms, able to be handled by children. They were lured by the prospect of booty, cars, homes, and televisions in Monrovia. To prove their loyalty, they often had to shoot their own parents, siblings, or friends. After the end of the civil war in 2003, programs of disarmament, demobilization, reintegration, and rehabilitation were launched. Youngsters who handed over their weapons received tools, food, and the prospect of training. In 2006, Ms. Johnson Sirleaf was elected president and awarded with the Nobel Peace Prize for her efforts to bring peace to the troubled country.

The Cooperation with the Lutheran Church

On the left can be seen a ruined Lutheran church. The picture on the right shows the reconstructed St. Peter's Lutheran Cathedral in Monrovia, where in 1990 a terrible massacre took place. (Privately owned)

The immigrant slaves mostly belonged to the Methodist, Baptist, and Episcopal churches. They distanced themselves from the local population and formed a small exclusive upper class. In 1906, the Americo Liberians finally granted the locals the right to vote. They started no missionary work, fearing the loss of their power if the indigenous people also became Christians. Only gradually did they let foreign missionary societies in the country. In 1860, Lutheran missionaries came from America and began missionary work in Bong and Lofa counties. In 1957, the Lutheran Church in Liberia (LCL) was founded. In 1975, Bishop Roland Payne asked DWM for help in the church's work in Palipo area in the southeast. Payne died in 1994 when he was forced to flee from the rebels during the civil war. Ronald Diggs became his successor in 1984 and also served 1990/91 as vice-president of the country. He was followed in 1995 by Dr. Sumoward Harris. Since 1998, DWM sent coworkers to LCL. The Lutheran church fell into the chaos of civil war. In its main church of St. Peter in Monrovia a terrible massacre of hundreds of men, women, and children took place in 1990. This probably was mainly rooted in ethnic backgrounds. The Western partners from USA, Denmark, Sweden, and DWM coordinate their cooperation with the church in the forum Partners in Mission (PIM).

LCL is a self-confident church which is heavily engaged in society and politics. It is active in the Christian Liberian Council of Churches and PROCMURA. Approximately seventy pastors, three hundred evangelists, and one hundred deacons work in about fifty congregations with a total of 70,000 members. During the civil war many Christians fled from the rural areas to Monrovia, where new churches were planted. The church also cares for Lutheran Christians who fled to the neighboring countries of Guinea and Sierra Leone, where they founded Lutheran congregations. It maintains many programs for disabled persons, trauma healing, reconciliation, education, and against AIDS. For former child soldiers, the program Under the Tree (UTT) was developed, where traumatized children and adolescents learn through play, practical exercises, and community experience how to live together peacefully. LCL has two major hospitals in Curran and Phebe, which were senselessly looted and destroyed by marauding soldiers. The Gbarnga School of Theology is now jointly operated with the Methodist and Episcopal churches and has been temporarily moved to Monrovia and integrated into the United Methodist University. In the Totota Lutheran Training Institute, courses for church workers are organized and the Bible is translated in the vernacular languages. The official language of Liberia is the strange Liberian English, which was brought by the founders from the American South. In addition, many tribal languages are spoken. In the services, the Lutheran liturgy is mixed with charismatic elements.

Relations with Other Churches and Organizations in Africa

West Africa

In 1964, the Lutheran radio station Voice of the Gospel, located in Cameroon, started with broadcasts in Fulfulde language. After the great drought in the Sahel zone in the early 1970s, the churches intensified their attention for the nomadic people called Fulbe or Fulani. It includes about 15 million people living in a belt that extends over ten countries from Chad to Senegal. Their religion is Islam but mixed with popular religious elements.

In 1979, the ecumenically oriented Joint Christian Ministry in West Africa (JCMWA) was founded. It comprises a total of twenty African churches and ten partners from USA and Europe. DWM cooperates on behalf of the United Evangelical Lutheran Church of Germany. The organization aims to offer a holistic service and foster cooperation between Christians and Muslims. Aggressive sounds are avoided and respect for the culture of the nomads is mediated. This is done through regional seminars, visits, and events. The executive secretary Robert Wandersee, sent by ELCA, was tragically killed in 1998 by criminals. The Fulani are suffering from natural disasters and tensions with the settled population. Churches and missions provide assistance in the field of development and agriculture. Some Fulani join a Christian church, although JCMWA pursues no direct missionary intention.

South Africa

Since the 1980s, relationships began between the Bavaria and South Africa, especially to the *Kenosis Community* in Pietermaritzburg. Kenosis Community pursues the vision of a life and service community of black and white Christians headed by Professor Gunter Wittenberg. He taught at the University of Natal and during the apartheid he fought for the black population. He sat for more than a year in prison, part of that time even in solitary confinement. DWM gave repeated subsidies to Kenosis Community and facilitated the contact with the Deaconess Community Ushirika wa Neema in Tanzania and Bavarian deaconesses. Kenosis cares especially for AIDS orphans. It maintains a kindergarten and a guest house and helps children whose parents died from AIDS to receive a qualified education and vocational training. The relationship with the Lutheran ELCSA Natal Diocese is difficult. It refused partly to encourage girls to enter the community.

In Pietermaritzburg, the School of Theology is associated with the University of Natal which was founded in 1988 for black and white students. The Lutheran Umpumulo Seminary was dissolved and transferred to Pietermaritzburg. Many students live in the Lutheran House of Studies, which was led by Rev. Georg Scriba, who studied in Erlangen.

Ethiopia

The Ethiopian Evangelical Church Mekane Yesu (EECMY) has long been considered the fastest growing Lutheran church in Africa. It includes about five million members with over one thousand pastors who are trained at the Theological Seminary Mekane Yesu in Addis Abeba. The church was founded in 1880 by Norwegian missionaries. In the 1930s, Hermannsburg Mission joined. Since 1987, DWM supported the scholarship fund of the church with a significant amount. The students were studying theology, social sciences, or agriculture in England and USA. Many of them did not return home; recently, almost all of the students do not return home. Therefore, DWM decided to end gradually the support of the fund.

The Program for Christian Muslim Relations in Africa

The Program for Christian Muslim Relations in Africa (PROCMURA) was founded in 1987 and has its headquarters in Nairobi. In 1993, DWM joined the organization. It works with churches in eighteen African countries, to enable them to do missionary work in Muslim societies, while mission is understood as proclamation in word and deed and peaceful coexistence with Muslims. It promotes initiatives for responsible Christian witness in multireligious societies through information and awareness-raising. For church workers, courses are offered in which prejudices are removed and ways are shown for careful dialogue. Other areas are explored that require joint actions by Christians and Muslims, for example HIV / AIDS, civil society, and good governance.

Latin America

Brazil

General

Brazil is the largest country in Latin America and has a wealth of resources that are unevenly distributed. Religion plays a major role. Although the Roman Catholic Church is still the largest, most powerful and influential church, it continually loses members who join Protestant sects and churches. Thus, the Pentecostals who promise money, healing, and miracles, are increasing more and more. African slaves brought with them the Candomblé cult, in which African deities mingle with Christian saints. One half of the population is black or mixed race, the other half are whites with a European background. Originally, there were about five million indigenous Indians living in Brazil. However, they were decimated by disease, slave labor, and systematic extermination to a population of 300,000 today. Only in 1989, the government granted them civic rights, including the right to vote, as they were previously under the guardianship of the Indian affairs office. They have been allocated certain areas which they had possessed before, according to documents. The contrasts between rich and poor can be seen everywhere. Favelas are located close to high-rise buildings.

The Cooperation with the Evangelical Church of the Lutheran Confession in Brazil

In the southern states of Rio Grande do Sul, Santa Catarina, and Paraná, European immigrants were settled at the beginning of the nineteenth century. They developed the land, pushed back the natives, protected the borders with the neighboring countries of Argentina and Paraguay, and "brightened" the population. The first large group of Germans arrived in Sao Leopoldo on July 25, 1824. From there later immigrants settled in the Serra Gaucha mountain range, where they laboriously cultivated their allocated land under the motto "first generation death, second generation distress, third generation bread." Other immigrants from Germany settled in the mid-eastern state of Espirito Santo. The predominantly Protestant immigrants were allowed to build churches, but at first could not have a tower. Each congregation included a school, in which pupils were taught in German until the 1930s with a break during the First World War. The Protestants in the villages preserve partially until today their German dialects originating from Hunsrück and Pomerania.

In Porto Alegre in the southern state of Rio Grande do Sul the headquarters of the Evangelical Church of the Lutheran Confession in Brazil (IECLB) is located. (Privately owned)

Soon after their immigration the Protestants founded congregations, the first in 1824 in Nova Friburgo and Rio de Janeiro, and in 1827 in Sao Leopoldo. They received support from the Protestant church in Berlin and the Basel Mission, since they mostly came from union or Reformed churches. On October 31, 1897 Rev. Otto Kuhr was sent by the Bavarian Lutheran Treasury of God to Brazil to work among German immigrants. He was a graduate of the Neuendettelsau Mission Seminary, like 140 colleagues who followed him until 1985.

German immigrants were closely related to their church. The founder of the Rio Grande Synod, Rev. Wilhelm Rotermund, said at a synodical assembly in 1916: "If you cease feeling and thinking evangelical, you cease to be a German. Conversely, whoever denies German language and German character, will even be lost from our church. Germaneness and gospel are linked for life and death." Numerous congregations also maintained schools which taught for many decades in German. Pastors from

Germany prompted the Lutherans to take care of their German heritage that merged with Brazilian elements.

It is, therefore, not surprising that Nazism among German Brazilians found many supporters, including pastors of the Lutheran church. Since 1924, the German Evangelical Church Federation was responsible for the sending of pastors abroad. Its bishop, Dr. Theodor Heckel, who later became dean in Munich, particularly sent pastors to Brazil who were inclined to the Nazi-oriented movement German Christians. Against this movement, the Brazilian government in the 1930s set up a program of integralism and banned in 1938 the German language in schools and in public. As Brazil entered the Second World War in 1942 on the side of the allies, the German language was banned altogether, even in worship, though many pastors and church members could hardly speak Portuguese. "The majority of the pastors went to jail, partly because they were Germans, partly because they had openly expressed their sympathies for Hitler's Germany." (U. Fischer) Many pastors, however, joined the Confessing Church and enabled the new start after the war.

During the military dictatorship of President Ernesto Geisel (with German origin) in the 1970s, the church boldly resisted interventions of the state, campaigned for detainees, and called for the observance of human rights.

In 1886, the Rio Grande Synod was founded. In 1905, the Lutheran congregations in Paraná, Sao Paulo, Espiritu Santo and Santa Catarina joined to a Lutheran synod headed by Rev. Otto Kuhr. It was called the "Treasury of God Synod" because many pastors who worked there came from Neuendettelsau. In 1932, it joined the German Evangelical Church Federation in Berlin, after negotiations with the Bavarian church to become a church district had failed. Its 50,000 parishioners were supervised by thirty-five pastors, of whom thirty-one had been trained in the Neuendettelsau Seminary. The Neuendettelsau graduate Wilhelm Fugmann made the first translation of the liturgy into Portuguese. Another seminarian, Rev. Friedrich Wüstner (1903–1996), was the last president of the synod. After the founding of the EKD in 1947, its office for foreign affairs assumed responsibility for pastors sent from Germany in which also the Martin Luther Association as successor of the Lutheran Treasury of God has been involved.

After the Second World War, the synods grew ever closer into a national church. On October 25, 1968 the Igreja Evangélica de Confissão Luterana no Brasil (IECLB)—Evangelical Church of the Lutheran

Confession in Brazil—was founded and based on a centralist constitutional order. The church is divided into historically different synods, while its name distinctly expresses its Lutheran character. More conservatively oriented congregations that had been established by the Lutheran Church–Missouri Synod formed the Igreja Evangélica Luterana do Brasil (IELB)—Evangelical Lutheran Church of Brazil. However, there are regular contacts between the two churches. IECLB has over 700,000 members, IELB about 230,000. While IECLB has long been a member of the Lutheran World Federation, IELB belongs to the International Lutheran Council. Both churches together make up only 0.65 percent of Brazil's population of more than 200,000,000.

The picture shows the installation of deaconess Hildegard Mathes as head of the Lutheran retirement home Lar Elsbeth Koehler in Blumenau by synod pastor Marianne Beyer Ehrat. (Privately owned)

In 1980, at the occasion of the 450th anniversary of the Reformation, ELCB signed a partnership agreement with IECLB which was renewed in 2010. Regular consultations, in particular on missionary concepts, grants, and exchange of pastors and other church employees were agreed upon.

Most church members of IECLB live in the three southern states and are predominantly ethnically of German origin. Until the 1960s, the lectures at the Theological Seminary founded in 1946 in Sao Leopoldo (Escola Superior de Teologie—EST) were held in German. There, most pastors of the church are trained. The church has established congregations in the north and west of the country, where many church members have migrated. A missionary action plan named "Mission of God—Our Passion" was adopted, which has the motto: "No congregation without mission. No mission without a congregation." The church understands mission as a comprehensive witness of Christians. "Where diaconal work starts, because people are suffering and need help, there acts God and builds a congregation and makes his work visible for the sake of human dignity." Therefore diaconic-social projects, schools, and daycare centers in the slums are important for the church. The church is committed also to small farmers, landless people, indigenous peoples, and other minorities. Currently, only a few German-language services are held. Rather, IECLB has become a very Brazilian church; however, it does not deny its German roots.

The Lutheran church is congregationally structured and emphasizes the local responsibility of its congregations. It is an outspoken parish church that practices the universal priesthood of all believers. Normally about 15 percent of church members attend the Sunday service. The congregations levy from their members a contribution, of which 10 percent goes to the national church. In the 1,800 congregations and preaching stations, over 700 pastors, eighty catechists, 140 deacons and deaconesses, and twenty missionaries are at work. The church maintains about fifty schools with about 35,000 pupils, twenty hospitals, and twelve nursing homes.

The church council is the supreme decision-making body, which elects the church president and the church leadership, which have their headquarters in Porto Alegre ("Happy Harbor"). The eighteen synods are headed by a synod pastor. Church President Dr. Nestor Friedrich succeeded Dr. Gottfried Brakemeier, Huberto Kirchheim, and Dr. Walter Altmann. In 1997, a new constitution was adopted which emphasizes the responsibility of the local congregations.

IECLB teaches the doctrine of the fourfold office, consisting of the pastoral, diaconal, catechetical, and missionary office. The training for the first three offices is done at the Theological Seminary in São Leopoldo and at the Facultade Luterana de Sao Bento do Sul in Teologia, which has a pietistic tradition. Missionaries are trained in a mission seminary in Curitiba.

IECLB is a diaspora church that is challenged by the mulitreligous context and a large Catholic majority. The number of Pentecostal churches mostly coming from USA and Afro-Brazilian cults is growing rapidly.

The graduates of the Neuendettelsau Seminary who were sent to Brazil were associated with the Protestant church in Germany. But they were paid from the beginning by the local congregations and were given the status of a pastor, in contrast to missionaries working in New Guinea, who only received an allowance from the mission. The pastors with Bavarian origin frequently held contact with the Mission Institute in Neuendettelsau and regarded it as their theological home without being employed by it.

The church maintains several institutions that are partially supported by the Bavarian church. The deaconess community, which was founded in 1939 on the Spiegelberg in Sao Leopoldo, comprises sixty sisters, who may be married or divorced. Among the indigenous people of Brazil, the Indian Mission Council COMIN works. It defends their rights to land, education, and health. It does not aim primarily to conversion but wants to practice reconciliation in the sense of a "silent mission" or "implicit evangelization." The office of CAPA works among small farmers.

The church receives grants from Bavaria and other German churches, from Martin Luther Association, Gustavus Adolphus Work, and from districts and congregations. The partner organization Obra Gustavo Adolfo (OGA) is based on the Spiegelberg near Sao Leopoldo. In particular, finances for scholarships, diaconal and missionary activities, and disaster relief are provided.

Central America

General

The Central American countries were colonized by Christopher Columbus after landing from Spain at the beginning of the sixteenth century. The Spaniards enslaved the ancient civilized peoples and exploited their rich gold treasures. With the soldiers came Catholic missionaries, especially Jesuits and Franciscans. They converted, partially by force, the natives to Christianity. In 1822, Central America fought successfully for its independence from Spain and belonged for a short time to Mexico. Then there was for some years a Central American republic, which split up in 1838 in the countries of Guatemala, El Salvador, Honduras, Nicaragua, and Costa Rica. The inhabitants of El Salvador are 90 percent mestizo, i.e., mixed Spanish and Indian heritage. Since the nineteenth century, the USA interfered regularly in the political and economic life of Central America. The USA treated the countries like colonies, installing and dismissing governments according to its will. After an American businessman in 1870 discovered that bananas from Honduras mature on the trip to New York and can be sold at a high profit, huge banana plantations were started. Banana companies like the United Fruit Company degraded Honduras to the first "banana republic" by bribing politicians and controlling the government. The United States still determines what is happening in Central America. It was alarmed when, in 1979 in Nicaragua, the leftist regime of the Sandinistas came to power. The result was civil war between soldiers and guerrillas in El Salvador, Nicaragua, and Honduras, which ended only in 1999. Violence and terror are commonplace today. Youth gangs, whose leaders were expelled from the United States, are terrorizing neighborhoods and demand protection money.

Countries are torn apart by huge social tensions between rich and poor. In many cases, a few families, who often live outside the country, own a large portion of the land. US corporations determine the economy. Industrial companies settle in free trade zones (Zonas Francas), where they are not bound by state laws regarding minimum wages and unions. El Salvador has been "dollarized," and in the other countries the dollar is seen as an unofficial payment. Civil wars have caused migration. Six hundred thousand refugees from Nicaragua live in Costa Rica and have to do mostly low-paid work. Many people emigrated to the United States; Los Angeles is the largest Latin American city on the continent. The remittances, that is, payments of emigrants to their relatives at home, are vital to many people and are important foreign exchange earnings. The USA imposed unfavorable trade agreements. Many people, especially young people, are unemployed. Earthquakes and other natural disasters impede development.

The Roman Catholic Church still has great influence in politics and society. Its members include the majority of people, even though numerous sects unfold their missionary activities. Pentecostal churches are springing up like mushrooms.

The Cooperation with the Lutheran Churches in El Salvador, Nicaragua, Costa Rica, and Honduras

At the beginning of the twentieth century, many Lutheran Christians from Germany came to Central America. However, their congregations started no specific missionary work among the native population. This began after the Second World War by the Lutheran Church–Missouri Synod which opened a Lutheran seminary in Mexico, among whose graduates were Medardo Gómez and Guillermo Flores.

In the second half of the twentieth century, four small Lutheran churches have emerged in Central America. They formed in 1988 the Communion de Iglesias de Luteranas de Centroamérica (CILCA). At the Regensburg Synod of 1995, ELCB signed a partnership agreement with CILCA, in which the IECLB was also included. The churches agreed in a so-called three-party-agreement to send Brazilian pastors to CILCA, for whom ELCB provides the financial resources. Both contracts were renewed in 2005. Since 1983, an office of the Lutheran World Federation in San Salvador supported the diaconal work of the churches. CILCA has a total of about 20,000 Christians who belong to the following churches:

The Salvadoran Lutheran Church (Sinodo Luterano Salvadoreno—SLS) has about 10,000 members in sixty congregations. It grew out of the missionary work of the Missouri Synod and was established in 1971 by Bishop Medardo Gómez. Controversies about the theology of liberation, ecumenism, and women's ordination led in 1986 to the break with the Missouri Synod. Bishop Gómez is heavily engaged in his country, politically and socially. Some consider him as the successor of the Catholic Archbishop Oscar Romero, who was murdered in 1980. Gómez was instrumental in the 1992 peace accord, which ended the more than decade-long civil war. He emphasizes the concept of an "integral mission" integrating proclamation and social work. In his "theology for life" (teologia por la vita) he stands up prophetically for the rights of the poor. Through social projects of sustainable agriculture, health, and education of children and young people, the church tries to react to the catastrophic situation.

Bishop Medardo Gómez officiates at an installation in Honduras with delegates from ELCB and IECLB participating. (Privately owned)

The spiritual office in the church is built in stages on the catechetical, evangelistic, diaconal ministry, and the office of the reverendo or reverenda. Only the pastor reverendo is permanently entrusted with the administration of the sacraments and must have a theological education. The Lutheran University, founded by the church in 1991, is now independent. In 2001, Deacon Helmut Köhler was sent as the first Bavarian church worker to El Salvador.

Bishop Victoria Cortez founded in 1990 the Lutheran Church of Nicaragua Faith and Hope and also served as vice-president of the Lutheran World Federation.(left) The church is particularly active in the field of health services. In front may be seen the general secretary Rev. Ilo Utech, originating from Brazil. (right) (Privately owned)

In Nicaragua the Lutheran Church of Nicaragua Faith and Hope (Iglesia de Nicaragua Luterana Fey y Esperanza—ILFE) was founded in 1990 by Victoria Cortez and is led by her since then. Cortez, who was for a period also vice president of LWF, came as a refugee in the 1980s from El Salvador to Managua and started to build a Lutheran church. In 2004, she was installed as the first bishop of the church. ILFE comprises about seven thousand parishioners. They often live under poor conditions. In 1998, the hurricane Mitch caused major damage and nearly 10,000 people died. ILFE maintains health centers and particularly appeals to young people. In rural areas it supports, within the concept of integral mission, small farmers in sustainable agriculture and accompanies them pastorally. In 1996, a partnership agreement with the church district of Nuremberg was signed. Volunteers and theologians from Bavaria work in the church.

In 2001, due to controversies over leadership, understanding of ministry, and structure of the church, the Nicaraguan Evangelical Lutheran Church (Iglesia Evangélica Luterana Nicaraguense—IELNIC) split from ILFE.

The Lutheran Church of Costa Rica (Iglesia de Luterana Costa Rica—ILCO) was founded in 1988 by Melvin Jiminez, who was its president since 2000 and was introduced in 2008 as bishop. Under his leadership, the church realizes a "pastoral popular" with an integral service of word, sacrament and service. It is particularly committed to the rights of indigenous people of Costa Rica and cares for the immigrants from Nicaragua, for the landless, plantation workers, and for marginalized groups. In the so-called casas abiertas, children from the poverty belt of San José are cared for. The church counts about two thousand church members in fourteen congregations. In 2002, a partnership agreement with the Bavarian church district of Aschaffenburg was signed. In 2014, Bishop Jimenez went into politics and resigned. Rev. Gilberto Quesada was elected as the new president.

In 1983, the Christian Lutheran Church of Honduras (Iglesia Cristiana Luterana de Honduras—ICLH) was founded by Guillermo Flores. It includes about two thousand church members in ten congregations. The Brazilian pastor Armindo Schmechel worked for several years to help build up the church. With church services, congregation visits, evangelism among children, and women's programs, the church is dedicated to the most disadvantaged groups. Because of the recurrent conflicts in the country, the church growth is severely limited. In addition to drug wars there are massive conflicts over land ownership and political issues.

Recently the newly founded Lutheran Church in Guatemala joined CILCA. The young Lutheran churches in Central America combine piety with music, and lively worship with social commitment. Their temperament and zeal for life help them on their way to a hopefully better future.

Relations with Other Lutheran Churches in Latin America

During the nineteenth and twentieth centuries, emigrants came from German-speaking areas of Europe—Germany, Switzerland, Austria, Volga region, and Bessarabia—to Argentina, Paraguay, and Uruguay. They brought with them their customs and their Protestant faith. Where they settled, they founded schools and congregations. Many of them merged in 1899 into the German Evangelical Synod of Rio de la Plata (Sinodo Evangélico Alemán del Rio de la Plata). Over time new congregations joined, the descendants of the first immigrants were open to their country's culture. In 1965, from the Sinodo Alemán del Rio de la Plata, the Evangelical Church of the Rio de la Plata (Iglesia Evangélica del Rio de la Plata) emerged. It works in partnership with neighboring IECLB and includes about 45,000 members in forty-two parishes with 200 congregations. The church intensifies the congregation building and works among street children. It is also committed to human rights and protecting the environment.

Since 1974, Bavarian pastors sent through the Evangelical Church in Germany are active in Argentina. Lately volunteers are sent by Mission One World to work in particular in diaconic projects of IERP.

The Evangelical Lutheran Church in Chile dates back to the period around 1860, when the first German Protestants emigrated to Chile. Since the separation of church and state in 1925, the Lutheran congregations formed a union, which led in the 1930s to the establishment of the German Evangelical Church in Chile. In 1959, the church changed its name to the Evangelical Lutheran Church in Chile (Iglesia Evangélica en Chile—IELCH). In the 1960s, IELCH began a process of "chilenization" and the formation of new Spanish speaking congregations. It also supported the government of Salvador Allende in his struggle for the oppressed and marginalized people. After the seizure of power by the military government of Pinochet in 1975, church president Helmut Frenz and other pastors were expelled. Almost all German speaking congregations withdrew from the IELCH and founded the Lutheran Church in Chile (Iglesia Luterana en Chile—ILCH). Lately, a rapprochement takes place through joint activities at the congregation level and common parish conferences to prepare a reunion. IELCH includes about three thousand members, who are cared for in twelve congregations by eleven pastors.

Since the 1990s, Bavarian pastors worked in IELCH and have recently been sent by Mission One World. Volunteers from Bavaria also work in the church.

3

Priorities and Developments of Bavarian Mission Work in the Twentieth Century

Understanding of Mission

The term mission has only been in use since the sixteenth century to denote the effort to win unbaptized people for the Christian faith. In Germany the term mission is controversial, even today inside and outside the church. It is more likely attributed to sects and evangelicals and sometimes regarded as "religious trespassing." On the background of the amalgamation of mission and colonialism, the word often has a negative undertone. In the secular world it is, however, often used for a specific philosophy of an enterprise or associated with a task that requires special effort. Many critics forget that Europe was once missionized. Without mission modern Europe would not be as it is, where Christianity unfolded enormous effects in the field of politics and society, culture and science. The missionary mandate of Matthew 28:18–20 was aimed at a small group of disciples who did not think in the least that their message would lead to a world religion. It was also originally not associated with any political aspirations. Without mission there would be no Christians in the world.

In his discourse *Three Books of the Church*, published in 1845, Loehe summarized his understanding of mission with the following words:

> The church of the New Testament, no longer a national church, but a church of all peoples, a church that has its children in all lands and gathers them out of all lands, the one fold of the one shepherd brought together from many a flock (John 10:16), the

> universal, the really Catholic church which flows through all the ages and into which all people pour–this is the great thought which is still in process of fulfillment, the work of God in the last hour of the world. It is the favorite thought of all the saints in life and death ..., the thought, which must permeate mission, or it does not know what it is and what it should be. Mission is therefore nothing else than the one church of God in its motion—the actualization of the one universal Catholic church. Where mission penetrates, fences collapse that separate nations from nations.

Thus, mission is not an aspect of church action, but its essence. Its overriding goal is the eschatological church, which only God himself can realize. It is a salvation-historical movement that reaches into eternity. A church without mission is dead. Mission sets the church in motion, crosses borders, and has the unity of the worldwide church as its destination.

In his essay on "Inner Mission in General" from 1850, Loehe described the unity of inner and outer mission:

> For the work of mission is nothing other than the task to call the church of Jesus, to gather, to enlighten, and to preserve for eternal life.... Outer mission is what can be done to reach the unbaptized,—inner mission comprises everything which is done towards the baptized.... The difference is only the areas: the outer mission operates among the unbaptized, the inner mission among the baptized. The two are not separated, but innermost connected, have the same dignity and honor, love and fidelity, and equal value.

Both are part of the same movement and are differentiated only by baptism. The baptized are committed to mission among the unbaptized. Home mission is followed by Gentile mission. Loehe understood the Lutheran church as a sending church. The sending originates in the congregation. He saw his missionary work always as a service to the church, though it was institutionally separated from the church.

The Neuendettelsau Mission worked on the basis of Loehe's understanding of mission and linked world mission with mission at home. It saw itself as a decidedly Lutheran missionary institution that tried to contribute to the establishment and consolidation of Lutheran churches everywhere.

Since the 1960s, heavy disputes began between evangelicals and so-called ecumenists in Germany regarding the understanding of mission.

Gradually, the controversy between mission and development work, word and deed could be clarified. In 1999, the synod of the Protestant churches in Germany put its meeting in Leipzig under the main theme "Speaking of God in the World—The Missionary Task of the Church at the Threshold of the Third Millennium." In its final address to the congregations it emphasized:

> Mission is not done for the church's sake. The church is taken into the mission of God. We have a mandate to open people's eyes to the truth and beauty of the Christian message. We want to win them that they bind in freedom to Jesus Christ and adhere to the church as the community of believers.... We are on the threshold of the third millennium. This is a time when the urgency of the missionary task is newly recognized everywhere in the churches and brought to the fore. We need for this all skills and all the strength we can muster.

Important for the development of the understanding of mission was the concept of *Missio Dei*, which stood in the center of the Fifth World Missionary Conference in Willingen in 1952. It was drafted by the Neuendettelsau missionary and later professor at Augustana Theological Seminary, Georg F. Vicedom. Accordingly, all missionary work is based on God's mission. In its missionary work, the church shares in God's own mission to save the world. Not the church, but God is the subject of mission. In his mission, the triune God turns to the world. God acts as creator, redeemer, and reconciler in global dimensions. His salvatory will refers not only to the individual but to the whole of creation. Thus, the concept of the conciliar process as a commitment to justice, peace, and integrity of creation is closely linked to the eschatological goal of worshipping the triune God in eternity.

Former New Guinea missionary Dr. Georg F. Vicedom (1903–1974) worked until 1956 in the Mission Institute and then took over the newly established missiological chair at the Augustana Theological Seminary, where he taught until 1972. He became one of the most important mission theologians of the twentieth century, especially because of his book on the concept of Missio Dei. (Archive Mission One World)

LWF has made this concept also the basis for its mission document adopted in 1983 by the Seventh General Assembly in Budapest in 1984 and published in 1988 under the title *Together in God's Mission: An LWF Contribution to the Understanding of Mission*:

> Participation in mission is the central objective of the church. The mission of the church derives from God's own mission and is enshrined in the self-revelation of God. . . . Mission is the continuing work of salvation of God the Father, the Son, and the Holy Spirit. Mission is God's order to his people to participate in his ongoing work of salvation. . . . A missionary church is always looking to find its way beyond its borders. This is part of its nature. Anyone who has received the message of the gospel, must pass on the good news of salvation in Christ to those who have not heard or who can not yet answer or have forgotten or been estranged from it. The actual mandate of mission is where faith in Jesus Christ meets with unbelief, repudiation, or rejection of Christ. This is the case even among the members of the church. . . . Mission is the joint responsibility of all Christians, of all congregations and of all the churches; mission at any location is the privilege and the common responsibility of the worldwide church.

Mission is here understood as trinitarian and not based solely on Christ. It must not be limited to areas outside Europe and starts not only "where the palm trees grow." It begins rather on the doorstep and reaches into all corners of the world. It must be understood as theologically functional and not geographically. It is aimed at Christians as well as "pagans" overseas and "neo-pagans" in Europe. It is necessary everywhere where faith meets unbelief, i.e., for everybody. Home mission and world mission belong together.

While at the Fourth General Assembly of LWF in Helsinki in 1963, mission was still understood primarily as proclamation and conversion, the Sixth General General Assembly in Dar es Salaam in 1977 emphasized a holistic understanding of mission. Proclamation also includes advocacy and service. Within the ecumenical movement the key words justice, peace, and integrity of creation enriched the mission concept. The Ninth General Assembly of LWF in 1997 in Hong Kong called for a renewed commitment to common witness in each place. This should be realized in the unity of mission and evangelism.

LWF published 2004 a new mission document titled *Mission in Context: Transformation, Reconciliation, Empowerment—An LWF Contribution to the Understanding and Practice of Mission.* It is based not on the Great Commission of Matthew 28, but on the Emmaus story in Luke 24: Mission is described as a common way. The document unfolds mission under the three keywords: transformation, reconciliation, and empowerment.

> These focal points of the mission . . . describe mission as the participation of the church in the mission of the Triune God in creation, redemption, and sanctification. They also reflect the holistic and contextual nature of mission, i.e a mission which is led by the Holy Spirit, to go the "way of the Son" as the way of incarnation, cross, and resurrection. Mission is the reason for the existence of the church. It springs from the nature of the church as a witnessing community, a gift of gracious justification of God for mission and invitation to mission.

These three terms are, therefore, on the one hand, the work of God as creator, redeemer, and sanctifier and, on the other hand, the threefold way of Christ in incarnation, crucifixion, and resurrection. At the same time, the mission document describes, on the basis of the Emmaus story, a "hermeneutical spiral approach." It begins with the description of mission contexts that change and challenge the churches, then brings the mission theology in dialogue with these contexts and goes over to the mission practice that reflects and influences both the theology and the context.

ELCB in its Church Law on Mission and Ecumenics of 2006 describes in its preamble that mission and ecumenism belong together:

> The Evangelical Lutheran Church in Bavaria lives in the communion of the one holy and apostolic church. With the Christian churches in the worldwide ecumenical movement it has to share with them the God-given task to spread the reconciling and peace-making message of God in Jesus Christ in word and deed. Mission and ecumenism are the main characteristics and expressions of the life of the church. . . . Through partnership work and development services, ELCB takes the responsibility to share the spiritual and material goods entrusted to it with others and to work towards just structures in society and economy.

In 2007, guidelines were formulated for the work of the newly founded Center Mission One World–Center for Partnership, Ecumenics, and Mission, which summarizes its mission and objectives:

> - We practice and promote Christian life in a worldwide perspective and work together with our partners for more justice, peace, and integrity of creation in the one world.

- We build our partnerships with churches in Africa, Latin America, East Asia, and Pacific by encounters, personnel exchanges, and financial support.

- We promote ecumenical and global learning and are committed to the concerns of our partners.

- We are committed to human rights so that women, men, and children can live in dignity and freedom.

- We are called by God in his mission and encourage people to carry on the message of Jesus by faith, hope, and love across all borders.

Thanks to the efforts of missionaries and missionary organizations, the gravity of Christianity shifted increasingly from North to South. While at the beginning of the twentieth century 90 percent of the Christians lived in the North, at its end more than 60 percent live in the South. They raise their voices more clearly. Christianity still exerts in Africa and Asia a great fascination and appears for many people in combination with Western civilization as attractive. However, the traditional confessional churches are losing influence in favor of charismatic sects and churches.

DWM invites every year representatives from Lutheran churches for an international summer school to strengthen the communion between Christians in the North and in the South. (Archive Mission One World)

Mission theology is taught at several institutions of higher learning in Bavaria. Since 1820, the (Reformed) professor Christian Krafft held mission historical lectures at Erlangen University at irregular intervals. At the end of 1861, the former Leipzig mission director Karl Graul (1814–1864) came to the faculty of theology in Erlangen, which in 1854 had conferred on him an honorary doctorate. In 1864, he qualified as a university lecturer as the first German mission scholar with the famous lecture "About the Importance of Mission within the Science of the University." Because he died suddenly in November of that year, he could not take the honorary professorship requested. It would have been the first Protestant mission professorship in Germany. Nevertheless, Graul is considered a founder of missiology in Germany.

Dr. Karl Graul (1814–1864) was the first director of Leipzig Mission. In 1861, he joined the faculty of theology in Erlangen and is considered a founder of missiology in Germany. (Archive Leipzig Mission)

At the faculty of theology in Erlangen, missiological lectures were repeatedly held, for example, by the Neuendettelsau mission director, Dr. Friedrich Eppelein. In the 1950s and 1960s, the professors Dr. Gustav Stählin and Dr. Wilhelm Maurer tried to establish a mission chair, which eventually was occupied in 1967 by Dr. Niels-Peter Moritzen. At the Augustana Theological Seminary in Neuendettelsau the former New Guinea missionary Dr. Georg F. Vicedom taught beginning in 1956 as professor of missiology. To avoid the Christian claim for exclusivity and superiority in recent years, the term intercultural theology is used. Within this discipline, research is done on theories of culture, religion, society, and reason. Its goal is to analyze mission and religion in the context of secularism, post-colonialism, and globalization.

Mission and Church

Missionary work in Bavaria did not develop "from above" but "from below." Individuals and groups started missionary activities in the early nineteenth century. The Bavarian government and the church which was under its rule prohibited or hindered for a long time all missionary initiatives. Only in 1843, the Bavarian Central Missionary Association was officially approved. However, since 1841, Wilhelm Loehe, as a parish pastor, trained missionaries in Neuendettelsau and sent them to America. As a private initiative Friedrich Bauer in 1846 founded the Mission Preparation Institute in Nuremberg. Finally, in 1849, the Society for Inner (since 1888: and Outer) Mission in the Sense the Lutheran Church was founded. It thereupon employed Friedrich Bauer, who had previously earned his living as a teacher of religion in Nuremberg. Loehe understood the foundation of the Society as an interim solution until the church becomes "the society of societies in which all true societies merge."

The missionary work operated by the Society was, for over a hundred years, not an institutional part of the Bavarian church. While working in and for the church, it was legally independent. However, there were many personal relations between mission and church. The Mission Institute initially received no grants from the church budget and had to rely on donations and collections from the congregations and from individuals. In the 1960s, however, some mission buildings in Neuendettelsau were built from church funds.

Since the merger of the World Council of Churches with the International Missionary Council in 1961, initiatives in Germany developed to unite the mission centers with the regional churches. It was a lengthy process with many negotiations that led to different solutions in the churches. In Bavaria, the integration of church and mission was completed at the meeting of the General Synod in Bayreuth in October 1971. In the newly established Department for World Mission the missionary work of Neuendettelsau Mission in New Guinea was combined with the missionary work in Tanzania by Leipzig Mission and the church headquarters in Munich. Missionary work became a task for the whole church and its congregations.

The integration of church and mission brought significant changes for the missionary work itself. Now many other church services and institutions started in Bavaria, and the former special position of the Mission Institute as the biggest institution in the church, was considered in the relationship to other institutions. However, missionary work needs a free space, which should not be unduly limited by church regulations. Between an internationally operating mission center and a regionally working church there will always be tensions that must be endured and constantly clarified. To meet the risk of a "domestication of mission," it must preserve its necessary "autonomy and freedom" as a service center with worldwide missionary and ecumenical dimensions. Although mission now received a stable financial basis and a firm stand in the church and its congregations, it lost part of its independence.

LWF has developed, in recent years, the concept of communio. The tenth LWF General Assembly in Winnipeg in 2003 decided to change the name to the Lutheran World Federation—A Communion of Churches. Comunion means more than solidarity and accompaniment. It is based on the Holy Scriptures, baptism, Lutheran confession, and the joint celebration of Holy Communion. LWF is understood not merely as a sympathy community but faces a common task and obligation. The partnership programs between churches and congregations should be embedded in the communion. For this purpose, the General Synod of the United Evangelical Lutheran Church of Germany stated, in a resolution in 2004:

> Within the Lutheran world community, we are confident that the joint Lutheran confession overcomes the boundaries of peoples, races, cultures, languages, and social classes and makes possible for us the experience of God-given unity. The Lutheran World Federation has included in its name the word communion to mark the increased global connectedness of the Lutheran churches. It is not meant as a separation from other denominations but intended to strengthen the Lutheran communion as a viable pillar in the house of all Christendom.

LWF offers a platform for mutual exchange that is important in particular for the many small Lutheran churches which often live their faith in minority situations and under difficult conditions. Thus, the Lutheran identity of the churches could be strengthened. DWM worked in recent decades closely together with LWF. The directors and secretaries were represented in important committees of LWF and the United Evangelical

Lutheran Church of Germany. Also, good contacts were established with the World Council of Churches.

The concept of communion was also taken up in a document adopted by the Bavarian General Synod in 2006 entitled "External Relations of ELCB—A Contribution to the Worldwide Communion":

> ELCB is . . . really church, but not the whole church of Jesus Christ. . . . ELCB is part of the mission community of all called and sent for Christ's sake. . . . . This is realized in common witness, ecumenical learning, and the common commitment to justice, peace, and integrity of creation. Lutheran confession on the one hand and ecumenical openness on the other hand thus form the cornerstone of the understanding of ELCB . . . The global relationships of the Bavarian church are exemplary implementations of communion among all Christians.

People in God's Mission

Mission is done by people. The Mission Seminary was, from the beginning, the center and heart of the Neuendettelsau missionary work. The missionaries studied for many years in a spiritually oriented fellowship, and this fellowship then continued overseas. They were sent overseas, originally for their entire lives, and ordained for missionary service. During their studies it was strictly forbidden to have relations with young women. When leaving, however, a bride should be available. Sometimes, young women notified the Mission Institute and agreed to marry a missionary. In any case, the missionaries could only be married with the consent of the mission director. The missionary's wives played an important role in the missionary work. They were particularly active in the education of girls and women. Since the 1970s, an intensive debate about the status of "accompanying wives" took place.

The first woman directly sent from Neuendettelsau was the teacher Emilie Heumann, who in 1902 was sent to teach missionary kids in New Guinea. She later married the missionary Christian Keysser. Then nurses and female doctors followed. More recently, female psychologists, teachers, theologians, and development workers were sent together with their male colleagues.

The missionaries were allowed to return permanently to Germany only in case of illness or other special circumstances. After their return they could not easily become pastors in Bavaria, because the Bavarian church had agreed with the goverment in 1924 to employ only academically trained pastors, who also had the right to teach religious instruction in public schools. Gradually it became possible that missionaries could become "assistant pastors" (Pfarrverwalter) after an examination.

The First World War, and even more the Second World War, brought an incision in the missionary work. The connections were interrupted. The missionaries often had to leave the country or were interned. To everyone's astonishment, the spiritual life in the mission churches did not break down, but the missionary work was continued by indigenous personnel. In the 1930s, the first indigenous pastors in Tanzania and PNG were trained and ordained.

The World Missionary Conference in Bangkok in 1972 called for a moratorium with regard to personnel and money. The churches of the South had to refrain, for a time, on personel and finances from the North in order to gain their independence. But it turned out soon that the churches of the South continue to rely on the human and financial assistance from the North for their large range of facilities in health and education. The financial resources and the number of persons sent from Germany diminished considerably in recent decades.

"We are an autonomous church," Bishop Dr. Wesley Kigasung said at a conference with Bavarian missionaries in January 2001 in PNG. As early as 1999 he had stated: "We do not depend on the missionaries but must stand on our own feet with our own resources. Our church must believe in itself and its own workers. It needs to consider whether it really needs missionaries or calls them only because of material goods. If we really go ahead in the work, then we can cooperate with overseas churches and build the church together in today's world." Kigasung also did not conceal his discomfort with the dominance of some former missionaries.

Regularly, the coworkers of DWM meet at regional conferences to exchange information about their work and to strengthen their fellowship. The picture shows a staff conference in Alexishafen (Papua New Guinea). (Privately owned)

The fields of work for the missionaries were in particular: church planting, training, and qualification of local coworkers, theological education, instruction in crafts and music, health, construction, diakonia, vocational training, (financial) management, and technical services. More than half were non-theologians and partly received the official status of a development worker or were financed by the German Federal Ministry for Economic Cooperation and Development. These were architects, doctors, teachers, social workers, technicians, agricultural advisers, and pilots next to pastors, deacons, and religious educators.

The partner churches expect that a missionary works much but interferes little in the church policy. His advantage is that he comes from outside and leaves again. He is not involved in local commitments and networks. The human and financial support of DWM should not interfere with the independence of the partner churches. DWM examined carefully whether a clear job description for the posting of a missionary existed. It should be avoided that the missionary is required only because of his car, money, or relations. The living and working conditions of the missionaries became overall worse, not least because of the increase in crime since 1970. In addition, their role had been earlier clear as heads of mission stations and facilities. Now they had to subordinate to the local authorities.

At the same time the period of pioneering mission and long-term missionaries ended. Missionary service was now limited to a certain period of time. The former bringers of the gospel became consultants and partners. Instead of long-term missionaries increasingly short-term employees were sent, e.g. as senior experts. Some mission agencies have replaced the term missionary by the term ecumenical coworker to avoid associations with the colonial era.

The challenges for missionaries are varied, whether they are going alone or as a family. They must find their way in a new culture and build a new network of relationships. They must learn to cope with a work environment which is mostly unfamiliar. They often suffer from vague job descriptions and unclear decision-making structures. Some do not find the balance between criticism and solidarity. The return to Germany is not always easy. The supposed home has become strange and they have to accommodate again.

Since the turn of the millennium, the interest in working overseas decreased in general, for which the following reasons played a role:

- Non-theologians fear for their professional future and possible unemployment. Pastors are concerned about losing the connection to their home church.

- Employment of spouses. DWM paid since 1991 for the accompanying spouse the minimum amount in the pension system, but the wives wanted to exercise their profession independently. For theologians, job-sharing has not been successful, since "half" pastors in job sharing are yet unknown overseas.

- Decreasing ability to engage in a different culture and language.

- Strong dependence on a particular home region, closeness to family and friends.

- Education of children whom parents do not like to send to boarding schools.

- Security problems due to the increasing crime.

- Fear of climate and tropical diseases.

- Receding interest in the Third World and skepticism about solving its problems.

People are more important for ecumenical-missionary relations than clever statements and negotiations at conferences. They are the actual bridge builders. On the background of their experience and change of perspective, they can give important impetus for the church's work at home on their return. Conversely, it is important that staff from the partner churches fulfill a service in Bavaria. As the first African pastor, Zephaniah Mgeyekwa worked from 1979 to 1982 in Coburg. Only in 1998, the first exchange pastor from New Guinea, Baafecke Bamiringnu, came to serve in the parish of Dietenhofen. It may appear inappropriate that DWM takes away from the partner churches the best people for its exchange program. But the returnees are prepared to take over responsible tasks in their churches and share their experiences gained in Germany. The newly elected head bishop of ELCPNG, Jack Urame, worked as an exchange pastor in Germany while the new Presiding Bishop of ELCT Dr. Frederick Shoo received his doctorate from Augustana Theological Seminary.

In addition to the posting of full-time employees DWM, in cooperation with the church headquarters, promoted the exchange of scholarship holders with the partner churches. Lately, numerous volunteers are deployed who are funded by the program "Weltwärts" of the federal government. It is important that young people live for a while in another culture and share their experiences in their future personal and professional life. Recently the program was extended for young people coming from the South to the North.

While interest in a longer work overseas has declined sharply, young people, e.g., after graduation, like to go for a year as a volunteers overseas. The picture shows a volunteer at a New Guinean village. (Mission One World)

Mission and Partnership

The word partnership does not appear in the New Testament. It rather speaks of koinonia or communio as the Christian community. Within church and mission, the concept of partnership was first formulated in 1947 at the Fourth World Missionary Conference in Whitby (Canada) under the theme "Partnership in Obedience." The traditional parent-subsidiary relationship between North and South needed to be replaced by a new form of partnership. The churches in the South were on the road to independence but wanted to continue to work in partnership with the churches of the North. But this kind of partnership should be done with respect to the one Lord in obedience that forms the benchmark for the fraternal cooperation. The experience during the time of the Second World War played an important role, in which the Christians in the South discovered that they could carry on the missionary work themselves that was begun by the missionaries. This was realized by the representatives of the North. The churches in the South wanted to be involved in the common missionary task in the future, in particular with regard to preaching, personnel, and finances. The so-called younger churches or mission churches became partner churches. The New Guinean Bishop Kigasung defined partnership as "walking side by side."

In the nineteenth century the Englishman Henry Venn and the American Rufus Anderson had independently developed the concept of the three-self for the churches resulting from the missionary movement: self-propagating, self-governing, and self-supporting. In the twentieth century David Bosch added as a fourth principle self-theologizing. Already during the First World Missionary Conference in Edinburgh in 1910, the independence of the churches in the South was demanded. The first independent churches emerged in the 1920s in India. In 1963, at the seventh World Missionary Conference in Mexico City, the program of mission in six continents was adopted. This meant that mission moves no longer only from North to South, but also from South to North, from South to South, and from East to West.

Since the 1950s, the former "mission fields" became independent churches. Thus, the missionary societies were obliged to define their role in relation to the so-called younger churches. The development of an equal partnership between North and South and the indigenization of church and theology were the focus. The mission statement of the LWF Assembly in Budapest emphasized in 1983 that the main responsibility for the mission lies in the local church and continued: "If it has not sufficient resources, it should seek cooperation with neighboring and other churches. This expresses the unity of the worldwide church." Klaus Schäfer wrote in a report to the EKD General Synod in Leipzig 1999 that the "crisis of mission" turned into the "success of mission, because everywhere younger churches arose that now strive for independence."

At the same time, since the 1960s in Bavaria, district partnerships developed that extended into congregation partnerships. In Coburg in 1963, the first partnership program with the district in Chimala in southern Tanzania was started. Zephaniah Mgeyeka, as the first African pastor, worked from 1979 to 1982 at the Moriz Church in Coburg. Often these partnership programs were connected with a missionary who came from the district or returned to it. The first "brown" New Guinean Christians came in 1957 to Neuendettelsau. Previously no Bavarian Christian had ever seen a Christian from New Guinea. Before that time only missionaries made the connections between Christians in Bavaria and in Africa or PNG. Now mission "received a face" when visits began in both directions. This was a new movement in the mission scene that left extremely blessed footsteps. Many people today are involved on a district and parish level.

DWM has supported and promoted this development from the beginning. Meanwhile, almost all Bavarian districts have commissioners for partnership, development, and mission who bring the concerns of the global church into the congregation work. They accompany the development-related and missionary work and coordinate the activities of the individual parishes. They communicate information and ideas and keep in touch with the overseas partners. Partnership agreements are recommended. In the congregations, the commissioners for mission and partnership are committed to ensuring that the voice of partner churches can be heard at festivals, district synods, special church services, or in personal encounters. Visits in both directions are important and financially supported by ELCB. Since the 1980s, annual meetings of the commissioners are held in Neuendettelsau.

Through the Church Law on Mission and Ecumenism of 1995, the mission conference was created to which all districts delegate a pastor and a lay person as commissioners. They should reinforce the wishes of the basis and accompany critically the work of DWM and ELCB church governing bodies through requests and statements. It serves as a forum for mutual consultations and exchange of experiences. DWM tries to expand the increasing bilateralism through the perspective of multilateralism and the networking with partnership groups, also outside of Bavaria.

According to the ELCB constitution, the Bavarian church sees its commitment "to participate in world mission and in the worldwide ecumenical partnership." In the statement on the external relations of 2006, ELCB describes its partnership relations as concretization of relationships within the communion of the universal church. The partners should meet "in principle on an equal footing" as independent churches and decide on the use of resources and people:

> The priorities are therefore visits, conversations, sympathy, mutual sharing of church life, joint celebration, and especially worship. . . . Money should not be the first, but also not the last aspect. The partnerships of ELCB are experienced as communities of learning and sharing, cooperating and growing together. . . . From this experience flow witness and orientation (martyria), experience of God and self-reflection (leiturgia), communion (koinonia), and assistance and accompaniment (diaconia) as basic dimensions of the mandate of the church. . . Unilateral dependencies should be avoided and rifts between churches and cultures overcome. The goal of ecumenical learning is the 'reconciled diversity' and mutual spiritual and theological enrichment. . . . Even in times when resources are scarce, partnership work in all dimensions belongs essentially to the being of the church, because we are only the church of Jesus Christ in communion with the other Christians through all times and in all places.

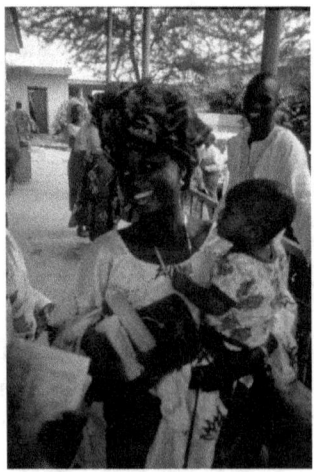

Bavarian Lutherans experience a different kind of church service during their visits in partner congregations. In Africa, everybody should come to church with a Bible and read the texts which are explained. (Privately owned)

Partnership also includes advocacy. DWM considered itself as an advocate of its overseas partners in Germany. In 1992, it protested publicly against a broadcast advertisement of the German Mail, in which PNG was presented as a country of cannibals. After an open letter, this advertisement was withdrawn immediately. It also protested against a board game "Jump into the Boat or into the Boiler." As a partner of the churches in the South, DWM saw as its task to raise the public awareness of foreign cultures and break down prejudices.

There are partnership programs which are not channeled through DWM, but by the ELCB headquarters in Munich or church regions and districts. Some years ago, the regional bishop of Ansbach-Würzburg started a partnership with ELCA Upper Susquahanna Synod and was followed in 2000 by the Augsburg region which began a companionship program with ELCA Southeastern Synod. Within such North-North partnerships no financial support is involved. Rather they comprise mutual encounter, theological exchange, and practice of spiritual community.

Up to a "partnership of equals" with most churches in the South, the Bavarian church still has to travel a long path. Its partner churches frequently were founded only a few decades ago and differ in organizational, financial, and theological aspects from ELCB. They live in different political, social, and cultural contexts. Nevertheless, it is important to express through partnership the unity of the church of Jesus Christ. Our partners in the South often can not understand that homosexuality is now widely accepted in our culture as well as divorce even among church employees. Also, there are different viewpoints regarding the evaluation of other religions. In partnership dialogue, such differences should not be concealed but openly verbalized. We must study together the Holy Scriptures and strive for its meaning in our present time.

Mission and Money

The "nodding negro" was until the 1960s an important popular figure of mission. The figures of plaster or paper mache were set up in churches, kindergartens, and schools, and moved the head after insertion of a coin. (Mission One World)

The missionary work had to rely on donations and collections from the outset, as it was not part of the church's finances. The Neuendettelsau Mission operated frequently on the border of bankruptcy, e.g., during the Nazi period, when public collections were banned, and currencies were locked. Often it could not pay the salaries and pension contributions on time.

Fundraising and mission journalism are closely interlinked. Loehe financed his missionary work by selling his mission journals. In 1922, Maria Drexel founded the Neuendettelsau Small Collection (Neuendettelsauer Kleinsammlung). That same year, the former New Guinea missionary Johann Stössel began with the highly successful collection Mission Help (Missionshilfe).

With the establishment of DWM in 1972, ELCB took over full responsibility for the financing of missionary work. The budget of DWM became a part of the church budget. The percentage of funds for DWM dropped in twenty years from 2.8 percent to 2.2 percent. Nevertheless, it is still the largest single item in the budget which, of course, sometimes provoked covetousness. Approximately 85 percent of DWM finances come from church taxes, only 15 percent from donations and collections. The collections in all congregations at Epiphany and harvest thanksgiving Sunday are earmarked for missionary work.

Through DWM, substantial funds flowed into the partner churches. The local congregations in Africa or PNG are self-sufficient and self-financing. For the regional institutions, particularly schools and hospitals, funds from overseas are often needed. Not only the church members, but the entire population will benefit from these subsidies. It is estimated that half of all hospitals in Africa are church-run. This support from Germany is possible only because DWM receives significant funding from church taxes. If the church tax system was abolished, not only the churches in Germany but also those overseas would suffer.

In consultations with the partners, the delicate issue of corruption plays an important role. In some partner churches there is corruption at various levels. For church leaders it is often difficult to distinguish between private and church funds. Salaries are not enough in many cases to feed a large family, to pay money for school and hospital. Therefore, there is great danger to divert funds from overseas to the private sector or not use them for the intended purpose. It must also be remembered that the handling of money represents something new and unknown for people who have been confronted only recently with modernity.

Missionary work has been funded from the outset by many small donations. Director Vorländer thanks the Neuendettelsau Deaconess Henriette Mühlschlegel for the donations which she had collected for many years for mission. (Archive Mission One World)

Mission and Media

Mission and journalism went hand in hand from the beginning. Not only information on the work of the missionaries should be given through publications, but also revenue being generated, and donors being won. Often there were only few reports about critical aspects and problems, but mainly on successful conversions by the missionaries.

Already in 1710, the first mission journal appeared in Germany. It was edited by August Hermann Francke under the title "The Royal Danish Missionaries from East India Sent in Detailed Reports." It was published in a high circulation and scored good revenue for the Danish-Halle Mission. In 1816 in Basel, the Magazine for the Latest History of the Protestant Missionary and Bible Society, or in short, the Basel Missionary Magazine appeared which became widespread in Bavaria. Since 1836, the Dresden (later Leipzig) Mission published a handout which is called, since 1846, the Evangelical Lutheran Mission Journal. From 1844 on, the Nuremberg Mission Journal appeared, published by the Central Missionary Association. "Until about the end of the nineteenth century, missions in broad sectors of the population almost had a monopoly on reporting from distant parts of the world. Mission journals stood in high regard not only in circles of mission friends," Martin Keiper observed. Those who wanted to see pictures from other parts of the world had to look into missionary magazines; Basel Mission trained missionaries before leaving in the use of the new photography.

Since his student days, Wilhelm Loehe was interested in the dissemination of religious pamphlets and already in 1830 belonged to two tract associations. In 1841, he founded a tract association himself to spread home missionary writings on the basis of the Lutheran church. In 1849, it was taken over by the newly founded Society for Inner Mission in the Sense of the Lutheran Church. It published under various names—Self-Publication of the Society, Mission Publisher, or Publisher of the Mission House—until about 1930, when the name Free Mouth Publisher (Freimund-Verlag) came into use. This is the oldest publishing house in the Bavarian church.

In addition to the dissemination of tracts Loehe published regularly in particular in the *Nördlingen Sunday Journal* (*Nördlinger Sonntagsblatt*). It was published by the C.H. Beck's bookstore in Nördlingen, which was transferred in 1889 to Munich and still exists as one of the most prestigious publishing houses in Germany. The Nördlingen pastor and talented publicist Friedrich Wucherer (1803-1881) was one of Loehe's closest friends and took over, in 1829, the editorship of the *Nördlingen Sunday Journal* and, since 1835, as publisher. With up to eight thousand subscribers, it was widespread even beyond Bavaria. In 1841, he published Loehe's call to find "emergency helpers" for the emigrated Germans in America. From 1844 to 1860, he helped in the publication of Loehe's *Church Communications from and about North America* (*Kirchliche Mittheilungen aus und über Nord-Amerika*). In the first year it reached a circulation of eight thousand and gave Loehe substantial revenue for his missionary work. The information on the development of the Lutheran synods in the USA was presented with their theological and political disputes and described as the ideal Lutheran church which is free from government control. Since 1910, the journal appeared as *Neuendettelsau Mission Journal* (*Neuendettelsauer Missionsblatt*), which was later edited by Christian Keysser.

In 1850, the Mission Society founded the *Correspondence Paper* (*Correspondenzblatt*). Wucherer printed the *Free Mouth* home calendar (*Freimundkalender*) since 1851 with a circulation of six thousand copies. According to his words, he wanted to "make propaganda for the kingdom of God by awakening determined Christian spirit and mind and promote sound and joyful courage rooted in God." From 1914 to 1995, the journal *Concordia* was published as an information organ of the Society for Inner and Outer Mission. Its successor, *Confessio Augustana—Lutheran Magazine for Religion, Society and Culture* (*CA*) is published since 1996. The ecclesiastical and political weekly *Free Mouth* (*Freimund*) scored long runs especially after the First World War. By publications, revenue and donations were generated for the Mission Institute.

In 1855, Wucherer also founded the Free Mouth Church and *Political Weekly for Town and Village* (*Freimunds Kirchlich Politisches Wochenblatt für Stadt und Land*), which at the same time acted as an organ of the Mission Society. From Wucherer came also the symbol of the publication, namely the wanderer before the Janus head with the town of Nördlingen in the background. In the 1930s, the weekly magazine had a circulation of up to 20,000 copies. Mission inspector Helmut Kern described, in 1933, its task as follows: "The Free Mouth is a distinct evangelistic and training journal, which with a free mouth from the standpoint of Lutheranism takes position on the issues of the day and therefore stands in the center of the fight." In 1929, under Eppelein's influence, it was subtitled as *Organ of a Public Mission from the Standpoint of Evangelical Lutheran Christianity*, and in 1933 renamed *Lutheran Weekly for Church and People*. It was read not only in Germany but also in the overseas churches related to the work of the Neuendettelsau Mission, namely, in the Americas, Australia, and New Guinea. Additional booklets partly achieved millions of copies in the 1930s.

The anti-Semitic and anti-democratic tendencies of the *Free Mouth* journal since the end of the First World War were already described. Its anti-Semitic diatribes helped to prepare the population for the systematic exclusion of the Jews by the Nazi regime and their eventual murder in the holocaust. The *Free Mouth* journal came into compliance with National Socialism for a backwards feudal society in which law and order, sacrifice and discipline, should determine the life of the Christian people. The pogroms of November 1938 were not mentioned. On April 20, 1939 an article appeared in which God's grace is praised, which was given to the German people with Adolf Hitler. With the beginning of the war, allegedly imposed by the enemies, the journal called to fight for the honor and freedom of the German people. Although some issues were banned by the Nazis, the *Free Mouth* journal was totally friendly-minded towards the Nazi regime.

In 1941, the newspaper received a reprimand with the threat that it would be prohibited in a repeated case. In the same year all missionary magazines had to be stopped, "to free people and material for other important war purposes," as stated in the communication from the Nazi government. In the last issue of the *Free Mouth* journal on May 29, 1941 it is stated: "We thank God . . . and joyfully bring our sacrifice for the Reich in its struggle for survival." Other publications were also banned. After the war in 1948, the military government allowed the Mission Institute to publish books and magazines. The weekly *Free Mouth* appeared still until 1957.

In 1910, the first *Neuendettelsau Children's Journal* (*Neuendettelsauer Kinderblatt*) was issued, for which Maria Drexel was later responsible and partially achieved long runs. It ended in 1990. In the following period, the Mission Institute published various magazines, e.g., *World Mission*, which in 1963 was replaced by *Word and Mission* as a supplement to the Sunday papers *The Word in the World*, *Call into the World*, *Children's Letters from Mission*, *Three Minutes Mission*, *Intercession Calendar*, and in particular since 1989 *Time for Mission*. Since 2003, six mission organizations from Germany, Switzerland, and Austria publish a joint magazine, each with regional parts. The Bavarian issue appears under the name *InSight* (*EinBlick*).

The Neuendettelsau Mission used, since the 1950s, the new media, namely, slides and films. Many films about the partner churches were produced by Manfred Perlitz, Martin Lagois, and Klaus Wölfle and partially broadcasted on television.

In 1995, DWM took over the publisher of the Evangelical Lutheran Mission Leipzig (Verlag der Ev. - Luth. Mission Erlangen), founded in 1897. The publisher has been continued since 1965 in Erlangen, under the energetic leadership of Rev. Christoph Jahn. Under the slogan "The World that Speaks to Us," it has published numerous materials and manuals, missiological discourses, etc. It was continued under the name Erlangen Publisher for Mission and Ecumenics (Erlanger Verlag für Mission und Ökumene) as demand publishing.

The Evangelical Lutheran Central Association of Foreign Mission also published materials, especially under the leadership of Rev. Walther Ruf (1910–1997), who succeeded Rev. Steck in 1946. As a follow-up of the *Nuremberg Mission Paper*, the association published *View into the World* (*Blick in die Welt*) as a supplement to the ELCB *Church Information Journal*. The association also worked intensively on mission pedagogical issues in its own mission pedagogical association and published mission folders.

Today, missionary magazines are in fierce competition with the electronic media, television, and the Internet. Nevertheless, magazines are still important to raise awareness that Christians in Germany are part of a global community and the churches can enrich one another through their global relationships and contribute to world peace. "Behind the bell tower there is more." This motto for the mission press was formulated by Martin Keiper.

The publication of a missionary magazine forms a fine line between objective information and fundraising. Missionary work relies on donations. However, not only success stories may be published, but there must also be reports on problems and crises. In no case should the myth of uncorrupted people in the South Pacific or in Africa be spread. However, certainly it needs to be portrayed that the Christians in the South are often closer to the biblical message than the complicated Christians of the North. It is important to disseminate arguments against the accusation that mission was closely linked to colonialism and cultural destruction.

Mission and Development Service

In Germany in the 1960s, awareness of the need for development aid grew. The WCC assembly in Uppsala in 1968 called for a stronger commitment of the churches in the fight against poverty, which is not only an economic but also an ethical problem. Since 1959, the action Bread for the World, the Protestant Association for Development Aid (EZE), the Service Overseas (DÜ), and the Church Development Service (KED) were founded. In 1973, the EKD issued a memorandum on development as the church's ministry. Therein the relationships between rich and poor were revealed, and the churches were admonished to work towards fairer structures in the economy. In 1971, the Bavarian Church Development Service was founded in Nuremberg.

In Bavaria and in the rest of the German Federal Republic, a heated debate arose about how mission and development service relate to each other. Is development service a new form of mission? Some persons engaged in development work criticized the mission institutes as dusty, patriarchally oriented institutions. Their close relationship with the partners prevents a critical cooperation. The missions repeatedly pointed out that their missionaries were the first development aid workers. They sent not only theologians, but also doctors and nurses, architects and farmers. The missionaries promoted the cultivation of coffee and coconut trees, they explored the indigenous languages and cultures, established schools and health centers. Later, they built airfields to allow the supply in inaccessible areas.

An important boost brought in 1974 the request of the Ethiopian Evangelical Church Mekane Yesus to clarify the relationship of mission as proclamation of faith and Bread for the World as development assistance. The church wanted to know why the Western churches suddenly spend more money for development aid than for mission. An LWF consultation in Nairobi formulated in response the concept of a holistic understanding of mission. Evangelical groups have criticized the, from their view, one-sided social-political commitment of Bread for the World and founded as a counter-organization Help for Brothers. Even in the Frankfurt Declaration of 1970, the evangelicals expressed fear that development aid takes the place of the missionary testimony. At the World Council Assembly in Melbourne in 1990 poverty was addressed as a theological problem.

Since the 1990s, the conviction has widely prevailed that mission and development work belong together. The polemic has lost, on both sides, focus and polemics. Mission is understood holistically because Jesus himself announced not only salvation but also brought healing and fed the hungry. The people in the South have little understanding of the Western separation of body and soul. DWM therefore, with considerable resources and staff, supported development-related work in hospitals, schools, training centers, and agricultural projects. In its policy paper of 2002 DWM stressed its mission: to cooperate in combating the negative effects of globalization, because "the global players stand increasingly against local sufferers." Mission in a holistic sense includes evangelization, service to those in need, and commitment to justice, peace, and integrity of creation.

In 1995, DWM was intensively involved in cooperation with the Church Development Service on the preparation and organization of the meeting of the ELCB General Synod in Regensburg. Under the theme "Global Responsibility in Dialogue with Partner Churches" particular development issues were discussed. The final declaration included demands on politics, society, and church in regard to environmentally friendly production, promoting sustainable agriculture and rural development, debt relief, and strengthening of civil society.

DWM emphasized again and again that God created only one world and not a first, second, third, or fourth world. From the Millennium Development Goals of the UN, namely the halving of poverty by 2015, the global community is still far away. In 2007 on the occasion of the G-8 summit in Heiligenhafen, DWM called on local congregations to invite, with the ringing of their bells, prayers for peace and justice.

Mission and Colonialism

Between mission and colonial government there was an agreement in so far that the German government put education almost entirely in the hands of the missionaries. Thus, in New Guinea 600 schools were operated by the missions, but just two by the colonial government. Similar figures have been released from the colonies in Africa. In 1913, State Secretary Wilhelm Solf said in the Berlin Reichstag: "Colonization is missionizing, namely missionizing in the high sense of education for culture. But not to European culture, but a culture that can hold in the ground and is rooted in the life of the natives and is adapted to their spiritual and mental character." Solf thus entered against the criticism of the colonial policy of the German Reich, which was particularly inflamed by the bloody crackdown of the uprisal of the Hereros in South West Africa in 1904/1905, and in 1906 led to the dissolution of the Reichstag.

When mission inspector Johannes Deinzer in 1886 asked the New Guinea Company in Berlin to allow Johann Flierl's entry to Guinea, he described the mission as an "ally of the colonizing efforts of the present." The Neuendettelsau missionaries were not naive stooges of the colonial government. They were, however, dependent on the directives of the colonial government and would stand out as interpreters and mediators. The provisions of the New Guinea Company for the missionaries stated: They have to teach in German or a native language, rather than in English. The establishment of mission stations is subject to approval by the governor. Although the missionaries receive their instructions only by their missionary societies, they should be committed to support the administration with the best endeavors and rend pro bono services. They have, in particular, the task to accustom the natives to regular work and to teach handcrafts, gardening, and agricultural work. They can, if the public order requires it, be expelled from the country. In return, they can buy food and trade goods for their personal use according to the discounted rates for the Company's officials. Even the construction of buildings and the holding of schools required its approval. However, the German colonial administration since 1891 was so far away from the working area of the Neuendettelsau Mission that the missionaries had a pretty free hand.

There have always been conflicts because of the partially rigid recruitment methods of the Company. So the company's director, Adolph von Hansemann, in a letter dated March 3, 1898 to the director of the Mission Institute, criticized that the missionaries deterred the natives from recruitment with gifts:

> We believe that there can not be the intention of the management of the missionary society that their emissaries hinder the activity of the Company. We therefore take the occasion to contact you directly and take your mediation for an adjustment of opinions. If the missionaries based in Simbang are of the assumption that the recruited workers are treated indecently on the plantations of the Company, it is their duty to bring what they hear to the attention of the provincial governor, so that

abuses may be eliminated and the guilty can be punished. The directorate maintains emphatically that the native workers undergo humane and careful handling and can recognize it only with thanks, when it is supported in the implementation of this principle.

Rudolf Ruf emphasized in his thanks for the national donation of 1913 the importance of the missionary work for the promotion of culture: "Through the service of our missionaries the beginnings of culture in the uncivilized country have come. . . . In serving the culture we serve the kingdom of God." He referred to the numerous schools, which contribute to the "cultural uplift of the Papuans."

In the 1920s, mission senior Johann Flierl protested to the Australian colonial government repeatedly against the rigid recruitment methods by government officials. Obviously, he and his companions, after initial mistrust, soon gained the trust of local people. No Neuendettelsau missionary was killed by locals in New Guinea. Ten Catholic missionaries and missionary sisters suffered a different fate when they were killed in 1904 at the island of New Britain by the tribe of Bainings because they did not agree with their missionary methods. However, Flierl and his colleagues had never questioned the colonial system of their time.

With the First World War, the German colonial rule ended. The German missionaries could partially remain in the country or had to return home. Most German missionaries were interned and deported to Australia at the beginning of the Second World War. It is amazing that, with the withdrawal of the German missionaries, the proclamation of the gospel did not stop. In many cases, the number of Christians grew significantly. Missionary societies from other countries like the USA and Scandinavia continued the missionary work until the German missionary societies were able to resume the cooperation.

In Australia, in particular, the Neuendettelsau missionary Carl Strehlow fought for the rights of the Aborigines and defended them against the land claims by settlers and authorities.

The DWM position paper on "Our Christian Witness" of 2002 dealt with the amalgamation of colonial power and the mission. "Where injustice was exercised and where spiritual or physical violence was used, the church finds itself guilty." However, blessings should also come up for discussion, which came to the people overseas by sharing the gospel and was recorded mostly thankful by them. The mission has made a significant contribution to the political, economic, and social development in countries of the South. While the colonial powers in particular pursued economic goals, it was the mission's primary goal to proclaim the gospel.

Mission and Culture

Mission is often brought into connection with cultural destruction. Culture is a complex concept, not fixed, but a constantly changing process. Certainly, the missionaries were often hostile to indigenous cultures. They condemned, in particular, polygamy, vendetta, initiation and dance rituals, cannibalism, witchcraft, and idolatry. This was also related to experiencing an alien culture that they often experienced as a culture shock.

From the beginning, the encounter of the local culture is an important aspect of the task of a missionary. Johann Flierl initially studied the culture and language of the New Guineans for many years before he began preaching. Only after thirteen years, the first two locals were baptized. Even otherwise, Neuendettelsau missionaries spent a lot of time to get to know the indigenous religion and culture. They have not simply destroyed the local culture but imbued it with the Christian faith. Some missionaries were groundbreaking in the ethnological research. So, Hermann Strauss and Wilhelm Bergmann received honorary doctorates for research into the cultures and languages in the highlands of New Guinea. Neuendettelsau missionaries encouraged the indigenous languages by putting them into writing and thus preserved them from destruction. The indigenous music was recorded and processed in hymns. In Australia, Carl Strehlow (1871–1922) achieved great merit in exploring the mythology of the Aborigines. Unlike many anthropologists of his time, he assessed the spirituality of the natives positively and published its myths, legends, and fairy tales. His insights into totemism among the peoples of Aranda and Loritja were taken up by Sigmund Freud, Émile Durkheim, and Claude Lévi-Strauss, the founder of modern structuralism.

In the course of the history of mission, it was more and more realized that the culture is to be understood from that particular context. In New Guinea, in particular, Christian Keysser pursued the concept of linking the gospel with the indigenous culture; in Tanzania the missionary Bruno Gutmann, sent by Leipzig Mission, went a similar way. It is, however, not all good, what is self-evident in another culture. The penetration of Christianity in Africa or PNG has changed the indigenous cultures. Initially the converts should carry Western clothes and accept

Western morals. But gradually the missionaries realized that the local Christians do not have to simply accept the Western lifestyle. Western culture would have come even without the work of the missionaries to Africa, Asia, and the Pacific. The Christian faith can, rather, help people to find a meaningful future between tradition and modernity.

Mission, Religions, and Interreligious Dialogue

In 1910, the goal was formulated at the First World Missionary Conference in Edinburgh to evangelize the whole of mankind in the next generation. Mission was understood as a fight of the gospel against other religions. But the goal to reach or even to convert the whole of mankind with the gospel was not achieved, since the First World War made further joint missionary activities naught. The bloody battles of the Christian countries in the North have left their mark on the people in the South. They asked: How credible is the missionary proclamation of peace in Christ, if such a massacre of Christians is possible?

Currently, more than one third of mankind belongs to a church. In Europe, the number of Christians decreases significantly, while it increases in the South. Also, other religions, especially Islam, unfold their missionary activities. Here religion often serves as a means in disputes which are about power, politics, ethnic and economic interests in the first place. Islam shows itself in a fundamentalist shape and is often equated with terrorism.

Until the beginning of the twentieth century other religions in the area of mission had a mostly negative assessment. They were often seen as an expression of man's sin and the devil's tools in order to justify the need for conversion to the Christian faith. In the second half of the twentieth century, a more positive assessment of other religions has prevailed. In 1991, the Protestant churches in Germany published a statement with the title "Religion, Religiosity, and Christian Faith." It emphasizes that religions are not an expression of demonic powers, but a product of God's action in the world.

> They cannot simply be dismissed in the lump as human efforts, although they belong to the facts of history by which man turns the conditioned into the unconditioned and thereby demonizes it. Also, in the religions and behind them God appears in his world action with the aim that mankind finds him. God stands with his divinity at the target point of all religions, as he fulfills

their origin; at the same time, people contradict to the action of God according to their will.

On many international conferences, the topic of interreligious dialogue was discussed intensively. Already in 1989, the World Missionary Conference in San Antonio came to the conclusion: "We know of no other way of salvation than Jesus Christ. At the same time, we can set no limits to the saving power of God." In 1997, LWF General Assembly in Hong Kong formulated: "We recognize that all people are created by the one God who is at work in the world, including their religions and cultures." Tolerance does not mean indifference, but the quest for a peaceful coexistence. On the Catholic side, Hans Küng emphasized in his book "Global Ethic Project" that there would be no religious peace without religious dialogue, no world peace without religious peace and no global peace without global ethic. According to Theo Sundermeier, the coexistence of people of different faiths must today be determined by "mutual assistance, mutual learning, and common celebrations."

The predominant religious pluralism in many places is a reality which the missionary work can not overlook. Mission can therefore only be done in dialogue with people of other faiths, even if dialogue for many Christians has become a stimulus or insult. Interreligious dialogue does not replace mission. Rather, both are very closely related, as Jürgen Moltmann noted at the synod of the Protestant churches in Leipzig 1999: "Without interreligious dialogue no one will understand. Through interreligious dialogue no one has become a Christian."

The ministry of Jesus already included witness and dialogue. Jesus not only preached but conducted intensive dialogues with his Jewish opponents and with people of other faiths. About a Roman centurion, he said respectfully: "I have not found anyone in Israel with such great faith" (Matthew 8:10). Heretical Samaritans he put to the eyes of his listeners as models of true charity and gratitude.

Established with the support of the Department for World Mission, the Center for Christian-Muslim Encounter "Bridge-Köprü" in Nuremberg was headed by Rev. Hans-Martin Gloel (left). (Bridge)

In 1993, the Center for Christian-Muslim Encounter ("Bridge-Köprü") in Nuremberg was established. In the agreement between DWM, the Finnish Evangelical Lutheran Mission (FELM), and the Nuremberg congregation of St. Johannis, it was identified as an objective "to begin a testimony service among Muslim fellow citizens in Nuremberg." It is intended "to preach the gospel of Christ in witness and service to non-Christians, especially Muslims, to listen with inner respect towards people of other faiths, be ready to invite them to participate in the communion with Christ, and to encourage in German congregations the understanding of non-Christians and foreigners and to promote the Christian witness service among them." In the beginning FELM made available most of the money and staff. Then it withdrew more and more from the responsibility and handed over the work to the Bavarian church. By January 1, 2008 the Bridge was taken over by the district of Nuremberg. On December 16, 2007 a Bridge Festival took place with Bishop Johannes Friedrich in Nuremberg. The Bridge still represents a unique project within the churches in Germany.

In the last twenty years Christian-Islamic dialogue grew into a self-evident aspect of the deliberations of the church. Certainly, the danger of Islamic fundamentalism and the exploitation of Muslims for political purposes persist. The encounter between Christians and Muslims is determined by proximity and distance. Nevertheless, it is necessary to work together for more mutual respect and tolerance. Here, the words of the Apostle in 1 Peter 3:15f. serve as a guide: "Always be ready to answer to every man that asks of you an account of the hope that is in you, but do it with gentleness and fear of God."

Mission in Germany

A missionary institution not only fulfills tasks abroad but also at home. In recent decades, many immigrants arrived from abroad to Germany. To come into conversation with the Muslims among them, DWM in cooperation with the Finnish Evangelical Lutheran Mission founded the Center for Christian-Muslim Encounter, "Bridge-Koprü," in Nuremberg. At the same time, numerous Christians from Africa, Asia, and Latin America meet in international congregations all over Germany.

In cooperation with the ELCB headquarters in Munich, DWM built contacts with the congregations of other languages and origins. Their representatives feel called by God, not only to preach the gospel to their compatriots, but also to bring it to the many unchurched people in Germany. They want to return to the mission, what they themselves have received from European missionaries in their countries. They asked DWM to organize a theological course for congregation leaders. This was the starting signal for the project MISÜNO (Mission Süd-Nord–Mission South-North). For the first time in 2005, such a course was organized, which lasts for one year and covers important topics of faith and theology on weekends. Leaders of congregations with Latin American, African, or Asian background are supported through the course for their work and enabled to develop their congregations in the German context. The course is designed for pastors, but also for lay persons. Meanwhile the Protestant churches of Württemberg, Baden, and the Palatinate participate in this theological qualification program for migrant churches. Another purpose is to improve the contact between the different congregations and to the German churches. This is done by mutual visits, exchanges and joint operations.

Representantives from congregations of other languages and origins participate in a theological course organized by DWM. (Archive Mission One World)

In 2013 the German-Indonesian couple Dr. Ati and Markus Hildebrandt Rambe were installed as consultants for the relationship of ELCB to congregations of foreign language and background in Bavaria.

Mission and Diakonia (Social Services)

In 1854, Loehe grabbed a new task at home. On the one hand he was moved by the distress in the families and wanted to provide a remedy. On the other hand, he noticed that many girls and young women in rural areas had particularly few educational opportunities. Many of them had to remain unmarried because the family could not provide dowries for marriage. They were kept in the house as cheap laborers for their parents or brothers. So, he founded in 1854 the Association for the Female Diaconate under the auspices of the Mother Society in Neuendettelsau. Its so-called board of helpers (Helferkollegium) functioned as a supervisory body for the Deaconess Institute, where young girls were trained to become deaconesses majoring in nursing. In 1974, the board of helpers was transformed into the board of trustees.

In 1854, Wilhelm Loehe founded the Deaconess Institute in Neuendettelsau to provide a remedy for the distress in many families and offer educational opportunities for young women. (Central Archive of Diakonia Neuendettelsau)

Between the Mother Society for social services and the Mission Institute, there were personal connections but not an institutional link. Friedrich Bauer officiated, after Loehe's death in 1872, a few months as rector of the Deaconess Institute. Later, the rectors of the Deaconess Institute were members of the governing boards and committees of the Mission Society, while, conversely, the directors of the Mission Institute belonged to the board of helpers of the Mother Society. Today the Diakonia Neuendettelsau operates many schools, hospitals, homes for old and handicapped people and employs more than 7000 persons.

During a visit to Neuendettelsau in 1857, the president of the Iowa Synod Georg Grossmann took with him the first two deaconesses to Dubuque. They were followed by other deaconesses. They worked in schools and congregations. All got married and withdrew from the deaconess community. Later, no deaconesses were in the service of the Neuendettelsau Mission. In the 1950s the formation of a deaconess community was considered but never came about.

In the overseas partner churches mission and social services (diakonia) belong closely together. Through diaconic work new church members are won. Mission is understood holistically and includes diakonia. Already Loehe summed inner and outer mission as a service to body, soul, and spirit. The Bavarian church supports this service by its institutions and congregations in many ways through money, staff, and consultation.

4

Summary

NEARLY TWO HUNDRED YEARS ago, the history of the Lutheran mission in Bavaria began. It was initiated not by the official church, but by individuals and congregations. Under the influence of Pietism and the Lutheran renewal movement the interest in mission grew, similar to other regions of Germany. At first suspiciously eyed by state and church authorities, mission groups supported Basel Mission since 1819. Wilhelm Loehe in 1842, as a private initiative within his congregation in Neuendettelsau, sent the first "emergency helpers" to North America. As a friend and supporter of his missionary work, he met Friedrich Bauer, who in 1846 in Nuremberg founded the Mission Preparation Institute for Fort Wayne, which was transferred in 1853 to Neuendettelsau. The nearly 900 graduates of the seminary formed the backbone of the Bavarian missionary work first in North America, and later in Australia, New Guinea, Brazil, Africa, Asia, and Latin America.

Loehe fought heavily for the Lutheran character of the Bavarian church. Therefore, he based his missionary work on the Lutheran confession. His vision was to be able to form a free Lutheran church independent from the state, which he hoped to accomplish in America. His immediate successors Johannes and Martin Deinzer taught their students in the seminary dogmatics and ethics on a Lutheran basis. The missionaries took with them the teachings of their teachers and applied them to the practice of missionary work. They helped founding Lutheran churches overseas on this basis.

For Wilhelm Loehe and Friedrich Bauer, the following aspects of the Lutheran confession were important: Liturgy, Holy Communion, preaching of the word of God in the Bible, church discipline, personal confession, and understanding of the pastor's office as a direct call by Christ through ordination.

The Society of Inner and Outer Mission in the Sense of the Lutheran Church up to 1972 functioned as a vehicle of missionary work and followed a conservative Lutheran course. Its members commit themselves to a clear Lutheran confession. By integrating church and mission since 1972, the perspective of the new missionary organization opened into ecumenism. The ELCB Department for World Mission (DWM) was now part of a big regional church in which different directions are adjacent. Bavarian missionary work is embedded in the Lutheran World Federation and supports primarily Lutheran churches. It wants to strengthen the identity of the Lutheran churches in the South in their respective contexts. As a member of the World Council of Churches, ELCB also participates in its work and sends representatives to the world missionary conferences. Employees of DWM are members of various international committees and coordinate with them the Bavarian missionary activities.

The missionary work organized in associations saw itself always as a service to the church without being an organizational unit. Therefore, it was for some missionary friends initially not self-evident to go along the path of integration of church and mission. They feared the total absorption of the mission and emphasized its independence. However, the integration brought more advantages than disadvantages. In 1972, the new Department for World Mission (Missionswerk) received the status of "freedom and mobility necessary for its service." Also, the Center Mission One World, established in 2007, kept its previous "self-responsibility and freedom." However, the fundamental questions of concept, personnel, and finances are now decided by the church's governing bodies and the church headquarters in Munich. Missionary work is embedded in international bodies and developments and needs a certain flexibility and dynamism. It must not be overly constrained by church regulations that are based on the terms of a regional church and its congregations.

In the first hundred years of the Bavarian mission history, the church leadership in Munich did not participate directly in the missionary work but left this to the missionary organizations. In 1962, the decision of ELCB to participate directly in the missionary work in southern Tanzania meant a break. "Mission and church are inseparable," formulated the guidelines for church life of the Lutheran churches in Germany. The church needs mission and mission needs church.

Missionary work is done by men and women who are sent to missionary service. At first these were mainly graduates of the Neuendettelsau Mission Seminary and so-called lay workers. As fewer and fewer graduates of the seminary went overseas, since the 1960s increasingly pastors were sent by the church. In 1985, the training of the Mission and Diaspora Seminary finally ended. The time of lifelong missionaries had past and was replaced by the "temporary missionary." The work overseas was now considered for professional, family, and personal reasons only an epoch in the life planning. Also, it became complicated for the missionaries to find their role in the partner churches. Therefore, the interest for a service overseas decreased.

The Neuendettelsau Mission has always sent so-called lay missionaries who worked in hospitals, schools, agricultural projects, and trade organizations. As a result of the call of the World Council of Churches at Uppsala in 1968 to reduce poverty, the Bavarian church intensified efforts in the field of development aid. Increasingly, aid workers were sent who were partly financed through the newly established Protestant Association for Development Aid (EZE) from church and state funds. DWM worked increasingly with other development organizations such as Bread for the World. This also led to the foundation of the Bavarian Church Development Service (KED), which has been integrated in 2007 into the new Center Mission One World. A period of euphoria was recently followed by disillusionment. However, young people in particular cannot be put off going increasingly as volunteers for a year overseas.

The missionary work was initially strongly influenced by the conversion thought. This was linked with a devaluation of the pagan religions. Their practices were often judged to be dark to allow the light of the gospel shine all the brighter. In recent decades, the understanding of other religions has grown. The realization that mission and dialogue belong together gained acceptance.

The time of "pioneering mission" is over. The overseas churches have assumed responsibility for missionary work in their own hands. They operate their own mission in their countries. Actually, the term "missionary" when used only for a white person is obsolete. Therefore, many mission agencies are now using the term "ecumenical coworker." Mission as a one-way street from North to South has since been replaced by the two-way traffic between South to North. Pastors from the partner churches do service in Bavarian congregations.

As people from other continents came to Bavaria, African and Asian congregations developed. Their leaders consider themselves missionaries who want to bring the gospel not only to their countrymen, but also to the Germans. They are looking for the contact with the German churches and like to attend training courses within the program "Mission South-North."

Since the World Missionary Conference of 1947 in Whitby, the term "partnership" was introduced into the mission theology and missionary cooperation. Due to the two world wars, the connections between the Western mission agencies and their overseas work areas were often cancelled. Amazingly, the missionary work continued under indigenous leadership. The self-confidence of local church leaders grew, and they increasingly demanded the independence of their churches. The former mission fields became independent churches, but mostly wanted to continue to work together with the Western missions. Therefore, the concept of "partnership in obedience" was developed. The mother-daughter relationship became a partnership of equals in common obedience towards Christ as the Lord of church and mission. Since then, the fruits resulting from the work of Bavarian missionaries became independent. Although they often receive further grants, fewer and fewer missionaries work in their institutions and do not exercise a leadership role in any case. The churches determine autonomously their church life. Overseas employees are bound by their instructions.

On a congregation and district level, a large network of partnerships has emerged in Bavaria. Whereas previously the connection to the mission mainly happened by the missionary, it is now more often by direct encounters of Bavarian Christians with their overseas partners. Mission received a face, so to speak. These partnerships require monitoring and networking.

As part of the public relations work, DWM took over more and more the task of being a mouthpiece for the Christians in the South and drawing attention to the political, social, economic, and religious developments in their countries. It participated in the conciliar process for justice, peace, and integrity of creation. It addressed issues of globalization and climate. This was to counteract a declining interest in the issues of the so-called Third World, because God created only One World.

The churches in the South increasingly raise their voices in the ecumenical concert. An intense, honest dialogue about differences is called for. The traditional denominations are losing influence. The independent churches that are mostly charismatically oriented attract more and more people. Therefore, it is important to strenthen the Lutheran identity of Lutheran churches worldwide. In recent decades the influence of other religions, to which two thirds of mankind belong, grew. Because of that the efforts in interreligious dialogue must be intensified and ways explored for a peaceful coexistence of people of different faith.

"Mission is the one church of God in its motion." With these words Wilhelm Loehe has described the essence of mission. Mission moves the church to keep it in motion. In recalling the history of mission in Bavaria during the last two hundred years, readers are encouraged to join this worldwide movement and participate in the Christian witness of our time. The famous Neuendettelsau missionary Christian Keysser was guided for his missionary work by Psalm 98:3, "All the ends of the earth have seen the salvation of our God."

Entrance to the Center Mission One World in Neuendettelsau. (Privately owned)

Appendices

Chronologies

Bavaria

1808 February 21 Wilhelm Loehe (Löhe) was born in Fürth
1812 June 14 Friedrich Bauer was born in Nuremberg
1815 Foundation of the Basel Mission
1819 Foundation of the first Bavarian missionary association in Erlangen
1827 November 10 Wilhelm Loehe starts a mission circle in Fürth
1836 Foundation of the Dresden Mission, since 1848 Leipzig Mission
1837 August 1 Wilhelm Loehe becomes pastor in Neuendettelsau
    July 25 wedding of Wilhelm Loehe and Helene Andreä
    Foundation of the Catholic Ludwig Mission Society
1840 Beginning of the friendship between Wilhelm Loehe and Friedrich Bauer
1841 Wilhelm Loehe publishes pastor Wynecken's call for help for the Lutheran co-religionists in North America in the *Nördlingen Sunday Journal*
    The first "emergency helpers" Adam Ernst and Georg Burger are trained by Loehe
1842 July 11 Farewell service for Adam Ernst and Georg Burger
1843 January 17 Foundation of the Protestant Central Missionary Association
    First edition of *Church News from and about North America*
    November 24 death of Helene Loehe

1844 First edition of the *Nuremberg Mission Journal*

1845 First mission festival in Nuremberg

    Foundation of the mission colony Frankenmuth, Michigan under the leadership of pastor August Crämer

    Beginning of missionary work among Native Americans

1846 April 23 Opening of the Mission Preparation Institute for Fort Wayne in Nuremberg by Friedrich Bauer

1849 September 12 Foundation of the Society for Inner (from 1888: and Outer) Mission in the Sense of the Lutheran Church in Gunzenhausen

    Friedrich Bauer becomes full-time employee of the Mission Preparation Institute

1850 First mission festival of the Society for Inner Mission

    First edition of the *Principles of High German Grammar for the Lower and Middle Classes of Higher Educational Institutions* by Friedrich Bauer

1851 January 1 First edition of the *Free Mouth Calendar*

    Visit of Dr. Carl Walther und Friedrich Wynecken from the Missouri Synod in Neuendettelsau

1853 April 15 Transfer of the Mission Preparation Institute to Neuendettelsau

    Renaming of the Protestant Central Missionary Association to the Evangelical Lutheran Central Missionary Association

1854 May 9 Foundation of the Deaconess Institute in Neuendettelsau by Loehe

1855 First edition of the *Free Mouth Church and Political Weekly for Town and Village* (*Freimunds Kirchlich Politisches Wochenblatt für Stadt und Land*)

1858 Foundation of the mission students' association Corcordia

1860 Foundation of the Lutheran Treasury of God in Bavaria for Beleaguered Co-Religionists in Hersbruck, later the Martin Luther Association

    July 23 Murder of the missionary Moritz Bräuninger by Native Americans

    October 23 Johann Meischel is sent to Australia

1861 Dr. Karl Graul starts missiological lectures at the University of Erlangen

Friedrich Wucherer succeeds Loehe as chairman of the Society for Inner Mission (–1891)

1864 Johannes Deinzer becomes teacher at the Mission Institute

1865 The first Bavarian brass band is founded by Loehe in Neuendettelsau

1866 October 17 Twenty-fifth jubilee of the North America Mission in Neuendettelsau

1867 Dedication of the new mission house in Neuendettelsau

1872 January 2 Death of Wilhelm Loehe

1874 December 13 Death of Friedrich Bauer in Rothenburg on the Tauber

1875 Johannes Deinzer becomes mission inspector and head of the Mission Institute

Johann Stolz is sent to Australia

1878 Johann Flierl is sent to Australia

1879 Journey of Johannes Deinzer to America to attend the twenty-fifth jubilee of the Iowa Synod

1884 Foundation of the Bavarian Mission Conference

1886 January 25 Foundation of the Society for Evangelical Lutheran Mission in East Africa in Hersbruck, called Hersbruck Mission

July 12 Johann Flierl starts missionary work in New Guinea

1897 January 25 Death of Johannes Deinzer, who is succeeded by his brother Martin Deinzer as the head of the Mission Institute

November 20 Otto Kuhr is sent to Brazil by the Lutheran Treasury of God in Rothenburg on the Tauber

1903 October 28 Dedication of the new seminary building "Kosthaus" in Neuendettelsau

1904 Journey of Martin Deinzer to America to attend the fiftieth jubilee of the Iowa Synod

1909 Foundation of the Bavarian Association for Medical Mission in Erlangen

1911 July 12 Twenty-fifth jubilee of the New Guinea mission

1913 "National Donation for Christian Missions in our Colonies and-Dependences" on the occasion of the twenty-fifth jubilee of the reign of Emperor William II

Celebration of the hundredth birthday of Friedrich Bauer

1914 Foundation of the journal *Concordia* as the official information magazine (published until 1995)

Journey of mission inspector Karl Steck via India and Australia to New Guinea

1917 December 25 Death of mission director Martin Deinzer

1919 March 6 Classes in the Mission Institute are resumed after the First World War

Beginning of the home mission work of the Society for Inner and Outer Mission by professional workers

1920 Rudolf Ruf becomes mission director

Karl Steck returns from Australia

1922 Foundation of the Small Collection of the Neuendettelsau Mission (Kleinsammlung der Neuendettelsauer Mission) and the Neuendettelsau Mission Help Association (Neuendettelsauer Missionshilfe)

Christian Keysser becomes teacher at the Mission Seminary

Visit of Dr. Reu from Dubuque, Iowa

Dedication of the mission museum in Neuendettelsau

First sendings to Brazil and North America after the First World War

1925 Foundation of the New Guinea Home for Missionary Children in Neuendettelsau

1927 First direct sendings to New Guinea after the First World War

1928 Resignation of mission director Rudolf Ruf and beginning of the work of his successor Dr. Friedrich Eppelein

1929 Journey of Dr. Friedrich Eppelein und mission inspector Adam Schuster to New Guinea and Australia

1930 Dedication of the conference center in Neuendettelsau (now House Luther Rose)

Beginning of the training of pastors for the Lutheran diaspora congregations in Ukraine, which led to the name Mission and Diaspora Seminary (MDS).

1931 Meeting of coworkers of the Mission Institute with leaders of the Nazi Party

1932 Journey of Dr. Eppelein to Columbus (USA) for negotiations to return the responsiblity for the New Guinea mission

1933 Dr. Eppelein and Dr. Keysser join the Nazi Party and the "German Christians"

Rev. Johann Langholf starts his work at the desk for Brazil

1934 The first mission airplane in the world, *Papua*, is shipped to New Guinea

The Nazi government forbids public collections

1935 Celebration of the seventy-fifth jubilee of the Martin Luther Association in Hersbruck with Bishop Hans Meiser

1936 July 14–15 Celebration of the fiftieth anniversary of the beginning of the New Guinea mission in Gunzenhausen with Bishop Hans Meiser

The collection for mission work at Epiphany is introduced in ELCB

1937 Dr. Eppelein is excluded from the Reich Press Chamber

1938 Johann Flierl returns to Neuendettelsau

1941 The Nazi government forbids all writing activities of Friedrich Eppelein

The publications of the Free Mouth Publisher cease.

1944 Closure of the Mission and Diaspora Seminary

1945 October Dr. Eppelein resigns from office

1946 Beginning of the work of Dr. Woldemar Schilberg as mission director

February 3 Reopening of the Mission and Diaspora Seminary

Confession of guilt by the Society for Inner and Outer Mission

1947 Foundation of the Augustana Theological Seminary

September 30 Death of Johann Flierl

The first missionaries are allowed to return from Australia to New Guinea

1950 Dr. Woldemar Schilberg steps down and Hans Neumeyer becomes mission director.

1953 Sr. Maria Horn is sent as the first missionary after the Second World War to New Guinea

1955 November 4 Dedication of the new building of the Mission and Diaspora Seminary

1956 Journey of mission director Neumeyer to New Guinea to attend the foundation ceremony of the Evangelical Lutheran Church of Papua New Guinea

1957 August 29 First visit of Lutheran Christians from New Guinea in Neuendettelsau (Christian Gwang und Mufuanu Quewai)

1961 July 12 Celebration of the Seventy-fifth jubilee of the New Guinea mission with Bishop Hermann Dietzfelbinger

December 14 Death of Christian Keysser

The Mission and Diaspora Seminary become a separate institution under the leadership of Dr. Oswald Henke (until 1975)

1962 Rev. Hagen Katterfeld becomes mission director (until 1964)

1963 First partnership program between Coburg district and Tanzania

1964 Rev. Hans-Gernot Kleefeld as the first missionary of ELCB is sent to Tanzania

1964 Dr. Wolfram von Krause becomes mission director (until 1972)

1970 Foundation of the Bavarian Church Development Service in Nuremberg

1971 October 21 Passing of the Church Law on World Mission and Ecumenicall Work by the ELCB General Synod in Bayreuth

1972 April 1 Beginning of the work of the Department for World Mission (Missionswerk)

June 1 Director Horst Becker, DD, starts his work and is installed by Bishop Hermann Dietzfelbinger on July 12 during the mission festival in Gunzenhausen.

The Association of Diaspora Services (Arbeitsgemeinschaft der Diasporadienste) as a cooperation of the Martin Luther Association and the Bavarian branch of the Gustavus Adolphus Work is founded in Neuendettelsau

1974 Opening of the permanent exhibition World Mission Today

1975 The DWM regional offices in Bayreuth—later Munich (1980), Würzburg (1986), and Altdorf (1991)—begin their work

DWM becomes a member of the newly founded Association of Protestant Churches and Missions in Germany (EMW)

Dr. Won Yong Ji from Korea works until 1978 as the first ecumenical coworker of DWM and translates Luther's works into Korean

1977 Contacts begin to develop with Asian churches

1978 Zephania Mgeyekwa from Tanzania comes to Bavaria and works as the first exchange pastor until 1982 in Coburg

1979 The DWM Institute of Mission Studies (Missionskolleg) starts its work

The first seminar for theologians from East Asia is held

April 30 The ELCB General Synod decides that no further applicants for the Mission and Diaspora Seminary will be accepted

1980 DWM becomes a member of the Joint Christian Ministry in West Africa (JCMWA)

1981 Rev. Walter Lupp is sent as the first Bavarian coworker to Zaire

1982 The ELCB General Synod in Weiden deals with the topic of mission and ecumenism with the participation of Bishop Sir Getacke Gam (PNG), Rev. Gabriel Kimirei (Tanzania), and Church President Dr. Gottfried Brakemeier (Brazil)

1984 Remembrance of the Africa conference in Berlin one hundred years ago

1985 Last examinations of the Mission and Diaspora Seminary are held

The first South South Seminar is held

Contacts with the Chinese Amity Foundation begin

1986 The DWM conference center is opened

Celebration of one hundred years of missionary work in PNG

Visits of Federal Minister for Development Dr. Jürgen Warnke and Prime Minister of Papua New Guninea Sir Michael Somare

1987 DWM starts the support of the scholarship fund of the Ethiopian Evangelical Church Mekane Yesu

1988 The first teacher is sent to Amity Foundation in Nanjing

The Pacific Network and the Pacific Information Center are founded

1989 Political changes in Germany: the EMW and the regional missionary centers in East Germany are reorganized

Dr. Wanis Semaan joins DWM as consultant for Islam

1990 The remodelled permanent exhibition World Mission Today is opened

1991 Celebration of one hundred years of missionary work in southern Tanzania

The study of the Starnberg Institute on Development and Environment—Economic and Ecological Development in PNG is published

October 31 Director Horst Becker ends his service

1992 January 31 Director Dr. Hermann Vorländer is installed by Bishop Dr. Johannes Hanselmann.

Crisis of missionary work in PNG in connection with the discussion on the Starnberg study and the Ok Tedi Mine

April 22 The Federal Minister for Development and Economic Cooperation and PNG Minister for Justice hold talks with DWM

July 12 DWM celebrates "150 years of missionaries sent from Neuendettelsau"

Wermer Strauss is sent as the first Bavarian missionary to the Seafarers' Mission in Singapore.

DWM joints the Program for Christian Muslim Relations in Africa (PROCMURA)

1993 January 1 The Center for Christian-Muslim Encounter ("Bridge—Köprü") starts its work in Nuremberg in cooperation with the Finnish Evangelical Lutheran Mission

1994 July 8–9 Consultation of the ELCB General Synod on mission and development

The first summer school on "Lutheran Theology in the Land of Martin Luther" is held

1995 January 1 DWM incorporates the Leipzig Mission Publisher under the new name Erlangen Publisher for Mission and Ecumenics, directed by Rev. Christoph Jahn

July 21–26 Consultation in Kainantu (PNG) about the cooperation of the ELPNG with its overseas partners

August: Visit of a delegation from Neuendettelsau and surroundings to the USA to attend the 150th anniversary of the foundation of Frankenmuth

Foundation of the China Information Office of the German missionary centers in Hamburg

The renovated conference center of the Society for Inner and Outer Mission is reopened under the name House Luther Rose

November 26—December 1 ELCB General Synods discusses in Regensburg the topic "Global Responsibility in Dialogue with Partner Churches"

A resolution and the revised Church Law on Mission and Ecumenism are passed

1996 May 15-18 Seminar on alternative energies in Africa with the topic "From Fossil Fire to the Sun"

1997 July 11 Twenty-fifth jubilee of DWM is celebrated with Bishop Hermann von Loewenich

September 9 Death of Johann Flierl fifty years ago is commemorated

October 10 The Leipzig Mission Publishers in Erlangen celebrates the hundredth anniversary of its foundation with Federal Minister Carl-Dieter Spranger and Bishop Volker Kress from Saxony

November 22 Service in Rothenburg on the Tauber with Bishop Hermann von Loewenich and Brazilian Church President Huberto Kirchheim to commemorate the sending of Otto Kuhr to Brazil one hundred years ago

1998 Rev. Horst Seeger is sent as the first Bavarian missionary to Mozambique

DWM joins the ecumenical student network Praynet

Baafecke Bamiringnu works as the first exchange pastor from PNG in Dietenhofen (until 2002)

1999 June 13 The ecumenical campaign "Jubilee 2000" is opened in a service in Nuremberg with Missio Munich

July 15–18 Symposium and day of encounter to commemorate the first baptisms in New Guinea one hundred years ago

September 12 The Society for Inner and Outer Mission celebrates its 150th anniversary

2000 Rev. Malte Rhinow is sent to Korea as the first Bavarian missionary

July lecture of Bishop Dr. Johannes Friedrich at the festival of the worldwide church about church and mission

Dr. Johannes Triebel becomes the first ELCB consultant on Christian-Muslim dialogue

July 16 The North-South Initiative for the promotion of alternative energies in Tanzania is founded

2001 The cooperation of ELCB and DWM with African congregations in Bavaria starts

DWM joins the Alliance against AIDS

2002 August 1–16 Bishop Dr. Johannes Friedrich visits the Lutheran partner churches in Singapore, Malaysia, PNG, and Australia to commemorate the first Lutheran Communion service in PNG one hundred years ago

2003 September 29–30 Dr. Vorländer participates in the first church leader conference of the Lutheran Mission Cooperation in Moshi (Tanzania)

May 26 Bishop Dr. Johannes Friedrich holds a visitation in DWM

Deacon Helmut Köhler is commissioned to El Salvador as the first DWM coworker

2004 September 26 A delegation from the Chinese State Administration for Religious Affairs visits DWM and is welcomed by Deputy Prime Minister of Bavaria Dr. Günther Beckstein

DWM participates in the state exhibition "Good Bye Bayern—Grüss Gott Amerika: Emigration from Bavaria to America since 1683"

2005 First seminar for congregations of foreign origin, "Mission South North"

Declaration of the German missionary centers in regard to the maji maji uprisal one hundred years ago in Tanzania

The new journal *InSight* (*EinBlick*) in cooperation with other missionary centers is launched

DWM cooperates with Missio Munich in the campaign "Bull's Eye—No Wars with Children" and hosts the visit of Chancellor Angela Merkel during the Protestant Church Rally in Hanover

Celebration of thirty years of independence of PNG with Sir Arnold Amet

August 7–24 Visit of Bishop Dr. Johannes Friedrich in Kenya and Tanzania

Foundation of the International Loehe Society in Dubuque, Iowa

Director Vorländer participates in the celebration of the twentieth anniversary of the Amity Foundation in Nanjing, China

2006 July 1 The consultant for Latin America, Dr. Wolfgang Döbrich, moves his office to Neuendettelsau

July 2 First Open Air Festival with African congregations in Nuremberg

November 30 ELCB General Synod passes the new Church Law on Ecumenics, Mission, Development Work, and Partnership in Rummelsberg

Foundation of the Association for New Guinea Culture

2007 January 14 Opening ceremony of the new institution Mission One World—Center for Partnership, Development and Mission of the ELCB with Bishop Dr. Johannes Friedrich and Bishop Dr. Medardo Gómez from El Salvador

Dr. Sigurd Kaiser is sent as the first lecturer on theology from Germany to the Union Theological Seminary in Nanjing, China

June 13 Opening of the exhibition God's Word in China, an exhibition about the history and distribution of the Bible, by the president of the Chinese Christian Council, Rev. Dr. Shengjie Cao, and the director of the Amity Foundation, Dr. Qin Zhongui

August 1–20 Journey of a delegation of the ELCB to China and Korea under the leadership of Bishop Dr. Johannes Friedrich and Synod President Heidi Schülke

Center Mission One World participates in the campaign of German missionary centers under the theme "Mission—for God's Sake and the World's Sake"

November 20–24 First Consultation of ELCB with its sixteen partner churches ending with a symposium and farewell to Dr. Hermann Vorländer

2008 January 1 The Nuremberg district takes over the responsibility for the Center for Christian Muslim Encounter ("Bridge—Köprü")

Director Peter Weigand begins his work

ELCB celebrates the two-hundredth birthday of Wilhelm Loehe

2012 In Neuendettelsau the two-hundredth birthday of Friedrich Bauer is celebrated

2013 Dr. Ati and Markus Hildebrandt Rambe begin to work as consultants of ELCB for congregations of foreign language and background

2015 Director Peter Weigand retires

    July 18 Dr. Gabriele and Hanns Hoerschelmann are installed as directors of Mission One World

Overseas

Pacific and East Asia

AUSTRALIA

1860 The Neuendettelsau missionary Johann Meischel begins his work in Australia

1875 Johann Stolz is the first missionary directly sent from Neuendettelsau

1878 Johann Flierl arrives in Australia

1921 Foundation of the Evangelical Lutheran Church in Australia (ELCA) and the United Evangelical Lutheran Church of Australia (UELCA)

    UELCA takes over the missionary work in New Guinea

1966 ELCA and UELCA merge to form the Lutheran Church of Australia (LCA)

NEW GUINEA

1884 North East New Guinea becomes a German protectorate under the name Emperor William Land and is governed by the New Guinea Company under the leadership of Adolph von Hansemann

1886 July 12 Johann Flierl arrives in Finschhafen

    October 10 The first mission station is founded in Simbang

1889 Foundation of the mission station on the Tami islands

1892 Foundation of the mission station on Sattelberg mountain

1899 Foundation of the mission station Deinzerhill

    August 20 Baptism of Kaboing and Kamungsanga by Johann Pfalzer

The German Empire buys back the sovereignty of New Guinea from the New Guinea Company

Arrival of Christian Keysser

1902 First Communion service in Obasega

The teacher Emilie Heumann (married Keysser) is sent as the first female missionary by the Neuendettelsau Mission

1903 Ceremony with big man Zake in Bore

1904 Foundation of the mission station Heldsbach

Uprisals against the colonial government in Madang region

1908 September 6 Indigenous missionaries start missionary work in Hube hinterland

1911 Foundation of the mission station Ampo in Lae

1913 May 5 Launching and dedication of the mission ship Bavaria in Rabaul

1914 Missionary conference in Heldsbach with mission inspector Karl Steck

August 2 The First World War starts, and the Australians occupy New Guinea

1921 May 12 The United Evangelical Lutheran Church of Australia (UELCA) and the Iowa Synod take authority over the missionary work of the Neuendettelsau Mission

1922 Evangelists are stationed in the eastern highlands

1925 The Australian government permits Neuendettelsau missionaries to continue work in New Guinea

1926 The UELCA forms a trust company for the missionary work in New Guinea

1927 Nurse Helene Moll is sent as the first missionary after the First World War

1930 Departure of Johann Flierl to Australia

1931 Foundation of the mission station Kaiapit as the starting point for the highlands mission

1935 Arrival of the mission aircraft *Papua*

1937 Foundation of a Nazi stronghold in Finschhafen

July 13 Foundation of the mission station Asaroka in the highlands

1939 September 1 Beginning of the Second World War and the deportation of many missionaries to Australia

1940 The first indigenous pastors are ordained

1941 Deportation of missionaries' wives to Australia

1942 The northern part of New Guinea is occupied by the Japanese

1943 Missionary Adolf Wagner is killed by Japanese soldiers

1947 The first interned missionaries are allowed to return to New Guinea

1950 Inspection tour of Georg Vicedom to take up contacts with the missionaries

1953 Foundation of the Lutheran Mission New Guinea by the Lutheran churches in Australia and USA

1953 Nurse Maria Horn is sent as the first missionary after the Second World War from Neuendettelsau

1956 The Evangelical Lutheran Church of New Guinea (ELCONG) is founded and John Kuder is elected as the first bishop

1959 Foundation of the theological seminaries in Logaweng and Ogelbeng

1968 Foundation of the Melanesian Institute in Goroka

Foundation of the Martin Luther Seminary in Lae

1973 Sir Zurewe Zurenuo is elected as the first indigenous bishop (–1982)

The Lutheran Mission New Guinea is dissolved and the New Guinea Coordinating Committee (NGCC) is founded

1975 Papua New Guinea receives its independence

1976 Foundation of the Evangelical Lutheran Church of Papua New Guinea (ELCPNG)

1982 Sir Getacke Gam is elected bishop (–1998)

1986 One hundredth jubilee of the Lutheran mission in New Guinea

1992 Discussion about environment in connection with the Ok Tedi Mine

1997 Consultation at Kainantu between ELCPNG and its partners

1998 Dr. Wesley Kigasung is elected bishop (died 2008)

1999 January 1 ELCPNG Partners Forum begins its operations succeeding NGCC

2002 August 8–16 Visit of Bishop Dr. Johannes Friedrich

2010 Giegere Wenge is elected bishop (–2016)

2016 Jack Urame is elected bishop

2017 Treaty between ELCPNG and ELCB

China

1841 Forcible Opening of China by the British government
1911 Revolution
1949 Mao Zedong takes over power
1965 Beginning of the so-called cultural revolution
1979 Opening of the first five churches
1980 Foundation of the China Christian Council
1985 Foundation of the Amity Foundation by Bishop K.H. Ting
1987 Foundation of the Amity Bible Printing Press in Nanjing
    DWM sents the first teacher to China
2004 Visit of Vice Minister Wang of the State Administration for Religious Affairs in Neuendettelsau
2007 August 1–14 Visit of a delegation from ELCB headed by Bishop Dr. Johannes Friedrich and Synod President Heidi Schülke
    June: A Bible exhibition of the China Christian Council is opened in Neuendettelsau by President Dr. Shengje Cao
    Dr. Sigurd Kaiser is sent as the first lecturer from Germany to teach at the Union Theological Seminary in Nanjing.

Hong Kong

1897 China leases Hong Kong to Great Britain as a crown colony
1954 Foundation of the Evangelical Lutheran Church in Hong Kong (ELCHK)
1992 Dedication of the new building of the Lutheran Theological Seminary (LTS)
    Dr. Karlhermann Mühlhaus is sent as the first professor from Neuendettelsau to LTS
1997 Ninth Assembly of the Lutheran World Federation in Hong Kong under the theme "In Christ Called to Witness"
    Hong Kong returns to China as a Special Administrative Region

Korea

1832 The German missionary Karl August Gützlaff visits Korea

1850 Beginning of the Christian mission

1905 Korea is occupied by Japan (–1945)

1950 Beginning of the civil war between North and South Korea

1953 Ceasefire

1958 Beginning of Lutheran missionary work by the Lutheran Church–Missouri Synod

1965 Foundation of the Lutheran Theological Seminary, now Luther University

1971 Foundation of the Lutheran Church in Korea (LCK)

2002 Dr. Malte Rhinow is sent as the first coworker from Bavaria

2007 August 15–19 Visit of the delegation from ELCB under the leadership of Bishop Dr. Johannes Friedrich and Synod President Heidi Schülke

Malaysia and Singapore

1953 Foundation of the Lutheran Church in Malaysia and Singapore (LCMS)

1992 Werner Strauss is sent by DWM as the first coworker for the Seafarers' Mission in Singapore

1998 Foundation of the Lutheran Church in Singapore (SCS)

2002 August 2–4 Visit of Bishop Dr. Johannes Friedrich

Africa

Tanzania

1891 The German Empire establishes the Protectorate German East Africa

1891 Bethel Mission starts missionary work in the Usambara Mountains and Berlin Mission in southern Tanganyika and coastal area

1893 Leipzig Mission sends missionaries to north Tanganyika

1920 German East Africa becomes a British mandate

1961 Independence of Tanganyika, which, under Julius Nyerere, unites with Zanzibar as the United Republic of Tanzania

1963 June 6 Foundation of the Evangelical Lutheran Church in Tanzania (ELCT)

1964 Hans-Gernot Kleefeld is sent as the first missionary by the Bavarian church to work in southern Tanganyika

1972 DWM takes over the work of the Leipzig Mission and ELCB in Tanzania

1973 Foundation of the Lutheran Coordination Service East Africa (LCS)

1983 The deaconess community Ushirika wa Neema in Moshi is founded

1998 Foundation of the Lutheran Mission Cooperation (LMC)

1999 January 11–15 Conference on renewable energies in Dodoma

2005 August 4–24 Visit of Bishop Dr Johannes Friedrich

2012 Treaty on Cooperation between ELCT and ELCB

2016 Dr. Frederick Shoo, a graduate of the Augustana Theological Seminary, is elected Presiding Bishop of ELCT

Kenya

1844 Missionary Johann Rebmann from Germany works in Mombasa and views as the first European the Kilimanjaro

1886 The Hersbruck Mission starts missionary work in southern Kenya

1960 Independence of Kenya

1968 Foundation of the ELCT Kenya Synod

1984 Volker Faigle is sent as the first missionary from DWM

1992 Foundation of the Kenya Evangelical Lutheran Church (KELC)

1997 Zachariah Kahuthu becomes the first bishop of KELC

2005 August 1–3 Visit of Bishop Dr. Johannes Friedrich

Congo/Zaire

1960 Independence and civil war; Mobutu seizes power

1997 Mobutu is deposed by Joseph Kabila

1977 Foundation of the Joint Commission for Zaire

1983 Foundation of the Église Luthérienne du Zaire

Walter Lupp begins his work as the first missionary from DWM
1992 Installation of Bishop Ngoy Kasukuti
1994 Dedication of the Lutheran cathedral in Lubumbashi
Foundation of the theological seminary in Kimbeimbe (IAFTA), now Luther University

Mozambique

1987 Foundation of the Joint Mission Board for Mozambique
1993 The Lutheran Church in Mozambique is registered by the government
2004 The Brazilian deaconess Doraci Edinger is murdered
2005 José Mabasso becomes pastor in charge and later bishop

Liberia

1822 Foundation of Liberia by former slaves from the USA
1860 Beginning of missionary work by American Lutherans
1957 Foundation of the Lutheran Church of Liberia (LCL)
1975 Bishop Roland Payne asks DWM for cooperation
1990 Massacre in St. Peter's Cathedral
1995 Dr. Sumoward Harris becomes bishop
1998 Marina Rauh is sent as the first missionary by DWM

North America

1842 Arrival of the first missionaries from Neuendettelsau, Adam Ernst and Georg Burger
1845 Foundation of the mission colony Frankenmuth, Michigan
Beginning of the missionary work among Native Americans
1846 October 10 Foundation of Concordia Theological Seminary in Fort Wayne by Dr. Wilhelm Sihler
Baptism of the first two Native American children in Frankenmuth

1847 Foundation of the German Lutheran Synod of Missouri, Ohio, and Other States, later called the Lutheran Church–Missouri Synod

1852 Foundation of the teachers seminary in Saginaw, Michigan, led by Georg Grossmann

1853 Foundation of Wartburg Theological Seminary in Dubuque, Iowa

1854 August 24 Foundation of the Evangelical Lutheran Synod of Iowa and Other States in St. Sebald by the Spring

1860 July 23 Murder of the Neuendettelsau missionary Moritz Bräuninger by Native Americans at the Powder River (Montana)

1864 Destruction of Lutheran missionary stations during the Civil War by Native Americans

1866 The Iowa Synod decides to end missionary work among Native Americans

1904 Fiftieth jubilee of the Iowa Synod

1925 The last missionary from Neuendettelsau is sent to North America

1930 The Iowa Synod joins the American Lutheran Church

1935 The teachers seminary in Saginaw is transferred to Waverly, Iowa, and named Wartburg College

1988 Foundation of the Evangelical Lutheran Church in America (ELCA)

Latin America

Brazil

1824 Arrival of the first German immigrants in Sao Leopoldo

1897 November 20 Sending of Otto Kuhr by the Bavarian Lutheran Treasury of God

Foundation of the so-called Treasury of God Synod

1968 Foundation of the Evangelical Church of the Lutheran Confession in Brazil (IECLB)

1980 Treaty on partnership between IECLB and ELCB

Central America

1822 Independence of Central America from Spain

1971 Foundation of the Salvadoran Lutheran Synod
1980 Murder of the Catholic Archbishop Oscar Romero in El Salvador
1983 Foundation of an LWF office in El Salvador
   Foundation of the Christian Lutheran Church of Honduras
1988 Foundation of the Lutheran Church of Costa Rica
   Foundation of the Communio de Iglesias Luteranas de Centroamérica (CILCA)
1990 Foundation of the Lutheran Church of Nicaragua "Faith and Hope"
1995 Treaties on partnership between ELCB, CILCA, and IECLB during the meeting of the General Synod of ELCB in Regensburg
2001 Deacon Helmut Köhler is sent as the first MWB coworker to El Salvador

Lists of Persons and Translations of Titles and Institutions

1. Church Presidents and Bishops of the Evangelical Lutheran Church in Bavaria

Dr. Friedrich Veit (1861–1948) 1921–1933

Dr. Hans Meiser (1881–1956)1933–1955

Dr. Hermann Dietzfelbinger (1908–1984) 1955–1975

Dr. Johannes Hanselmann (1927–1999) 1975–1994

Dr. Hermann von Loewenich (1931–2008) 1994–1999

Dr. Johannes Friedrich (born 1948) 1999–2011

Dr. Heinrich Bedford-Strohm (born 1960) 2011-

2. Heads of the Department for Mission and Ecumenics in the ELCB Headquarters in Munich

Kurt Horn (1910–1990) 1962–1975

Dr. Gerhard Strauss (1926–2001) 1975 -1991

Dr. Claus-Jürgen Roepke (born 1937) 1991–2001

Wolfgang Töllner (1940–2005) 2001–2005

Michael Martin (born 1959) 2005-

3. Heads of the Mission Institute, Department for World Mission, and Center Mission One World in Neuendettelsau

Friedrich Bauer (1812–1874) 1846–1874

Johannes Deinzer (1842–1897) 1875–1897

Martin Deinzer (1850–1917) 1897–1917

Rudolf Ruf (1868–1950) 1920–1928

Dr. Friedrich Eppelein (1887–1969) 1928–1946

Dr. Woldemar Schilberg (1911–1972) 1946–1950

Hans Neumeyer (1902–1992) 1950–1962

Hagen Katterfeld (1916–1964) 1962–1964

Dr. Wolfram von Krause (1914–1989) 1964–1971

Horst Becker DD. (born 1926) 1972–1991

Dr. Hermann Vorländer (born 1942) 1992–2007

Peter Weigand (born 1949) 2007- 2015

Dr. Gabriele Hoerschelmann (born 1968) and Hanns Hoerschelmann (born 1965) 2015–

4. Directors of the Mission and Diaspora Seminary

Dr. Oswald Henke (1910–2006) 1961–1975

Ernst Lippold (born 1935) 1975–1980

Dr. Hermann Reiner (born 1940) 1981–1985

5. Chairpersons of the Society for Inner and Outer Mission in the Sense of the Lutheran Church

Wilhelm Loehe (1808–1872) 1849–1861

Friedrch Wucherer (1803–1881) 1861–1881

Eduard Stirner Sr. (1812–1905) 1881–1895

Johannes Deinzer (1842–1897) 1895–1897

Wilhelm Eichhorn (1846–1923) 1897–1909

Eduard Sabel (1856–1928) 1909–1912

Eduard Stirner Jr. (1849–1927) 1912–1925

Konrad Wirth (1872–1941) 1925–1940

Heinrich Koch (1898–1974) 1940–1947
Friedrich Rupprecht (1892–1960) 1947–1955
Hans Luther (1910–1985) 1955–1959
Hermann Greifenstein (1912–1988) 1959–1965
Wilhelm Koller (1894–1988) 1965–1968
Werner Ost (1920–1995) 1968–1989
Dr. Wolfhart Schlichting (born 1940) 1989–2004
Detlef Graf von der Pahlen (born 1943) 2004–

6. Translations of Titles and Institutions

Dekanatsbezirk	church district
Diakonissenanstalt	deaconess institute
Kirchenrat	church official
Kollegium	executive board
Kuratorium	governing board
Landesbischof	bishop
Landeskirchenamt	church headquarters
Landeskirchenrat	supreme church council
Landessynode	general synod
Missionsanstalt	mission institute
Missionsseminar	mission seminary
Missionswerk	department for world mission
Oberkirchenrat	church executive

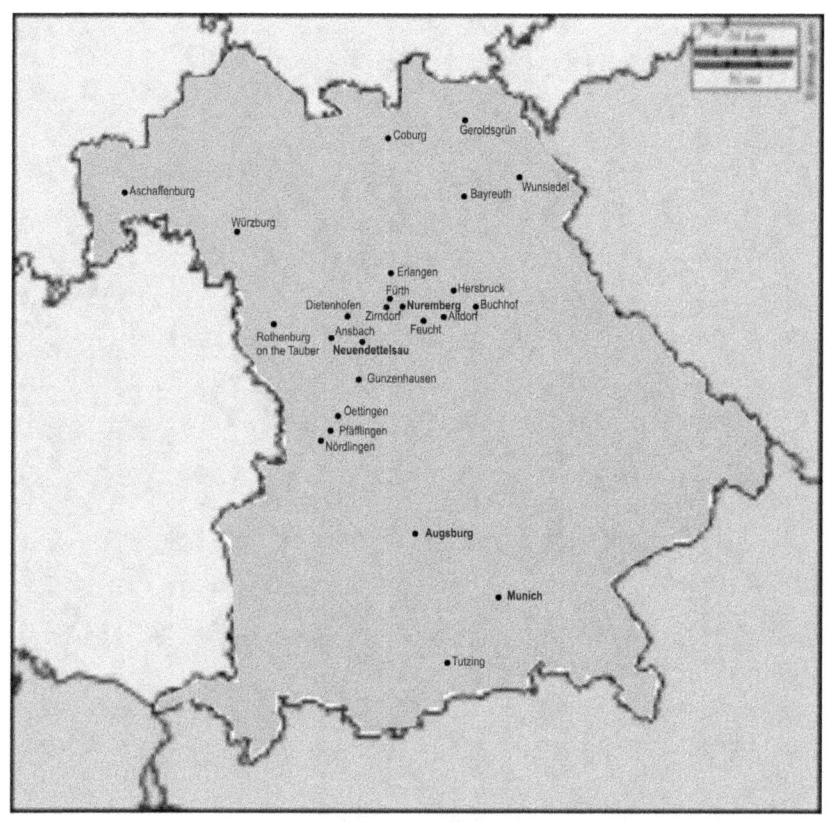

Map of Bavaria

Author Biography

HERMANN VORLÄNDER WAS BORN in 1942 in Moschin, Poland. He grew up in Württemberg and Bavaria. He graduated as an exchange student from Jonesville High School in Michigan and in 1962 from the Röntgen Gymnasium in Würzburg. After his military service he studied theology at Bethel Theological Seminary and the universities in Hamburg, Heidelberg, and Erlangen from 1964 to 1968. After his church entry examination, he worked as a teaching assistant at the University of Erlangen-Nuremberg, where he received his Doctor of Theology degree in 1971. In 1972, after his vicariate he passed the final church examination. From 1972 to 1976 he taught as a professor of Old Testament at the Near East School of Theology in Beirut, Lebanon. After his return due to the civil war, he worked from 1976 to 1981 as a pastor in Kaufbeuren. He was then called to the ELCB church headquarters in Munich, where he worked as the head of the department for examinations and continuing education. In 1988, he became dean of the southern district of Munich and pastor at St. Luke's Church. In 1992, he was appointed executive director of the ELCB Department for World Mission in Neuendettelsau. He retired in 2007 and continues to live in Neuendettelsau. Since 1968 he was married to the Rev. Dr. Dorothea, née Cyron, who died on January 17, 2018. She worked as a professor of church history in Beirut and pastor in Munich, Neuendettelsau, and Weissenbronn. They have four adult children and four grandchildren.

Rev. Dr. Hermann Vorländer headed the Department for World Mission from 1992 to 2007.

Bibliography

Bauer, Günter, ed. *Entstehung und Geschichte des Bayerischen Zentralbibelvereins.* Nürnberg: Zentralbibelverein, 1996.

Blaufuß, Dietrich ed. *Wilhelm Löhe—Erbe und Vision.* Gütersloh: Mohn, 2009.

Bosch, David J. *Transforming Mission: Paradigm Shifts in Theology of Mission.* American Society of Missiology 16. New York: Orbis, 1991.

Brandt, Hermann, ed. *30 Jahre Missionswissenschaft in Erlangen: Dokumentation eines Symposiums am 15. November 1997.* Erlangen: Erlanger, 1998.

Collver, Albert B. "Loehe: Mission Societies, The Church in Motion, and Missio Dei." In *Wilhelm Löhe und Bildung: Wilhelm Loehe and Christian Formation,* edited by Dietrich Blaufuß and Jacob Corzine, 171–82. Verein für bayerische Kirchengeschichte Nürnberg. Neuendettelsau: Freimund, 2016.

Dreher, Martin N. *Kirche und Deutschtum in der Entwicklung der Evangelischen Kirche Lutherischen Bekenntnisses in Brasilien.* Göttingen: Vandenhoeck and Ruprecht, 1997.

Durst, Friedrich. *Das andere Afrika.* 2nd ed. Erlangen: Erlanger, 2004.

Eppelein, Friedrich, ed. *Das Neuendettelsauer Missionswerk und seine 4 Arbeitsgebiete: Bericht 1933 der Gesellschaft für Innere und Äußere Mission im Sinne der lutherischen Kirche.* Neuendettelsau.

_____. *Lebenserinnerungen.* Manuscript. Landeskirchliches Archiv, MS 1302.

Eppelein, Friedrich, and Christian Keyßer. *Die politische Lage und ihre Auswirkungen.* 1945. Archive Mission One World Nr. 4.114a.

Eppler, Paul. *Geschichte der Basler Mission 1815—1899.* Basel: Missionsbuchhandlung, 1900.

Ernst, Manfred. *Winds of Change: Rapidly Growing Religious Groups in the Pacific Islands.* Suva: Pacific Conferences of Churches, 1994.

Farnbacher, Traugott, and Christian Weber. *Ein Zentrum für Weltmission Neuendettelsau: Einführung, Zeittafeln, Dokumente, Namen 1842-2002.* Neuendettelsau: Missionswerk der Evang.-Luth. Kirche in Bayern, 2004.

Farnbacher, Traugott, and Gernot Fugmann. *Johann Flierl (1858 bis 1947): Ein Leben für die Mission, Mission für das Leben.* Neuendettelsau: Erlanger, 2008.

Farnbacher, Traugott. *Gemeinde verantworten: Anfänge, Entwicklungen und Perspektiven von Gemeinde und Ämtern der Evangelisch-Lutherischen Kirche in Papua-Neuguinea.* Münster: LIT, 1999.

Fischer, Moritz. *Maasai gestalten Christsein*. Erlangen: Erlanger, 2001.
Fischer, Ulrich. *EKLBB—gestern, heute und morgen: Porträt einer Kirche in Brasilien*. Jahrbuch Evangelische Mission. Hamburg: Missionshilfe, 1977.
Fix, Karl-Heinz. *Glaubensgenossen in Not: Die Evangelisch-Lutherische Kirche in Bayern und die Hilfe für aus rassischen Gründen verfolgte Protestanten. Eine Dokumentation*. Gütersloh: Verlagshaus, 2011.
Fleisch, Paul. *Hundert Jahre lutherischer Mission*. Leipizig: Ev.-Luth. Mission, 1936.
Fontius, Hanfried. *Mission—Gemeinde—Kirche in Neuguinea, Bayern und bei Karl Steck*. Erlangen: Ev.-Luth. Mission, 1975.
Fuchshuber-Weiß, Elisabeth. "Von der Übersicht zur Einsicht—Friedrich Bauers Schulgrammatik." In *Friedrich Bauer 1812–1874: Pionier in der Weltmission, Wegbereiter des Duden*, edited by Claudia Jahnel and Hermann Vorländer, 77–134. Neuendettelsau: Erlanger, 2013.
Fugmann, Wilhelm. *Georg Pilhofer: Der Missionar*. Treuchtlingen: Wek, 2005.
_____. *Laß dein Brot übers Wasser fahren*. Treuchtlingen: Keller, 1996.
Geiger, Erika. *Wilhelm Löhe (1808–1872): Leben—Werk—Wirkung*. Neuendettelsau: Freimund, 2003.
_____. *The Life, Work and Influence of Wilhelm Loehe (1808–1872)*. Translated by Wolf Dietrich Knappe. St. Louis: Concordia 2010.
Grafe, Hugald. *One Hundred and Seventy-Five Years of Leipzig Mission*. Leipzig: Leipzig Mission, 2011.
Gremmels, Georg, ed. *Die Hermannsburger Mission und das „Dritte Reich": Zwischen faschistischer Verführung und lutherischer Beharrlichkeit. Quellen und Beiträge zur Geschichte der Hermannsburger Mission*, vol. 13. Münster, 2005.
Hauenstein, Philipp. *Fremdheit als Charisma: Die Existenz als Missionar in Vergangenheit und Gegenwart am Beispiel des Dienstes in Papua-Neuguinea*. Erlangen: Erlanger, 1999.
Henke, Oswald. "Geschichte und bleibender Ertrag des MDS." Concordia 3 (1985) 13–33.
Herzog, Albrecht I., and Schlichting Wolfram. "Gesellschaft für Innere und Äußere Mission im Sinne der lutherischen Kirche." In *. . . mitten unter euch: 200 Jahre Dekanat Windsbach*, edited by Horst Heißmann. Neuendettelsau: Erlanger, 2009.
Hiery, Joseph. *Die deutsche Südsee 1884–1914: Ein Handbuch*. Paderborn: Schöningh, 1984.
Jahnel, Claudia. "Friedrich Bauer als Wegbereiter theologischen Denkens und theologischer Ausbildung im weltweiten Horizont." In *Friedrich Bauer 1812–1874: Pionier in der Weltmission, Wegbereiter des Duden*, edited by Claudia Jahnel and Hermann Vorländer, 291–301. Neuendettelsau: Erlanger, 2013.
_____, ed. *Mi stori: Frauen erzählen Geschichte*. Neuendettelsau: Erlanger, 2012.
Ji, Won Yong. *Meines Bruders Hüter*. Erlangen: Ev.-Luth. Mission, 1979.
Kantzenbach, Friedrich Wilhelm. "Die Neuendettelsauer Mission und die Anfänge des Kirchenkampfes." ZbKG 40 (1971) 227–45.
Keiper, Martin. *Hinterm Kirchtum geht es weiter: Missionswerke und Öffentlichkeitsarbeit*. EMW Jahresbericht 2006/2007.
Kern, Helmut. "Das Arbeitsgebiet in der Heimat: Die Neuendettelsauer Volksmission." In *Das Neuendettelsauer Missionswerk und seine 4 Arbeitsgebiete: Bericht 1933 der Gesellschaft für Innere und Äußere Mission im Sinne der lutherischen Kirche*, edited by Friedrich Eppelein, 16–47. Neuendettelsau: Buchdr. der Diakonissenanst, 1933.

Keyßer, Christian. *Altes Testament und heutige Zeit*. Neuendettelsau: Freimund, 1934.
_____. *Das bin bloß ich: Lebenserinnerungen*. Edited by Wilhelm Fugmann. Neuendettelsau: Freimund, 1966.
Kittel, Manfred. *Provinz zwischen Reich und Republik*. München: Oldenbourg, 2000.
Koller, Wilhelm. *Die Missionsanstalt in Neuendettelsau: Ihre Geschichte und das Leben in ihr*. Neuendettelsau: Missionshaus, 1924.
Küng, Hans. *Projekt Weltethos*. München: Piper, 1990.
Liebenberg, Roland. "Testament eines biblischen Lutheraners: Friedrich Bauers Denkschrift und Anschreiben an die Synode von Iowa." In *Friedrich Bauer 1812–1874: Pionier in der Weltmission, Wegbereiter des Duden*, edited by Claudia Jahnel and Hermann Vorländer, 189–245. Neuendettelsau: Erlanger, 2013.
_____. *Wilhelm Löhe (1808-1872): Stationen seines Lebens*. Leipzig: Verlagsanstalt, 2011.
Löhe, Wilhelm. *Die Heidenmission in Nordamerika: Ein Vortrag in der Generalversammlung des protestantischen Zentralmissionsvereins zu Nürnberg den 2 Juli 1846*. In *Gesammelte Werke*, edited by Klaus Ganzert, vol. 4, 102–12. Neuendettelsau: Freimund, 1962.
_____. *Die lutherischen Auswanderer in Nordamerika: Eine Ansprache an die Leser des Sonntagsblattes*. In *Gesammelte Werke*, edited by Klaus Ganzert, vol. 4, 16–19. .Neuendettelsau: Freimund, 1962.
_____. *Drei Bücher von der Kirche*. In *Gesammelte Werke*, edited by Klaus Ganzert, vol. 6, 83–179. Neuendettelsau: Freimund, 1954.
_____. *Innere Mission im allgemeinen*. In *Gesammelte Werke*, edited by Klaus Ganzert, vol. 4, 178–88. Neuendettelsau: Freimund, 1962.
_____. *Vorschlag zu einem Lutherischen Verein für apostolisches Leben samt Entwurf eines Katechismus des apostolischen Lebens*. In *Gesammelte Werke*, edited by Klaus Ganzert, vol. 5, 213–52. Neuendettelsau: Freimund, 1954.
_____. *Zuruf aus der Heimat an die deutsch-lutherische Kirche Nordamerikas*. In *Gesammelte Werke*, edited by Klaus Ganzert, vol. 4, 68–85. Neuendettelsau: Freimund, 1962.
Mellinghof, Gerhard, ed. *Lutherische Kirche in Tansania*. Erlangen: Ev.-Luth. Mission, 1976.
Mensing, Björn. *Pfarrer und Nationalsozialismus: Geschichte einer Verstrickung am Beispiel der Evangelisch-Lutherischen Kirche in Bayern*. 3rd ed. Bayreuth: Rabenstein, 2001.
Moritzen, Nils-Peter. *Mission in Erlangen: Zur Vorgeschichte des Lehrstuhls für Missionswissenschaft an der theologischen Fakultät*. Akademische Reden und Kolloquien 14. Erlangen: Friedrich Alexander Universität, 1998.
_____. *Werkzeug Gottes in der Welt: Leipziger Mission 1836—1936—1986*. Erlangen: Ev.-Luth. Mission, 1986.
Mroßko, Kurt Dietrich. *Mission und Drittes Reich*. Manuscript. Neuendettelsau, 1986.
Müller, Klaus W. *Georg F. Vicedom as Missionary and Peacemaker*. Erlangen: Erlanger, 2002.
Nelson, H. N. "Loyalties at Sword-point: The Lutheran Missionaries in Wartime New Guinea 1939–45." *Australian Journal of Politics and History* 24 (1978) 199–217.
Nessan Craig I. "Friedrich Bauer zum 200: Geburtstag Genealogie eines vergessenen Vorfahren." In *Friedrich Bauer 1812-1874: Pionier in der Weltmission, Wegbereiter*

des Duden, edited by Claudia Jahnel and Hermann Vorländer, 245–64. Neuendettelsau: Erlanger, 2013.

———. "Theological Curriculum at the Missionsseminar Neuendettelsau in the 19th Century: The Contribution of Christliche Dogmatik and Christliche Ethik by F. Bauer, J. Deinzer / M. Deinzer." In *Wilhelm Löhe und Bildung: Wilhelm Loehe and Christian Formation*, edited by Dietrich Blaufuß and Jacob Corzine, 182–97. Verein für bayerische Kirchengeschichte Nürnberg. Neuendettelsau: Freimund, 2016.

Ngeiyamu, Joel, and Johannes Triebel. *Gemeinsam auf eigenen Wegen: Ev.-Luth. Kirche Tansanias nach 100 Jahren*. Erlangen: Ev.-Luth. Mission, 1994.

Perkins John. "The Swastika among the Coconuts: Nazism in New Guinea in the 1930s." In *Fascism Outside Europe*, edited by Stein Ugelvik Larsen, 287–309. Social Science Monographs. Boulder: Columbia University Press, 2001.

Pilhofer, Georg. *Geschichte des Neuendettelsauer Missionshauses*. Neuendettelsau: Freimund, 1967.

———. *Die Geschichte der Neuendettelsauer Mission in Neuguinea*. 3 vols. Neuendettelsau: Freimund, 1961–1963.

Rhinow, Malte. *Eine kurze koreanische Kirchengeschichte bis 1910*. Münster: Schöningh, 2013.

Rößler, Hans. "Friedrich Bauer—ein fränkischer Theologe und Schulmann mit weltweiter Wirkung." In *Friedrich Bauer 1812–1874: Pionier in der Weltmission, Wegbereiter des Duden*, edited by Claudia Jahnel and Hermann Vorländer, 11–76. Neuendettelsau: Erlanger, 2013.

———. *Unter Stroh und Ziegeldächern: Aus der Neuendettelsauer Geschichte*. Neuendettelsau: Freimund, 1982.

Rößler, Hans, and Mathias Honold. *Wilhelm Löhe und die Amerika-Auswanderung 1841–1872*. Neuendettelsauer Heft Nr. 5. Neuendettelsau, 2008.

Rößler, Hans, and Wolfgang Roth. *Die Luftmunitionsanstalt 2/XIII und das Munagelände Neuendettelsau 1934–1958*. Neuendettelsauer Heft Nr. 1. Neuendettelsau, 2003.

Roser, Hans, *Von Bayern bis Brasilien: Der Martin Luther Verein*; ein Stück bayerischer Kirchengeschichte, Rothenburg: Peter 1985.

Roser, Hans, and Keller, Rudolf. *Ich bin bereit: Lutherische Pfarrer in Brasilien 1897–1997*. Erlangen: Martin Luther, 1997.

Ruf, Walther. "Wegbereiter des Missionswerkes Bayern." *Jahrbuch Mission* 1986, 302–31.

Schmutterer, Martin. *Tomahawk und Kreuz: Fränkische Missionare unter Prärie-Indianern 1858–1866: Zum Gedenken an Moritz Bräuninger*. Neuendettelsau: Freimund; Erlangen: Ev.-Luth. Mission, 1987.

Schreiber, A. W. *Die Edinburger Welt-Missions-Konferenz*. Basel: Missionsbuchhandlung, 1910.

Schuster, Adam. *Aus tausend Jahren Neuendettelsauer Geschichte*. Ansbach: Brügel, 1963.

Seifert, Heinz. *Hersbruck 1886: Aufbruch nach Ost-Afrika*. 2nd ed. Hersbruck: Dekanat 1992.

Simon, Matthias. *Mission und Bekenntnis in der Entwicklung des Evangelisch-Lutherischen Zentralmissionsvereins für Bayern*. Neuendettelsau: Freimund, 1953.

Sommer, Wolfgang. "Freimund—Kirchlich.Politisches Wochenblatt für Stadt und Land." *Zeitschrift für bayerische Landesgeschichte* 76 (2013) 809–82.

Stadler, Jürgen. *Die Missionspraxis Christian Keyßers in Neuguinea 1899–1920: Erste Schritte auf dem Weg zu einer einheimischen Kirche*. Nürnberg: VTR, 2006.
Strehlow, John. *The Tale of Frieda Keysser*, vol. 1, *1875–1910: Frieda Keysser and Carl Strehlow: An Historical Biography*. London: Wild Cat, 2011.
Sundermeier, Theo. *Konvivenz und Differenz: Studien zu einer verstehenden Missionswissenschaft*. Erlangen: Erlanger, 1995.
Töllner Axel. *Eine Frage der Rasse?: Die Evangelisch-Lutherische Kirche in Bayern, der Arierparagraf und die bayerischen Pfarrfamilien mit jüdischen Vorfahren im "Dritten Reich"*. Stuttgart: Kohlhammer, 2007.
Triebel, Johannes. "Wechselvolle Geschichte: 170 Jahre Zentralverband für Äußere Mission." *Jahrbuch Mission* 2014, 201–6. Hamburg: Missionshilfe, 2014.
Ustorf Werner. *Mission im Nationalsozialismus*. Berliner Beiträge zur Missionsgeschichte, Heft 3. Berlin: Wichern, 2002.
VELKD, and Arnoldshainer Konferenz, eds. *Religion, Religiosität und christliche Glaube*. 2nd ed. Gütersloh, 1991.
Vicedom, Georg. *Missio dei: Einführung in eine Theologie der Mission*. München: Kaiser, 1958.
Vorländer, Hermann. "Bauers Umfeld und Erbe—Sein missionshistorischer Kontext und die Weiterentwicklung seines Werkes bis in die Gegenwart." In *Friedrich Bauer 1812–1874: Pionier in der Weltmission, Wegbereiter des Duden*, edited by Claudia Jahnel and Hermann Vorländer, 265–90. Neuendettelsau: Erlanger, 2013.
_____. *Kirche in Bewegung: Die Geschichte der evangelischen Mission in Bayern*. Neuendettelsau: Erlanger, 2014.
Wagner, Herwig, and Hermann Reiner. *The Lutheran Church in Papua New Guinea: The First Hundred Years 1886–1986*. Adelaide: Lutheran Publishing, 1987.
Weber, Christian. "Die Anfänge der Neuendettelsauer Mission unter Johann Konrad Wilhelm Löhe aus der Retrospektive nach 25 Jahren." In *Franken und die Weltmission im 19. und 20. Jahrhundert*, edited by Wolfgang Weiß, 129–42. Quellen und Forschungen zur Geschichte des Bistums und Hochstifts Würzburg, vol. 65, Würzburg: Schöningh, 2011.
_____. *Missionstheologie bei Wilhelm Löhe: Aufbruch zur Kirche der Zukunft*. Gütersloh: Mohn, 1996.
_____. "Weitblickend, konzentriert und ehrlich: Das missionarische Bildungskonzept Friedrich Bauers." In *Friedrich Bauer 1812–1874: Pionier in der Weltmission, Wegbereiter des Duden*, edited by Claudia Jahnel and Hermann Vorländer, 135–88. Neuendettelsau: Erlanger, 2013.
Winter, Christine. "The Long Arm of the Third Reich." *Journal of Pacific History* 38 (2001) 85–108.
_____. *Looking after One's Own: The Rise of Nationalism and the Politics of the Neuendettelsauer Mission in Germany, New Guinea and Australia (1921–1933)*. Berlin: Peter Lang, 2012.
_____. "The NSDAP Stronghold Finschhafen, New Guinea." In *National Socialism in Oceania*, edited by Emily Turner-Graham and Christine Winter, 31–47. Frankfurt: Peter Lang, 2010.
Zwanzger, Andreas, ed. *Tobias Kaboing der Erstling unserer Mission*. Lebens-Bilder 1. Neuendettelsau: Missionshaus, 1919.

Index of Persons

Allende, Salvador, 172
Althaus, Paul, 57, 113
Altmann, Walter, 166
Amet, Arnold, 224
Anderson, Rufus, 188

Baierlein, Eduard, 10
Bamiringnu, Baafecke, 79, 187, 223
Basano, 68
Bauer, Friedrich, 3, 20-29, 31, 36, 38, 47, 50, 76, 92, 107, 181, 210, 215-17, 225, 235
Bauer, Friedrich Wilhelm (Fred), 23, 28,
Bauer, Gottlieb, 23, 38
Bauer, James, 92
Bauer, John, 92
Bauer, Julie Dorothea, 21
Bauer, Levi, 92
Becker, Horst, 77, 80, 82, 94, 145, 220, 222, 235
Beckstein, Günther, 124, 224
Bedford-Strohm, Heinrich, 92, 234
Beer, Ludwig, 64
Bergmann, Wilhelm, 112, 202
Blumhardt, Christoph, 1
Bräuninger, Moritz, 11-12, 216, 233
Brakemeier, Gottfried, 166, 221, 231
Brandt, Heinrich, 8
Burger, Georg, 8-9, 85, 215, 232

Calvin, Johannes, 20
Cao, Shengjie, 127, 225, 229

Chang, Gideon, 136
Charles Prince of Wales, 100
Chou En Lai, 127
Columbus, Christopher, 167
Confucius, 122-23
Cook, James, 95
Cortez, Victoria, 170-71
Crämer, August Friedrich, 10, 216

Decker, Johann, 113
Deindörfer, Johannes, 14-15
Deinzer, Johannes, 22, 26, 28-31, 47, 102-3, 200, 210, 217, 235
Deinzer, née Bauer, Magda(lena), 23, 36
Deinzer, Martin, 22, 25, 31-37, 47, 105, 210, 217, 235
Delitzsch, Franz, 2
Deng Xao Ping, 124
Detzner, Hermann, 40
Dietzfelbinger, Hermann, 68-69, 72-73, 77, 116, 149, 220, 234
Diggs, Ronald, 84, 159
Dober, Johann Leonhard, 1
Doe, Samuel, 157
Döbrich, Wolfgang, 89, 225
Donigi, Peter, 84
Drexel, Maria, 38, 196
Duden, Konrad, 21-22
Durkheim, Émile, 202
Durst, Friedrich, 140, 157

Edinger, Doraci, 156, 232

INDEX OF PERSONS

Eichhorn, Wilhelm, 235
Eliade, Mircea, 96,
Elisabeth II. Queen of England, 95, 100, 119
Eppelein, Friedrich, 33, 41, 45–46, 48–60, 64–66, 110, 113, 180, 195, 218–19, 235
Ernst, Adam, 8–9, 85, 215, 232
Ernst, Manfred, 121

Faigle, Volker. 151, 231
Farnbacher, Traugott, 106, 117
Fetzer, Karl, 45
Fikenscher, Karl, 21
Finsch, Otto, 99, 104
Fischer, Ulrich, 74, 164
Flierl, Dora, 111
Flierl, Hans, 40
Flierl, Helmut, 109
Flierl, Johann, 30, 41, 64. 96, 101–11, 116, 201–2, 217, 219, 223, 226–27
Flierl, Louise, 111
Flierl, Wilhelm, 109
Flores, Guillermo, 169, 171
Fontius, Hanfried, 41
Forstmeyer, Wilhelm. 49
Francke, August Hermann, 1, 194
Frenz, Helmut, 172
Freud, Sigmund, 96, 202
Friedrich, Johannes, 85, 88, 90, 106, 124–25, 128, 134, 149, 205, 223—25, 228–31, 234
Friedrich, Nestor, 166
Fritschel, Gottfried, 14–15
Fritschel, Sigmund, 14–15, 18
Fugmann, Gernot, 83, 85
Fugmann, Wilhelm (PNG), 62, 113, 115–16
Fugmann, Wilhelm (Brazil), 164

Gam, Getacke, 84, 116–17, 221, 228
Garms, Werner, 50
Gareis, Gustav, 39
Geisel, Ernesto, 164
Gloel, Hans-Martin, 205
Göring, Hermann, 52
Götz, Frieda, 106

Götz, Justus, 54
Gómez, Medardo, 90, 169–70, 225
Graul, Karl, 180, 217
Greifenstein, Hermann, 236
Grieninger, Wolfgang, 136
Grossmann, Georg, 14, 208, 233
Grottke, Gotthard, 51
Gützlaff, Karl, 94, 122, 133, 230
Gutmann, Bruno, 202
Gwang, Christian, 68, 220

Haefner, Johannes, 50
Hänel, Richard, 54
Hanselmann, Johannes, 82, 222, 234
Hansemann, Adolph von, 99, 102—5, 200, 226
Hansemann, Ottilie von, 103
Harless, Adolf von, 2–3, 19, 21
Harris, Sumoward, 159, 164, 232,
Heckel, Theodor, 164
Hellenthal, Walter, 112–13
Hengstenberg, Ernst Wilhelm, 5
Henke, Oswald, 70, 76–77, 220, 235
Herrlinger, Jakob, 112
Heumann, Emilie, married Keysser, 106, 183, 227
Hildebrandt Rambe, Ati, 207, 226
Hildebrandt Rambe, Markus, 207, 226
Hindenburg, Paul von, 52
Hitler, Adolf, 45–46, 53, 55, 58, 60–61, 110, 112, 115, 164, 196
Höfling, Friedrich, 2
Hoerschelmann, Gabriele, 91–92, 225, 235
Hoerschelmann, Hanns, 91–92, 225, 235
Hoffmann, Ludwig, 20
Holz, Karl, 64
Holzschuher, Heinrich, 2
Hong Yin, 123
Hormess, Friedrich, 63
Horn, Kurt, 70, 234
Horn, Maria, 219, 228
Hsiao, Andrew, 130
Hunnius, Nikolaus, 22
Hwah, Tung Chee, 131

Ittameier, Karl, 30–31

INDEX OF PERSONS

Jacobsen, Volkher, 117
Jahn, Christoph, 81, 197, 222
Ji, Won Yong, 79, 94, 133, 220
Jiminez, Melvin, 171
Johnson, Prince, 157

Kabila, Joseph, 152, 231
Kabila, Laurent Desiré, 152
Kaboing, Tobias, 105–6, 226
Kahuthu, Zachariah, 151, 231
Kaiser, Sigurd, 127, 225, 229
Kamm, Georg, 148
Kamunsang, Silas, 105, 226
Kasukuti, Ngoy, 86, 153, 232
Katterfeld, Hagen, 69, 220, 235
Keiper, Martin, 194, 197
Kenyatta, Jomo, 140, 150
Kern, Helmut, 46–48, 54, 195
Keysser, Christian, 38, 40–41, 53, 56, 59–64, 96, 105–8, 113, 183, 202, 214, 218–20, 227
Keysser, Frieda, 96
Kibaki, Mwai, 150
Kibira, Josiah, 145
Kigasung, Wesley, 116, 119–20, 184, 188, 228
Kikwete, Jakaya, 142
Kimirei, Gabriel, 221
Kirchheim, Huberto, 166, 223
Kleefeld, Hans-Gernot, 144, 220, 231
Klein, Friedrich, 52
Koch, Heinrich, 59, 62, 65, 236
Köberlin, Theodor, 72
Köhler, Helmut, 170, 224
Koller, Martha, 42, 106
Koller, Wilhelm, 22, 46, 57, 236
Krafft, Christian, 2, 5, 180
Krapf, Ludwig, 30
Krause, Wolfram von, 69, 220, 235
Kress, Volker, 223
Kressel, Konrad, 72
Krüger, Wolfgang, 122
Kuder, John, 67–68, 116, 228
Küffner, Otto, 22, 34
Küng, Hans, 204
Kuhr, Otto, 31–32, 163–64, 217, 223, 233
Kweka, Erasto, 149

Lagois, Martin, 197
Laiser, Thomas, 147
Langholf, Johann, 51, 59, 219
Lee Kuan Yew, 137
Lehner, Stephan, 112–13
Lema, Agnes, 143
Levi-Strauss, Claude, 96, 202
Liebenberg, Roland, 28
Lippold, Ernst, 70, 235
Livingston, David, 139
Loehe, née Andreä, Helene, 5, 215
Loehe, Max, 97
Loehe, Paul, 97
Loehe, Wilhelm, 4–29, 36, 85, 91–92, 105–6, 181, 194–95, 207–10, 214–17, 225, 235
Loewenich, Hermann von, 32, 86–88, 116, 223, 234
Loscher, Hans, 44
Lossin, Franz, 37, 45–46
Ludwig I King of Bavaria, 4
Lumumba, Patrice, 152
Lupp, Walter, 153, 221, 232
Luther, Hans, 236
Luther, Martin, 13, 20, 59, 86, 124, 131, 153–54, 222

Mabasso, José, 156, 232
Magufuli, John, 142
Mao Zedong, 122–23, 229
Martin, Michael, 93, 117, 234
Marx, Karl, 124
Matiane, Palias, 119
Maurer, Wilhelm, 180
Maximilian King of Bavaria, 19
Meischel, Johann, 95, 216, 226
Meiser, Hans, 44, 46, 48, 50, 53–54, 59–60, 63, 65, 219, 234
Merkel, Angela, 224
Mgeyekwa, Zephania, 79, 150, 187, 189, 221
Mkapa, Benjamin, 142
Mobutu, Sese Seko, 152–53, 231
Moi, Daniel Arap, 150
Moll, Helene, 40, 106, 227
Moltmann, Jürgen, 204
Mondliane, Edmondo, 155
Moritzen, Niels-Peter, 180

INDEX OF PERSONS

Moshi, Stefano, 145
Mott, John, 35
Mühlhaus, Karl Hermann, 229
Mühlschlegel, Henriette, 193
Müller, Karl, 50
Müller, Ludwig, 54
Mukala, Daniel Kabamba, 154
Mushemba, Samson, 84, 153
Mwenegoha, Amani, 148
Mwinyi, Ali Hassan, 142, 146, 148

Narakobi, Bernard, 84
Neumeyer; Hans, 38, 67, 116, 219–20, 235
Noko, Ishmael, 139
Nyerere, Julius, 141–42, 148, 231

Ost, Werner, 72–73, 236

Pahlen, Detlef Graf von der, 236
Payne, Roland, 159, 232
Perlitz, Manfred, 197
Peters, Carl, 140
Pfalzer, Georg, 105, 226
Philemon, Bart 84
Pilhofer, Georg, 66, 70, 110, 112–14
Pinochet, Augusto, 172
Puyi Emperor of China, 124–25

Quesada, Gilberto, 171
Quewai, Mufuano, 68, 220
Quin, Zhongui, 127, 225

Rabe, Paul, 50
Rauh, Martina, 232
Raum, Hans, 109
Raumer, Karl von, 2
Rebmann, Johann, 30, 231
Reiner, Hermann, 70, 235
Reu, Michael, 28, 218
Rhinow, Malte, 133, 223, 230
Ritter, Leonhard, 59
Roepke, Claus-Jürgen, 234
Rössler, Hans, 25
Romero, Oscar, 169, 234

Rotermund, Wilhelm, 163

Ruf, Rudolf, 34, 37–39, 41, 48, 50, 201, 218, 235
Ruf, Walther, 197
Rupprecht, Friedrich, 236

Sabel, Eduard, 235
Salazar, Antonio de, 155
Sawaya, Geofrey, 156
Schäfer, Klaus, 189
Schemm, Hans, 46
Schilberg, Woldemar, 65–67, 219, 235
Schleiermacher, Friedrich, 5
Schleinitz, Georg von, 103
Schleinitz, Margot von, 103
Schlichting, Wolfhart, 236
Schmechel, Armindo, 171
Schmidt, Jakob, 12
Schmutterer, Gottfried, 58
Schmutterer, Magdalena, 58
Schneider, Johann, 36
Schneller, Hermann, 115
Schroth, Fritz, 88
Schülke, Heidi, 125, 225, 229–30
Schüller, Michael, 15
Schuster, Adam, 27, 37, 41, 48, 56, 59, 63, 218
Schuster, Wilhelm, 27
Scriba, Georg, 161
Seeger, Horst, 156, 223
Seiler, Gottfried, 34
Semaan, Wanis, 79, 221
Shoo, Frederick, 150, 187, 231
Sihler, Wilhelm, 232
Sirleaf, Johnson Ellen, 158
Söderblom, Nathan, 43
Solf, Wilhelm, 199–200
Somare, Michael, 100, 221
Spittler, Friedrich, 1
Spranger, Carl-Dieter, 84, 223
Stadler, Jürgen, 27, 31
Stählin, Gustav, 180
Stählin, Therese, 28
Steck, Karl, 31, 34, 36–37, 41–42, 107, 109, 197, 218, 227
Stirner, Eduard Sr., 31. 235
Stirner, Eduard, Jr., 37, 235
Stössel, Johann, 38, 46, 64, 192
Stolz, Johann, 96, 217, 226

Strauss, Gerhard, 234
Strauss, Hermann, 202
Strauss, Werner, 137, 222, 230
Strehlow, Carl F., 96, 201-2
Strehlow, Frieda, 96
Stürzenhofecker, Hubert, 113
Sumaili, Mwamba, 154
Sun, Yat Sen, 123
Sundermaier, Theo, 204

Tai, Nicholas, 130
Taylor, Charles, 157
Theile, Otto F., 39, 49-50, 97, 109, 112
Tholuck, August, 21
Thomasius, Gottfried, 2
Ting, K.H., 126-27, 130, 229
Töllner, Wolfgang, 234
Tolbert, William R., 157
Traunfelder, Adolf, 44, 61, 64-65
Tremel, Karl, 106
Triebel, Johannes, 223

Urame, Jack, 116, 187, 228
Usdorf, Werner, 66
Utech, Ilo, 170

Veit, Friedrich, 234
Venn, Henry, 188
Vetter, Konrad, 105
Vicedom, Georg F., 59, 63, 65, 67, 176, 180, 228
Vorländer, Dorothea, 239
Vorländer, Hermann, 82, 84-86, 88, 91, 193, 222, 224-25, 235, 239-40

Wacke, Karl, 57
Wacke. Magdalene, 57
Wacke, Siegfried, 57
Wagner, Adolf, 113-14, 228
Walther, Carl Ferdinand, 13-14, 216
Wandersee, Robert, 160
Wang, Zuoan, 124-25, 229
Warnke, Jürgen, 221
Weber, Christian, 23
Weber, Ferdinand, 28
Weigand, Peter, 91, 225-26, 235
Wenge, Giegere, 116, 228
Wenge, Luther, 119
William (Wilhelm) II German Emperor, 34, 217
Winter, Helmut, 82
Winter, Christine, 115
Wirth, Konrad, 235
Wittenberg, Gunter, 160
Wölfle, Klaus, 197
Wucherer, Friedrich, 7, 195, 217, 235
Wüstner, Friedrich, 164
Wynecken, Friedrich, 7, 14, 215-16

Yu, Thu En, 137

Zahn, Heinrich, 37, 106
Zake, 107, 227
Zehnder, Judy, 92
Zindel, Friedrich, 43
Zinzendorf, Nikolaus Ludwig Graf von, 1
Zurewe, Zurenuo, 116, 228
Zwingli, Huldrych, 20

Index of Places, Countries, Rivers

Addis Ababa, 149, 153, 161
Adelaide, 95, 97–98
Africa, 3, 30, 35, 42, 48, 77, 80, 86–87, 89, 95, 98, 138–61, 166, 179, 189–203, 193, 206, 210, 221–22, 230
Aha, 16
Alexishafen 104, 185
Alpirsbach, 64
Alsace (-Lorraine), 64
Altdorf, 78, 220
(North) America/USA 3–30, 36, 39, 50, 76, 85, 91, 94, 106, 115, 117, 129, 133, 138, 157–58, 160–61, 167–68, 195–96, 201, 210, 215, 217–18, 222, 228, 232–33
Ampo, 106, 117, 119, 227
Amron, 120
Amsterdam, 35
Ansbach, 1, 21, 54, 59, 62, 191,
Argentina, 162, 171–72
Arusha, 153, 156
Asaroka, 111, 227
Aschaffenburg, 67, 171
(East) Asia, 3, 35, 77, 80, 86–87, 89, 94–138, 179, 203, 206, 210, 221, 226
Astrolabe Bay, 103
Augsburg, 5, 14, 58, 143, 148, 191
Australia 12, 29–30, 36, 39, 41, 48–50, 62, 65, 67, 76, 84–85, 94–102, 106, 108–17, 129, 196, 201–2, 210, 216–18, 224, 226–28

Austria (-Hungary), 21–22, 76, 172, 196

Baden, 206
Bagamoyo, 141
Baitabag, 120
Baldingen, 8
Bangkok, 76, 78, 184
Bangladesh, 94
Banz, 120
Barossa Valley, 95
Basel, 1, 194
Bayreuth, 45–46, 48, 64, 72, 78, 181, 220
Beijing, 123–24, 129
Beira, 156
Beirut, 82, 239
Belgium, 138, 141, 152
Berlin, 5, 52, 99, 102, 113, 138, 163–64, 199, 221
Bessarabia, 172
Bethel, 239
Bong County, 157–58
Bonn, 83
Bore, 107, 227
Borneo, 134, 137
Bougainville, 100
Brazil, 31, 33, 39, 45, 50–51, 63, 67, 69, 73–74, 76, 80, 91, 156, 162–67, 170, 210, 217–19, 221, 223, 233
Brazzaville, 152
Bremen, 9, 71, 104

Brisbane, 49, 97, 110
Bruckberg, 55
Buchhof, 30, 101
Budapest, 177, 188
Bukoba, 145, 147
Bulolo, 111

Cambodia, 138
Cameron Mountains, 136
Cameroon, 160
Canada, 9, 117, 129
Canberra, 95
Caribbean, 1
Central America, 167–73, 233–34
Chad, 160
Chile, 91, 172–73
Chimala, 189
Chimmoio, 156
China, 94, 118, 122–38, 157, 224–25, 233, 229
Coburg, 79, 187, 189, 221
Columbus (Ohio), 9, 49, 110, 219
Congo/Zaire, 80, 82, 86, 150, 152–54, 221, 231–32
Cooktown, 102–3
Costa Rica, 167–68, 171, 234
Curitiba, 166

Dar-es-Salaam, 94, 145, 149, 155, 177
Deer Creek, 12
Deinzerhill, 105, 226
Denmark, 1, 145, 156, 159
Dietenhofen, 79, 187, 223
Dodoma, 231
Dormagen, 63
Dresden, 3, 5, 95, 215
Dubuque, 15, 18, 69, 74–75, 208, 218, 224, 233

East New Britain, 103
Edinburgh, 34, 41, 188, 203
Ega, 111
Eisenach, 15, 38, 74
El Salvador, 90, 167–71, 224, 234
Elim, 102
Elisabethville, 153
Emperor William Land, 99, 104, 226

England/Great Britain, 1, 99, 122, 129, 134, 138, 141, 161, 229
Erlangen, 2, 3, 5, 9, 21, 28, 40, 48–49, 57, 80–82, 113, 131, 161, 180, 197, 217, 222–23, 239
Espiritu Santo, 162, 164
Ethiopia, 161, 221

Feucht, 34
Fiji, 122, 130
Finke River, 96
Finschhafen, 42, 99–100, 103–6, 110, 112–13, 115–16, 226–27
Fly River, 83
Fort Wayne, 6, 10, 20–22, 210, 216, 232
France, 5, 138
Franconia, 2, 10, 18, 44
Frankenhilf, 10
Frankenlust, 10
Frankenmuth, 10–11, 216, 222, 232
Frankentrost, 10
Frankfurt, 5, 77, 198
Freising, 67
Fubilan Mt., 83
Fürth, 2, 5, 215

Gaza, 156
Gbarnga, 159
Geroldsgrün, 40
Ghounzhou (Canton), 123
Göggingen, 57
Göttingen, 9
Goroka, 121, 228
Gotha, 9
Greifswald, 66
Guatemala, 167, 172
Guinea, 157, 159
Gunzenhausen, 16, 44, 50, 68, 77, 216, 219–20

Hagen, 119
Hai, 149
Halle, 21, 194
Hamburg, 71, 129, 145, 222, 239
Hanover, 33, 80, 91, 224
Heidelberg, 239
Heiligenhafen, 199

Heldsbach, 41, 105, 107, 227
Helgoland, 31, 140
Helsinki, 145, 177
Hermannsburg (Germany), 66, 71, 76,
Hermannsburg (Australien), 96, 101
Herrnhut, 1
Hersbruck, 2, 30, 33, 216, 219
Hildesheim, 81
Holland, 99
Honduras, 167–68, 171, 234
Hong Kong, 93, 129–31, 138, 177, 204, 229
Hube, 106, 227
Hubei, 130
Hunsrück, 163
Huon Gulf, 108

Illinois, 15
India, 10, 80–81, 94, 188, 194, 218
Indonesia, 94, 99–100
Iowa, 15, 233
Ipoh, 136
Irian Jaja, 100
Iringa, 146
Ivory Coast, 157

Japan, 94, 132, 230
Jerusalem, 51, 115
Jonesville, 239

Kaiapit, 106, 227
Kainantu, 117, 222, 228
Kalemie, 153
Kambaidam, 111
Katanga, 152
Kaufbeuren, 82, 239
Kenya, 30–31, 80, 82, 150–52, 224, 231
Kidugala, 149
Kilimanjaro, 30–31, 143–44, 146, 148–49, 231
Kimbeimbe, 154, 232
Kinshasa, 153
Kirchenlamitz, 5
Kisi, 152
Kleinlangheim, 10
(South) Korea, 79, 94–95, 132–34, 220, 223, 230

Kota Kinabalu, 137

Lae, 67, 78, 106, 116–17, 119–20, 227–28
Laos, 138
Latin America, 35, 74, 89–90, 162–73, 206, 210
Lausanne, 78
Lebanon, 79, 239
Leipzig, 176, 189, 204
Liberia, 80, 156–59, 232
Locarno, 110
Lofa County, 158
Logaweng, 116, 228
London, 128
Los Angeles, 168
Lubumbashi, 153, 232

Macau, 123
Machame, 146
Madagascar, 136
Madang, 103–4, 109–10, 116, 120, 227
Mafinga, 149
Makumira, 146, 153
Malacca, 94, 138
Malaysia, 94, 98, 118, 129, 134–37, 224, 230
Malindi, 151
Malolo, 106
Managua, 171
Manono, 153
Maputo, 156
Marangu, 146
Masoka, 148
Massai Plains, 147
Mecklenburg, 82
Mekong, 131, 138
Melanesia, 109
Melbourne, 198
Mendota, 15
Meru, 148
Mexico, 167, 169
Mexico City, 188
Michigan, 10, 14, 18
Missouri, 12, 233
Mönchsroth, 1
Mombasa, 30, 151, 231

Mongolia, 138
Monrovia, 156–59
Montana, 12, 233
Morogoro, 141
Moschin, 239
Moshi, 143, 148–49, 224, 231
Mozambique, 80, 150, 155–56, 232
Munich, 2–3, 46, 69–70, 74, 78, 82, 91, 130, 164, 181, 191, 194, 206, 211–12, 220, 239
Mwanga, 149
Mwika, 146
Myanmar, 136, 138

Nairobi, 150–52, 161
Nanjing, 122–23, 126–28, 221, 225, 229
Natal, 160–61
New Delhi, 71
Neu Dettelsau (Ohio), 9
Neuendettelsau, 4–239
(Papua-)New Guinea (PNG), 12, 29, 34, 36–42, 45, 48–50, 53, 56–68, 73, 76, 78–80, 82–85, 94, 97–122, 137, 181, 184–85, 187, 189, 191–93, 196, 199–202, 210, 217–26, 221, 228
New Pomerania, 103
New York, 9, 63, 168
New Zealand, 97
Nicaragua, 167–68, 171, 234
Niederberg, 152
Nigeria, 139
Nimba County, 157
Njombe, 149
Nördlingen, 7, 194,
Nordheim, 41
Norway, 145, 161
Nova Friburgo, 163
Nuremberg, 2, 4–5, 11, 16, 21–22, 30, 44, 46, 48–49, 60, 64, 82, 85–86, 89, 101, 171, 181, 194, 197, 205, 210, 215–16, 220, 222–23
Nyassa Lake, 144, 153

Obasega, 106, 227
Oberstdorf, 67
Oettingen, 8, 63

Ogelbeng, 111, 116, 228
Ohio, 9, 12, 233
Ok Tedi, 83–84, 118, 222, 228
Oman, 140
Onerunga, 111

Pacific, 80, 84, 86–87, 89, 99, 100, 102, 112, 115, 121–22, 197, 203, 221, 226
Palatinate, 206
Palestine, 48, 51, 76
Palipo, 158
Papua, 100
Paraguay, 162, 171
Paraná, 162, 164
Petersaurach, 65
Pfäfflingen, 63
Philippines, 94–95, 132, 138
Pietermaritzburg, 160–61
Poland, 64–65, 239
Polsingen, 41
Pomerania, 163
Port Moresby, 79, 83, 100
Porto Alegre, 163, 166
Portugal, 138, 155
Poznan, 66
Powder River, 12, 233
Prussia, 95

Queensland, 95

Rabaul, 34, 103, 109, 113, 227
Raipinka, 111
Regensburg, 85–86, 169, 199, 223, 234
Reichenschwand, 30
Rhodesia, 155
Ricatla, 155
Rift Valley, 144
Rio de Janeiro, 163
Rio de la Plata, 171
Rio Grande do Sul, 162–64
Rothenburg on the Tauber, 28, 31–32, 217, 223
Rummelsberg, 88, 90, 148, 225
Rwanda, 138

Sabbah, 134, 137
Saginaw, 14, 233

Sahel zone, 160
Samoa, 99
San Antonio, 204
San José, 171
San Salvador, 169
Santa Catarina, 162, 164
Sao Bento do Sul, 166
Sao Leopoldo, 69, 162–63, 165–67, 233
Sao Paulo, 164
Sarawak, 134
Sattelberg, 105–7, 226
Saxony, 5, 12–13, 82
Scandinavia, 201
Sebastiansweiler, 61
Senegal, 160
Serra Gaucha, 162
Seoul, 132, 134
Shanghai, 123–24, 127
Siassi, 116
Sierra Leone, 159
Silesia, 95
Simbang, 49, 101, 105, 116, 226
Singapore, 129, 136–38, 222, 224, 230
South Africa, 69, 144, 155, 160
Soviet Union/USSR, 64, 157
Spain, 167, 233–34
Spiegelberg, 167
Starnberg, 82–83, 222
St. Sebald by the Spring, 15, 233
Stuttgart, 71
Sumatra, 98
Susquehanna, 191
Suva, 122
Swaziland, 149
Sweden, 145, 156–57, 159
Switzerland, 172, 196
Sydney, 112

Taiwan, 94
Tami, 105–6, 226
Tamil Nadu, 137
Tana River, 151
Tanganyika, 141, 144, 230–31
Tanunda, 111
Tanzania, 73, 77–82, 94, 138, 140–51, 155–56, 160, 181, 202, 211, 220–21, 224, 230–31

Tatura, 114–15
Thailand, 98, 130, 138
Thuringia, 63, 82
Torres Strait, 99
Totota, 159
Triesdorf, 21
Tübingen, 42, 45
Tutzing, 84

Uganda, 143, 150
Ukraine, 51, 76, 218
Umpumulo, 161
Union County, 9
Uppsala, 198, 212
Uruguay, 172
Usa River, 149
Usambara Mountains, 144, 230

Vatican, 129
Versailles, 39–40, 42, 52, 97, 109–10
Victoria, 114
Victoria Lake, 144
Vietnam, 136, 138
Volga region, 172

Wartburg, 74
Wasu, 119
Wau, 110–11, 121
Waverly, 15, 233
Weiden, 221
Weimar, 43
Weissenbronn, 239
West Papua, 56, 114
Whitby, 188, 213
Willingen, 176
Windsbach, 8
Winnipeg, 182
Württemberg, 1, 64, 206, 239
Würzburg, 2, 78, 191, 220, 239
Wunsiedel, 2
Wuppertal, 71

Zanzibar, 31, 140–41, 231
Zimbabwe, 139, 156
Zirndorf, 49, 60

Index of Institutions

American Lutheran Church, 15, 110, 116, 233
Association of Diaspora Services, 73–74, 220
Association of Protestant Churches and Missions in Germany (EMW), 71, 82, 220–21
Augustana Theological Seminary, 65, 67, 69, 150, 176, 180, 219

Basel Mission, 1–3, 5, 20, 130, 137, 163, 194, 210
Bavarian Association for Medical Mission, 42, 217
Berlin Mission, 71, 144–45, 230
Bethel Mission, 144–45, 230
Bridge – Köprü – Center for Christian Muslim Encounter, 82, 85, 205, 222, 225

Central (Evangelical Lutheran) Missionary Association for Bavaria, 3–4, 11, 19–20, 30, 41, 81, 181, 197, 215
Church Development Service (KED), 89, 128, 198–99, 212, 220
Concordia Theological Seminary Fort Wayne, 6, 10, 21–22, 210, 216, 232

Deaconess Institute, 207–8, 216
Department for World Mission (DWM), 71–88, 117, 128, 140, 161, 181, 197, 199, 207, 211, 220–25, 229–32, 235, 239
Dresden Mission, 5–6, 20, 95, 194, 215

Evangelical Church in Germany (EKD), 71, 91, 164, 189, 198
Evangelical Lutheran Church in America (ELCA), 15, 29, 160

Finnish Evangelical Lutheran Mission (FELM), 82, 85, 145, 153, 205, 222

Gossner Mission, 95
Gustavus Adolphus Work, 33, 74, 167, 220

Hermannsburg Mission, 69, 71, 76, 95–96, 101, 161
Hersbruck Mission, 30–31, 140, 151, 217, 231

International Lutheran Council, 116, 133, 165
Iowa Synod, 12, 14–15, 18, 27, 30, 110, 208, 217, 227, 233

Joint Christian Ministry in West Africa, 160, 221

Leipzig Mission, 3, 5–6, 10, 20, 30–31, 34, 41–42, 72–73, 77, 80–81,

117, 140, 145, 180, 194, 197, 215, 222–23, 230
Lutheran Church – Missouri Synod (LCMS), 4, 9–10, 12–14, 18–19, 22, 29, 97, 116, 120, 133, 138, 165, 169, 230
Lutheran Mission Cooperation (Tanzania), 146, 148, 224, 231
Lutheran Theological Seminary (LTS), 130–31, 229
Lutheran Treasury of God, 31–33, 163–64, 216–17
Lutheran World Federation (LWF), 78, 80, 94, 97, 115, 120, 130–31, 133, 138–39, 145, 149, 152, 155–56, 165, 170–71, 182, 188–89, 198, 211, 229, 234

Martin Luther Association, 32–33, 49, 74, 91, 164, 167, 216, 219–20
Mekong Mission Forum, 93, 98, 138
Mission One World – Center for Partnership, Development and Mission, 88–89, 91, 212
Mission (and Diaspora) Seminary (MDS), 6, 14, 22–28, 31–32, 34, 36–37, 40, 45, 47, 51, 58, 64, 67–70, 74–77, 91, 101, 107, 163–64, 183, 216, 218–21

Missionary Aviation Fellowship (MAF), 112, 117

Northelbian Mission Center, 117, 152–53,

Pacific Information Center, 122, 221
Pacific Theological Seminary, 122
Program for Christian Muslim Relations in Africa (PROCMURA), 159, 161, 222
Rhenish Mission, 103–4, 110, 130, 144

Society for Inner (and Outer) Mission in the Sense of the Lutheran Church, 16–17, 22, 41, 72–73, 76, 181, 194–95, 211, 216, 223

United Evangelical Lutheran Church of Germany, 77, 81, 160, 182–83

Wartburg College, 15, 233
Wartburg Theological Seminary, 15, 18, 69, 74–75, 233
World Council of Churches (WCC), 35, 71, 181, 198, 211–12

www.ingramcontent.com/pod-product-compliance
Lightning Source LLC
Chambersburg PA
CBHW071245230426
43668CB00011B/1594